TWILIGHT
GODDESS

TWILIGHT GODDESS

Spiritual Feminism and Feminine Spirituality

Thomas Cleary
and Sartaz Aziz

SHAMBHALA
Boston & London
2000

Shambhala Publications, Inc.
Horticultural Hall
300 Massachusetts Avenue
Boston, Massachusetts 02115
www.shambhala.com

9 8 7 6 5 4 3 2 1

First Shambhala Edition
Printed in the United States of America

⊗ This edition is printed on acid-free paper that meets the
American National Standards Institute Z39.48 Standard.
Distributed in the United States by Random House, Inc.,
and in Canada by Random House of Canada Ltd

Library of Congress Cataloging-in-Publication Data
Cleary, Thomas.
Twilight goddess: spiritual feminism and feminine
spirituality / Thomas Cleary & Sartaz Aziz.—1st ed.
p. cm.
Includes bibliographical references.
ISBN 1-57062-499-2 (alk. paper)
1. Goddess religion. 2. Women and religion.
I. Aziz, Sartaz. II. Title.
BL325.F4.C54 2000
291.2′114—dc21
00-021870

Contents

v

LIST OF ILLUSTRATIONS

A Note on Transliteration

THIS BOOK CONTAINS names and terms transliterated from a number of different languages. These languages belong to different linguistic families and are written by means of different systems. The phonetics of each of these languages differ from each other and from English, so there is no uniform way to represent sounds of all these languages in one system of Romanization. Various academic transliteration schemes have been developed for individual languages, but we have chosen not to adopt them in this context because their complications pose unnecessary problems for general readers without actually making accurate pronunciation possible, while specialists and students do not really need academic orthographic conventions to recognize the words.

TWILIGHT
GODDESS

Spiritual Feminism and Feminine Spirituality

A MONG THE MOST LIVELY and exciting trends in Western religious thought today is the renaissance of interest in traditional spiritual feminism, including Goddess worship, one of our most ancient modes of spiritual imagination. The widening appeal of Goddess theology and spiritual feminism in the present day may reflect perennial relevance in these traditions. The resurgence of these interests in the modern West is taking place in an era in which religious aspirations are dovetailing with social and scientific concerns about the rights of women and our relation to the earth. This convergence is redolent of a predilection of Goddess religion and spiritual feminism for wholeness and balance, and for harmony among the realms of the natural, human, and divine.

Religious conceptions of humankind in high antiquity appear to have spawned ideas of gods and goddesses, both as individuals and as partners. Often the gods and goddesses of human imagination were much like human beings in temperament and behavior, or like natural phenomena in their relationships to human society. Perhaps this was a natural reflection of primitive human psychology, but we have not entirely outgrown this habit. Even in modern cultures whose religions speak of a single deity, personal understandings of the deity may often continue to reflect

1

similar images or ideas of the divine in terms of human qualities or natural forces.

Even the oldest known religious literature, polytheistic as it may be
in appearance, nevertheless seems to contain visions of an essential and
transcendental divine unity. This vision of divine unity did not obliterate
the vision of divine plurality, however, just as the vision of divine plurality had not effaced the vision of divine unity. As a result, the image of
unity was sometimes called by one name, sometimes another, sometimes
yet another. Sometimes the gods and goddesses were envisioned as parents and children, sometimes as husbands and wives; sometimes a god or
goddess stood for an elemental fact of life, and sometimes envisioned
as absolute reality—or absolute reality was given the name of a god or
goddess.

This phenomenon seems to reflect the social, cultural, and intellectual
diversity of its milieu, whether or not deeper or higher truths about
human nature and objective reality are seen behind it. In the eyes of those
who strove to order and regulate society according to normative models,
which meant regularizing religious and political hierarchies, this degree
of diversity could seem threatening. Campaigns to suppress certain social
structures or religious beliefs may have been among the results of fearful
martial and priestly elites joining forces to establish the custom of maintaining their status and power through hereditary succession.

Nevertheless, even where patriarchal politics deprived women of political and legal rights, and the institutionalization of religions excluded
women, servants, outcastes, and independently inspired gnostics from
mainstream communal rites and privileges, the feminine and mystical
ways of spiritual knowledge have continued to operate as alternative or
underground traditions. Whether openly in moments of honor, or secretly in ages of oppression, these movements have influenced many cultures from the furthest East to Western Europe and the New World, both
in former times and in recent generations. It is natural, in this sense, that
a modern resurgence of Western interest in Goddess worship coincides
with growing involvement in studies of the mystical teachings of the
world.

In both monotheistic and polytheistic forms of religion, the divine is
envisioned as having both benevolent and terrifying aspects. This is not

difficult to understand, considering that life has both joys and sorrows, and for every birth there is a death.

The vision of the divine as both life-giving and death-dealing is characteristic of God religions as well as Goddess religions. The paradoxical nature of the divine as humanly perceived appears in both God- and Goddess-centered religions. The conceptual nuances and external manifestations of these human quandaries, however, may coincide and may differ in their expression in God and Goddess religions.

Twilight imagery of the Goddess, like personalized imagery of God, intertwining light and dark, may be a penetrating mirror of the human mind, which finds ambiguity in its experience of the world and projects intention on the universe at large. To peer into the personality of the hidden weaver beneath the warp and woof of religious culture, we can attempt to look through the seams of the images and shadows of the twilight Goddess of light and darkness.

Throughout history, all over the globe, religions of the Goddess, spiritual perceptions of the feminine, and the divine matrix of existence itself are to be found sometimes in the light, sometimes in the dark, now revealed, now concealed. It is not only because of social and political conditions that Goddess religion may reveal or conceal itself as the time requires; for there is spiritual time as well as terrestrial time.

Revelation and concealment are not only terrestrial tactics but also spiritual needs, because the Goddess reflects both our brightest hopes and our darkest fears, helping us to confront them both in their times with good grace and inner fortitude.

Twilight Goddess is named for this mirror of human hopes and fears; for this is a book of meditations and musings on spiritual visions of the Goddess of light and darkness, the Goddess of life and death, and on the many expressions of feminine spirituality and spiritual feminism inspired by such visions over the ages.

Historically, both in the East and the West, feminism has provided a more universal perspective on the human condition than have regional politics and the cultural biases they promote. Herein may be a clue to a possible role of spiritual feminism in the pursuit of world peace today. Just as spiritual feminism has linked outwardly different religious traditions in the past, so too it now reveals the common bonds that join all humanity with the planet we share.

3

1

The Divine Matrix
MOTHER GODDESS

G ODDESS WORSHIP as established religion in the present day exists primarily in India, but its current forms have emerged after many centuries of evolution. Goddess worship existed in India in most ancient times, as evidenced in the earliest collection of sacred hymns. Yet it was eventually suppressed and ostracized by elite Hindu priesthoods bent on establishing patrilineal caste and patriarchal rule.

Some believe it was aboriginal tribes in India who had matriarchal, matrilineal, and matrilocal customs—that is, women held positions of authority, families were traced through the maternal line, and husbands made their homes near their wives' families. These customs were contrary to those of the Aryans who conquered the aboriginal tribes and adopted them into the fringes of Aryan society to do the dirty work—in the literal sense of the word. This contradiction would have been one strategic reason for the suppression of Goddess worship, supposing that patriarchal Aryan invaders did in fact wage cultural warfare on matriarchal native tribes. The Aryan adoption of the divinities of other peoples, both gods and goddesses, however, suggests that the picture was far more complex than Aryan patriarchy versus non-Aryan matriarchy.

The existence of such matrifocal customs among some groups of Celts, who were also Aryans culturally related to the Hindus, suggests that matriarchal, matrilineal, or matrilocal customs did exist among the Aryans of ancient times, whether or not they were ever universal among them. Like the rule of hereditary caste, now known to have been a later development of Aryan culture nonexistent in the time of the Rigveda, normative patrilineal, patrilocal, and patriarchal customs may not have been an original or invariable feature of Aryan culture.

In time Goddess worship in India regenerated and reemerged with such energy that Hindu priests themselves eventually readopted it, albeit in their own modified forms. Parallel traditions of religious culture and spiritual development in which feminine elements are essential also lie at the heart of the mystical and esoteric teachings of Taoism, Buddhism, and Sufism.

Goddess worship seems to have existed since time immemorial. Ancient names of the Goddess—such as Infinity, among the oldest—are to be found in the Rigveda, a Hindu scripture thought to have been composed, or compiled, more than four millennia ago. Although this sacred text has been recited continuously for thousands of years, in the course of time Hindu women were forbidden by priests from hearing the scriptures and were excluded from the sacred rituals. Partly as a result of this and other imbalances in the structure of priest-centered Hinduism, protestant and reformist movements arose between three thousand and twenty-five hundred years ago, admitting women to their sacred recitals and their religious rites and regimens.

The most widespread and most influential of these counterbalancing movements was Buddhism, which as a consequence was opposed and suppressed by Hindu authorities when they rose to political power. Perhaps it was in response to the resurgence of patriarchal versions of Hinduism against egalitarian Buddhism that Goddess worship began to emerge as a distinct genre of religious momentum in India around fifteen hundred years ago.

The most creative period of Goddess religion may have been between 600 and 1600 CE. During that millennium Tantrism reached high levels of development in both Hinduism and Buddhism, producing religious movements of remarkable energy and power. Activity emanating from Tantrism's residual force has continued to the present day, attracting ever renewed interest from many quarters and many points of view.

The Divine Mother

Human beings are born in a state less developed than that of any other animal at birth, and so we need more nurturing than any other animal. It has been claimed that other animal species also have their own modes of worshiping the divine, but filial or parental imagery and sentiment in religious devotion have undoubtedly been developed to unique levels by human beings on account of the particularly long dependency of humans on parental nurture.

In terms of psychological development, the human mother also plays a more elaborate role than does the mother of other species, even though the latter is not thereby any less important. The mother is the first teacher of a human being, in formal perception as well as intuitive feeling, to say nothing of emotion, thought, and language.

These maternal roles may have inspired certain elemental imagery of goddesses and Goddess worship and propitiation. Visions of the earth mother, or Mother Earth, as the source of physical life seem perfectly natural. It has also been normal to associate goddesses with water and bodies of water, such as rivers, lakes, and wells, evoking the life-giving properties of water.

The disciplinary aspect of motherhood, nevertheless, is also envisioned of goddesses even in their life-source roles. Earth may quake, rivers may flood, wells may dry up; humans have both psychological and material needs for recognizing these facts of life and reconciling themselves with them, both as individuals and as societies. Many images of goddesses and Goddess worship therefore stem from the marriage of nature and culture.

Because psychological realities combine with material realities, goddesses have been envisioned in terms of the life-giving and death-dealing aspects of nature, and also as protectresses of culture. This can be seen in the traditional association of goddesses with towns and cities. This seems to be an expression of the cultural and constructive aspects of motherhood and the creative process, including the civilizing functions of protection, education, and the creation of boundaries.

The functional importance of mothers and motherhood was therefore recognized philosophically, in ways connecting the emotions of the individual with universal needs of humanity. Even in a nonreligious context,

the famous Hindu strategist Kauthilya, never known for sentiment judg-
ments, declared, "The mother is the most important of all teachers. The
mother is to be supported in all conditions of age."

This understanding of motherhood addresses the concerns of the evolution and maintenance of society as a whole as well as, or as an extension
of, the concerns of the development and livelihood of the individual.
Kauthilya also expands the meaning of "mother" to emphasize both personal and social significance in respect for mothers: "The leader's wife,
your teacher's wife, your friend's wife, your wife's mother, and your
own mother—these five are thought of as mothers."[1]

With the addition of religious and spiritual sentiments to instinctual
and social feelings, the image of the Mother Goddess exerted a powerful
influence over the minds of many Hindus, particularly the helpless, the
oppressed, the afflicted, and the aggrieved. Whether to throw themselves
upon her mercy, or to borrow her power to endure the unendurable, the
Mother Goddess has been worshiped with particular fervor by those to
whom the amenities and dignities of the mainstream culture have been
systematically denied.

Many means have been devised over the ages to summon the Goddess
in search of boons, whether of mercy or of knowledge. For us today the
most accessible method may be the ancient route of the names of the
Goddess, which were designed to focus the mind in particular ways.

These special ways of concentrating the mind were constructed to
foster evocations of elemental human perceptions and conceptions of the
divine. Goddess-summoning ceremonies might include recitation of as
many as a hundred to a thousand names of the Goddess, constructing
thereby the firmament of consciousness of her presence in the vision of
the meditator.

There are many names for the Goddess, especially in the still-living
Indian traditions of Goddess religion. Because they were made in a language in constant use for over four thousand years, their enciphered
meanings can be disinterred with relative ease in comparison to encoded
mantras whose origins were lost. The major Sanskrit names of the Goddess all derive from roots evoking both vivifying and mortifying aspects.

1. Thomas Cleary, trans., *The Art of Wealth* (Deerfield Beach, Fla.: Health
Communications, 1998), p. 156.

This gives an immediate clue to a quintessential pivot of Indian Goddess religion. The latent meanings of the Goddess names, brought to life with awareness, structure a mental space filled with images and visions of divine attributes and actions.

Here we will begin with the Mother Goddess names of Bhavani, Rri, Devi, Maya, and Kali, then go on to the emanations of Goddess and her many other faces.

Bhavani

The vision of Goddess as mother is perhaps most clearly expressed in the name Bhavani, a common name for Devi, or Goddess, in the rich traditions of Indian Goddess religion. Because invocation of names is so important in the practice of Goddess worship, it is natural for the meaning of the name to yield insight into the vision of the Goddess it invokes.

The name Bhavani, often seen as Bhowani or Bhowanee in older books, comes from the ancient Sanskrit root bhu, which means "being," "becoming," "living," "happening." These all evoke the primal existential and generative aspects of the Goddess; the Goddess is Being, the Goddess is Becoming; the Goddess is identified with creation, both as creative force and as the elemental universe itself.

In the causative verbal senses, the root bhu means "to call into existence," "to bring to life," "to animate," "to produce," "to cause," "to create," "to cherish," "to enliven," "to refresh," "to encourage." These names continue from being and becoming to invoke creation and nurture, essential functions fulfilled by mothers for infants and children, and for all beings by the earth and the universe.

As a noun with a long u, bhu means "space," "the place where being exists," "the world," "the universe," "the earth." In this sense, it is also used symbolically for the number one, standing for the primary, for wholeness, uniqueness. This is what mother is to the newborn infant, what the earth, the world, or the universe is to the primitive mind of humankind within the womb of existence.

The Goddess as Bhavani is all of this: identified with the creative principle, and also with existence itself, she gives life and grants boons. In the process, she is giving of herself, in traditional visions, for she is also life itself and she is Being itself.

This vision uplifts the devotee's relationship with self and society, and with the world and the cosmos, but it also lays a corresponding obligation upon the heightened consciousness. The process of fulfilling this spiritual obligation is symbolized in one way by ritual sacrifice of some kind, and in another way by acquisition of esoteric knowledge into the secrets of Being and Becoming, or existence and evolution. These two expressions of heightened consciousness were perhaps the original impulses of what we think of today as religion and science.

In this sense, religion and science, like spirit and matter, were born of the same mother. Seen from this perspective, the resolution of conflicts between religion and science, and between spirit and matter, may come not from a revolution so much as a restoration, a return to an interior wholeness of consciousness through which we can perceive the integrity of Being.

Rri

The mother goddess Rri is an ancient vision of the Goddess from the rich Indian traditions. Rri the Goddess is the Mother of the Gods, an exalted role in both spiritual and structural terms.

The disciplinary element in the educational aspect of motherhood can be seen Rri's role as chastiser, for Rri is also the name of the mother of the demons. And Rri is not only mother of gods and demons; a certain *bhairava*, or terror-causing being, and a certain *danava*, or demon, are named after Rri in Indian mythology to highlight these aspects of the human experience of nature, creation, and existence itself.

The root of the name of Rri is ri, which yields numerous meanings. "Movement," "rising," "reaching," and "obtaining" are meanings of the root ri, reflecting the enlivening, encouraging, fulfilling aspects of the Goddess. "To advance on an enemy," "to attack," and "to injure" are also meanings of the root ri, these reflecting visions of protection and also chastisement by the Goddess.

The root of the name of Rri, Mother of the Gods, is also the root of the term *arya*, which refers to a culture. This association appears to have been the original reason for the cultured classes of Hindu society to be called Aryas. The later distortion of this term into a racist label is based

10

on a misunderstanding of the original derivation, meanings, and associations of the word.

The Aryas were originally the descendants of the devotees of Rri, Mother of the Gods. The Aryan culture was constructed to imitate or embody the meanings of ri, the root of Goddess Rri's name, in the design of their civilization.

The prototype of the Arya civilization included a cultus of spiritual and emotional exaltation, a cultus of warfare and administration, and a cultus of trade and husbandry. Each of these specializations, furthermore, had its own particular versions of a general cultus of success and security. All of these occupations and concerns were addressed in some way through some form of Goddess worship. Speaking in terms of mantra, or the storage and evocation of energy and information in sounds and words, the significance of Rri as the mother of the gods may lie in the fact that the specialties of the three classes of Aryan culture are stored in the root of her name.

The primal goddess Rri of Indian tradition corresponds to the goddess Dana of Celtic Irish tradition. Ancient Irish paganism was related to Hinduism, and surviving myths display numerous cognate images and ideas. Dana is identified as De Ana, or Goddess Ana, who is called the mother of the Irish gods. The Irish gods are the so-called Tuatha De Danann, or People of the Goddess Dana, just as the Aryas are people of the goddess Rri.

In Irish mythology, the People of the Goddess Dana are both ancestors of the Irish people and tutelary divinities of Irish culture; they are represented as humans, as magicians, and as gods and goddesses. This is also true of the Aryas, who were human beings with a culture that included magical traditions as well as metaphysical and mythological ways of identifying the human and the divine, or envisioning the interpenetration of human and divine worlds.

In terms of its Irish root, the name of the goddess Dana is thought to be cognate with the Sanskrit *danu*, which primally means "moisture" and is thought to be the origin of the name of the great River Danube, through ancient Celtic. In Sanskrit, Danu is also a name of the Mother of the Gods, illustrating the life-giving image of the Goddess in the natural association of water with fecundity.

When Dana is identified as De Ana, or Divine Mother, it is customary to refer to her as the mother of the gods of Ireland, a creative or generative role characteristic of the enlivening vision of the Goddess. In the shadow of the name Ana, however, is another ancient Irish word, *ana*, meaning "attack" and "injury," both material and mental. This shadow word reflects the death-dealing, chastising vision of the Goddess as the immensity of Being itself, or the relentless cosmos, beyond the power of civilization to control.

The imagery of the Goddess's twilight nature as both enlivening and mortifying thus has its roots in remote prehistory. As the correspondence of Celtic and Hindu traditions suggests, such conceptions of the Goddess seem to have existed among the ancestors of the so-called Indo-Europeans before they had spread into either India or Europe. From this perspective, there is no reason to believe that Goddess worship was essentially adopted by the Indo-Aryans from indigenous tribal peoples in India.

As if in obedience to the goddess Rri in the sense of movement, her followers the Aryans were originally migratory peoples. Their countless subdivisions and far-flung migrations would have been sufficient to carry their versions of Goddess worship over vast areas; moreover, it was also their habit to adopt and absorb local deities wherever they went. When all is said and done, however, the extent of Goddess worship in ancient times around the globe need not be sought in historical connections, many though these be, but may be sufficiently explained by its natural basis in the realities of motherhood, beginning with fertility and nurture.

Devi

The name Devi is one of the most popular ways of calling to the Goddess or referring to the Goddess. The name means "The Divine in the Feminine Aspect," usually simply translated as "Goddess." The vastness of the scope of the name Devi for the Goddess may be a reason for its popularity.

The root of Devi is div, "sky," "heaven," which is also directly related to the English word *divine*. The root *div* also means "shine," "be bright," and the word *diva* means not only "heaven" or "sky" but also "day." This is reminiscent of the supremacy of the goddess Amaterasu Omikami in Japanese mythology. The name Amaterasu Omikami means "Sacred Goddess Illuminating the Sky," and she is identified as the sun, or the Sun

Goddess. In the same way the Goddess is also associated with sky, heaven, and light by the Sanskrit name Devi.

Closer examination of the root div reveals further dimensions of its vision of the divine. The root has meanings of casting dice, of playing or sporting, of trifling with someone or something. It also has meanings of spreading, increasing, and having free scope. There are also meanings of praising and rejoicing, of drunkenness and madness, and of sleeping and wishing. These meanings all convey some vision of the personality or presence of Devi in the minds of Goddess devotees.

From the perspective of the idea that there may be infinite possibilities, the way things happen to be is as but one of countless possibilities; in this respect life, or fate, resembles a game of chance, played out on a cosmic scale. From the perspective of enthusiasm and enjoyment, life has also been envisioned as a divine dance, or an epic adventure. From the perspective of disappointment and disaster, the power that rules the universe may seem to be toying with human feelings. This set of concepts contains both enlivening and chastening features of Goddess vision, illustrating the potency of the name Devi for prayer and meditation.

The root meanings of spreading, increasing, and having free scope externally belong to the enlivening, boon-granting aspect of the Goddess, while internally reserving her chastening, overpowering aspect. "Spread," "increase," and "freedom" all relate to the giving of life, the nurturing of life, and the full evolution of living potential. These meanings all emerge from the sense of the Goddess's boons to humanity and the natural world.

In the shadow of this "sense of spring" is the power of unlimited growth of the Goddess herself when she overwhelms the world and "swallows" the universe in demonstrating the impermanence of all things. This chastening aspect of the Goddess is manifest not only in disaster, disease, death, and the ultimate end of the world, but also in the consciousness of the devotee, who is thereby delivered from the snares of presumption and complacency, which lead away from the favor of the Goddess to bitterness and pain.

The meanings of praising and rejoicing latent in the root of the name Devi contain directions for worship and knowledge of the Goddess. "Praising" stands for the practice of remembering the attributes of the Goddess in order to train the mind to perceive the world in terms of divine will and action. "Rejoicing" stands for the consummation of the practice of praise, the recognition and acceptance of divine will and action, by which the devotee is infused with peace of mind. The underlying psychological nonresistance, or resignation, is considered the grace given by the Goddess. This "grace" energizes and empowers the devotee as a result of the relaxation of ingrained mental and physical inhibitions.

"Drunkenness" and "madness," also latent meanings of the root div of the name Devi, suggest further stages of psychological or spiritual development. Drunkenness is used in many traditions to symbolize the alteration of consciousness by meditative concentration, particularly in respect to taking the mind off external things and becoming rapt in inner bliss. Madness is a step beyond drunkenness, although the two are often closely related.

As in its mundane counterpart, metaphorical madness may be considered a kind of permanent derangement, often resulting from habitual drunkenness. In spiritual traditions, madness traditionally symbolizes consciousness gone beyond the limitations of conventional cognition and thought. The vision of liberated consciousness is incomprehensible to the conceptions of conventional thought, so it is called "madness" by those who repudiate it as well as those who espouse it.

In the context of Devi devotion, drunkenness and madness can refer to the states attained by the devotee through the intensity of devotion; but they can also refer to the wildness of specific visions of Devi in her terrifying, reason-defying aspect, when the world is in a state of chaos.

The last latent meanings of the root div of Devi, "sleeping" and "wishing," are also powerfully evocative of the vision of the divine in Indian Goddess religion. The conception of the universe or the world as we know it as being dreamlike, phantasmic, or illusory is common to both Hindu and Buddhist Goddess religions. These metaphysical qualities are aptly summarized in the images of sleeping and wishing, as are the devotional practices of entering trances and entreating the goddess Devi for boons of power, wish-fulfillment, happiness, or knowledge.

Maya

In Hindu tradition, Maya is one name for the Parashakti or Supreme Power. In ancient Sanskrit, the name Maya means "supernatural power," "wisdom," and "illusion." This last meaning highlights the metaphysical idea that the world as we know it is not an objective reality but a subjective illusion projected by our minds. This concept of reality is that subjective illusion entertains the notion, or feeling, that the description of the world we have learned through the process of socialization is identical to the real world itself. As we see reality through our illusions, in this sense, the Goddess as Supreme Power, or as the universe itself, is called Illusion, because for us illusion is our reality. Thus, as illusion personified, Maya is also called Durga, which means "Inaccessible," indicating the inaccessibility of the ultimate objective reality to the limited subjective intellect.

Maya also means "sorcery" and "magic." Both associations are related to the concepts of illusion and unreality, their nuances conveying the two main aspects of Goddess vision. Sorcery illustrates (in concrete practices) or symbolizes (in literary representation) the destructive or deadly power of illusion. Magic illustrates or symbolizes the constructive or creative power of illusion. Sorcery generally stands for intervention in the natural order seeking the destruction of others or power over others, while magic generally stands for creativity and wonder, for gifts, boons, and artistry. Symbolism is rarely fixed with absolute rigidity in Indian mythology, but in any case it might fairly be said that constructive imagination is perhaps the most vital element of Goddess religion practices.

The Goddess as Highest Power is also called Ma-Maya, or Mother Maya—Mother Illusion, or Mother Magic. In this sense she is also called Karani, or Creatrix, and even Omkari, Maker of Om, signifying the Goddess as the progenetrix of the divine trinity of Brahma, Vishnu, and Shiva. In her creative role she is also called Kriyashakti, or Power of Action. As the Highest Power envisioned as mother of the universe, the Goddess is also called Parabindu, or Supreme Seed.

The Goddess also has both terrifying and transcendental aspects as Highest Power. In her essential terrifying aspect, she is called Adi Bhairavi, or Primal Horror, often personifying death. The transcendental aspect of the Goddess, in which she is called Agocari, or Inaccessible, or Antari, Ultimate, may be considered a type of terrifying manifestation inasmuch as she transcends all conception. The transcendental aspect of the Goddess may also be considered a benign manifestation from the point of view of spiritual detachment from the world. In this case the Goddess is also called Jnanashakti, or Power of Knowledge, and Paravidya, or Supreme Knowledge. Thus the goddess Maya represents metaphysical motherhood, creating the sensation and perception of the world, and spiritual motherhood, leading the consciousness of the devotee beyond the boundaries of creation.

Goddess of Arts

While Hindu visions of the Goddess often relate directly to elemental nature, they concern culture as well. Civilization and the cultivation of the arts are associated with the goddess Sarasvati, She Who Has Many Pools. Sarasvati is an archetypal river goddess, like Dana of the Celts; the river symbolizes not only material fertility but also cultural fertility, with many streams of knowledge converging into a river of civilization. Sarasvati is the goddess of speech, eloquence, learning, and wisdom.

This vision of the Goddess also resembles the Celtic idea of Dana as De Ana, Mother of Gods, progenetrix of the magical Tuatha De Danann, or People of Divine Arts, Celtic deities of culture who included goddesses of poetry, medicine, and craft. These resemblances are not borrowings, of course, or coincidences, but remains of a common ancestry in remote antiquity.

The development of arts and sciences in ancient India is impressive even by modern standards, and much remains to be discovered of the Indian cultures of high antiquity. In terms of speech and culture in the context of Goddess religion, there is a great deal of Goddess-related literature in several classical and vernacular Indian languages as well as an enormous amount of concrete and abstract visual art to go with that literature. There are also daunting arrays of traditional skills associated with both orthodox and extraconventional feminine culture.

Sixty-four arts are listed in the *Kama-sutra*, India's most famous classic on the arts of love and romance, but other sources mention even more. The arts mentioned in the *Kama-sutra* include music, both vocal and instrumental; dance; drawing and stencil making; flower arranging and garland making; interior decoration; body decoration; perfuming; physical culture; manicure; massage and care of the body and hair; preparation of food and drink; sewing, weaving, and lacemaking; knowledge of gems and metals; woodwork and carpentry; machine making; basket weaving; arboriculture; animal husbandry; training pet birds to talk; and book-binding. Intellectual and literary arts include riddles and conundrums; replying to questions by classical quotations; completing quotations; storytelling; versification and meter; punning; foreign languages; regional languages and dialects; knowledge of Sanskrit equivalents of vernacular terms; and memory development. These are all part of the art of social intercourse, and the art of formal good manners is naturally included. The list goes on to encompass knowledge of games, both for amusement and profit, from children's games and toys to chess, dice playing, and even the art of cheating. The great game of political and military strategy is also on the list, as the art of worldly success. The uses of magic, drugs, spells, hypnosis, and this sort of thing are also among those of the sixty-four arts that could be used for entertainment or for vengeance or warfare.

The sixty-four arts are not all intended for everyone. It is said that half of them are suitable for the aims of conventional society, while half of them have a negative influence on character. All sixty-four, however, can serve the aims of courtesans, who are also human beings and have been cast in their role by forces greater than themselves. Because prostitution normally resulted from warfare, destruction, impoverishment, marginalization, and oppression, a prostitute's use of such skills as cheating, drugging, and mesmerizing, which would be considered immoral in conventional society, would be in a sense normal for someone outcasted by convention yet in a forced symbiotic interdependence with the same society that places her on the outer margin.

Women of orthodox Indian society were traditionally barred from learning the Vedas, the essential scriptures of Hinduism, and from administering the Vedic religion. That clearly does not mean that orthodox Indian women were uneducated or unskilled, but it does mean that women of professions or classes normally outcasted by the mainstream of Brahminic society would logically have no resistance to developing alternative cultural traditions and would be not entirely averse to artfully exploiting the people who systematically exploited them.

In this sense we may see a sociological and psychological element of the inner logic underlying the superficially paradoxical connection between the peaceful, benevolent goddess of arts and the terrifying, warlike goddess of dissolution. Thus it may not seem so strange, from the point of view of the whole spectrum of the sixty-four arts, that Matangi, the outcaste Goddess of the Dregs, is propitiated for poetic talent and divinatory knowledge as well as for victory over enemies and protection from kings and ghouls.

Goddess of Love

Visions of the goddess as the wife of the god and the progenetrix of the universe naturally evoke, in the human mind, sexual connotations and sexual imagery. Numerous examples of goddess names and epithets testify to this particular association in Goddess religions. It would not be true to say this is universal in all Indian Goddess religions, but the prominence of sexuality or sexual symbolism in certain aspects of Goddess religion is undeniable. In this context, what is particularly important to bear in mind is that the Goddess represents sexuality itself and not only female sexuality alone. The Goddess is not only in the *yoni*, or female sex, but also in the *lingam*, or male sex; and also in the intimate intercourse, or the union, of the female and the male. She is in eros, in desire, in emotion, and in enchantment.

Just as the Goddess represents both creation and destruction as two aspects of one reality, the Goddess also illustrates both creative and destructive potentials of sexuality. Thus, while both worldly and transcendental benefits are sought from the goddess of love, it is also accepted that dissolution and madness may ensue in the obsessive. This ambivalence may have served to instill a sense of respect for the power of sexuality that encompassed both emotional wonder and rational awe.

Although sexuality is in some sense a universal human experience, there are distinct cultural and historical differences in the understanding of sexuality. It is useful to bear this in mind when contemplating Indian Goddess religion, in order to avoid misconstruing its manifestations by projecting the values of one society onto that of another when interpreting cultural phenomena.

This problem often comes to the fore with particular poignancy in the context of sacred sexuality in Goddess religion. The gap between Christian antisexuality and Hindu eroticism may be one source of confusion when viewing Indian Goddess worship from a Western point of view. Certain aspects of Goddess religion may also be opaque from the perspective of the contemporary Western fashion of viewing interpersonal relations between members of the opposite sex in essentially political terms.

A prime example of the interference of a cultural gap in understanding Goddess religion may be seen in the interpretation of the popular icon of the goddess Kali sitting atop the god Shiva with his lingam in her yoni. Some modern Western writers take this to represent what they call male fear of female sexuality; others take it to symbolize the female taking control over the male, or the female being sexually dominant.

These interpretations are not to be dismissed out of hand, for at least they may serve to illustrate certain influential contemporary Western trends of thought about sexuality and gender relations. The suggestion that fear and struggle for power are primal realities of the relationship between men and women is certainly one of such profound implications that it cannot in any case be lightly ignored, no matter whether it is essentially true or false. In order to put this view into a larger context, however, it is useful to look more closely at the symbol of the embrace of the goddess and the god as perceived in Indian Goddess religion.

Generally speaking, there are two types of explanation for the image of the goddess sitting on top of the god in sexual intercourse: one is metaphysical, the other physical.

The metaphysical explanation is that Kali as the goddess of love and sexuality represents Shakti, or Power—that is, the Parashakti, or Supreme Power. The Supreme Power is therefore represented above the human plane, here symbolized by the god in anthropomorphic form. The shakti or power flows from a higher plane into the earthly plane through the union of the individual soul with the universal soul, here represented by intimate intercourse. The supine passivity of the male represents the internal suspension of the compulsive activity of the human mentality in order to become receptive to the divine influence of the higher power.

This also has a physical counterpart. The *Yoni-tantra* of the Left-Hand Path says, *Shaktirupa ca sa devi viparitarata yada* ("She, the goddess, is the form of Shakti when enjoying sexual intercourse in the inverted position"). This particular posture is one of the normal means of prolonging intercourse. The specific points of pressure it produces can be employed to control the male ejaculation, and the relative freedom from muscular exertion needed when the woman sits atop the man facilitates the internal circulation of sexually aroused energy.

The prolongation of intercourse is a normal technique of sacred sex, not only because it produces enhanced energy and bliss but also because it provides a basis for the conversion of physical and mental energy and bliss into more subtle states of awareness leading to purification of consciousness.

On this level, the image of passivity on the part of the male represents the state of inner calm required by sacred sexual intimacy. According to the Yoni-tantra, speaking in the context of sacred sex, ardently impassioned intercourse is wrong. In technical terms, this is because the dissipation of energy and attention through absorption in subjective excitement has two counterproductive effects. First, by internal distraction it obstructs the subtle union of consciousnesses on the spiritual plane of intercourse. Second, it short-circuits the accumulation and refinement of sexual vitality.

Expressed in terms of the religious practice of sacred sex as a mode of Goddess worship, to be carried away by subjective experience of ordinary excitement breaks the devotee's religious absorption in loving visualization and contemplation of the divine being in the woman with whom he is physically united in the most intimate way.

From the point of view of sacred sex, therefore, there is no reason to suppose that the position of the goddess atop her consort represents male fear of female sexuality. It may be employed as a method of cooperative mastery of combined sexual energy, but it is misleading to read the posture as female control of male sexuality, either in the practice of sacred sex in Indian Goddess religion or in the context of secular sexual mores in traditional Indian society.

In the context of the broad spectrum of sexual habits and mores in India described in the native classic Kama-sutra, there appears to be no reason to believe it was frightening or threatening or displeasing to a man to penetrate a woman with her sitting on top of him. The Kama-sutra describes far more aggressive behavior on the part of women, but even that is considered a type of play. To project a conflict-oriented interpretation on the posture of the active woman being penetrated by the supine man beneath her in Goddess iconography is, historically speaking, culturally inappropriate and sexually insensitive. The conflictive model of sexual relations may illustrate concern of conventional Western societies in modern times, but to project it on Indian Goddess religion obscures the nature and practice of traditional woman-worship and spiritualization of sexuality.

There is a parallel discrepancy between interpretations of other basic themes of Goddess mythology. One is the theme of the goddess being called in to subdue unruly demons the gods could not overcome; another is the theme of the goddess objecting to the god's habit of frequenting cremation grounds. Western interpreters see images of male impotence and marital discord in these myths, perhaps not without reason. The original religious context, however, suggests that the former image is essentially that of the female as the preeminent matrix of life, while the latter image is primarily a pragmatic warning about the sterility of attachment to asceticism.

Both of these visions, in which the matrix of life faces the depot of death, represent the triumph of the life-giving force over the death-dealing force. This is the primal vitality whose victory is repeated until the end of time, without which the universe itself collapses into nothingness. So in this sense, far from celebrating contest and conflict between male and female, these beautiful myths of the reviving and rejuvenating power of the savioress and seductress goddess are essentially affirmations of life.

Goddess of Enlightenment

Just as Goddess worship envisions a goddess in three forms—the gross, the subtle, and the ultimate—the aims of Goddess worship include corresponding material, magical, and spiritual levels of experience. Material aims might range from health, wealth, and security to secular authority, influence, and power over others. Magical powers sought through Goddess worship, though seemingly higher and more subtle, may also be directed to material aims such as these. The transcendental knowledge sought by those who worship the Goddess as ultimate is of a different order from material and magical knowledge, yet this higher knowledge subsumes all lower knowledge in its own way. For some people, therefore, spiritual knowledge is their prime concern in their approach to Goddess worship.

Among the most ancient of feminine Indian divinity figures is the goddess named Aditi. Also called mother of gods, Aditi's name is highly illustrative of *moksha*, or spiritual liberation: it means "unbound," "free," "infinite," "whole," "happy." Aditi depicts the ultimate felicity, connoting security, safety, immensity, inexhaustible abundance, and perfection.

In the masculine gender, the word *aditi* can mean "the devourer," used in specific reference to death. This contrast with the positive meanings of the feminine Aditi is, of course, fully consistent with the normal life-death polar imagery of Indian religion, seen in the names and epithets of every goddess vision.

Kali, whose dual nature in common Goddess worship has already been seen, often represents the highest reality in Tantric Goddess religion, going beyond the polarity of life and death. Accordingly, one tantra says that Kali is free from attributes, genderless, sinless, and imperishable. She is also identified with *sacchidananda*, or Being-Awareness-Bliss, the ultimate human realization of the divine. In the *Mahanirvana-tantra*, Kali is a common epithet for the primordial shakti or universal power.

Thus, in the iconography of the goddess of enlightenment, Kali's sword stands for knowledge, which cuts off ignorance and false consciousness, represented by the severed heads she wears or strews about. When Kali is depicted holding a bleeding head, this is also interpreted as the flowing out of passionate qualities, ultimately resulting in purification. She is portrayed with a lolling red tongue and white fangs, representing passionate qualities being overcome by spiritual qualities. Her skin color is black, symbolizing the formless, attributeless ultimate reality.

As a representation of ultimate reality or an image of the process of spiritual enlightenment, the Hindu Goddess as Aditi the Infinite or as Kali the Black One or Kali Mother Time comes closest to rapprochement with Buddhist metaphysics. Buddhism is commonly thought of as a derivative of Hinduism, but in the realm of Hindu Goddess worship, it would appear that Buddhism contributed significantly to the later development of Hinduism.

2

Tantric Goddess Worship

THE INFLUENCE of Buddhism on Hinduism appears on the higher abstract levels of spiritual or metaphysical intuitions and insights, as well as in the context of the secretive Left-Hand Tantra. Knowledge of the Left-Hand Tantra is explicitly attributed to the Hindu deity Vishnu, protector of the world, in the incarnate guise of Buddha.

Generally speaking, Tantric worship uses material substances, physical objects, sensory and perceptual impacts, and mental imagery and association—things such as geometrical figures, gestures, words, and sounds, combined with visualizations, meditations, and contemplations—to generate mental spaces inhabited by Goddess consciousness. These practices are found fragmented or isolated here and there in fine arts, song and dance, drama, ritual, and self-calming techniques. The individual elements may be regarded as interesting or valuable cultural artifacts in themselves, but their comprehensive use in the structuring of sacred sensory and perceptual spaces in Goddess worship depends on their coherent coordination.

Tantric worship is ordinarily divided into several categories, including those conventionally called Right Hand and Left Hand. The main difference between these two forms of worship is that the Left-Hand rites include meat, fish, wine, grain, and sexual intercourse. The Left-Hand Tantra has long been derided and condemned by orthodox Brahminists and devotees of the Right-Hand Tantra, but it is said to be very secret, and there is always the possibility that cults known well enough to be censured were actually not, or no longer, authentic Left-Hand Tantrics. There is also the possibility that the most vocal opponents of the Left-Hand rites were themselves practitioners in private, hiding behind a public posture of condemnation.

According to the legend of the origin of Left-Hand Tantra in Indian Hinduism, once the sage Vasishtha, whose name means "Master of Every Material Object," spent "ten thousand years" practicing austerities in devotion to the goddess Tara. After all that time and effort, however, the sage obtained no results; so he asked Brahma, the creator god, for a mantra, or magical spell, to help him in his quest.

Thus importuned by the sage, Brahma extolled Tara, saying that she represents the essential power through which Brahma creates, Vishnu protects, and Shiva destroys the world. Tara is the source of all light, effused Brahma, and the revelatrix of the Vedas, or "orthodox" bodies of Brahminic Hindu lore.

Brahma then gave Tara's mantra, her mnemonic invocation, to the sage Vasishtha to help him propitiate the goddess. With this Vasishtha went to a Goddess shrine to evoke Tara with the mantra.

After a thousand years of devotion to the mantra, Vasishtha still obtained no results. He began to get angry, whereupon the earth trembled and the gods became anxious. Finally Tara appeared to him and explained that his rites had not worked because he did not understand her and did not know how to worship her, because her manifestation as China Tara cannot be fostered through yoga and ascetic practices.

Tara told Vasishtha that knowledge of her way of worship was known only to Vishnu in the form of Buddha, adding that he could learn this only in China.

Vasishtha then went to Tibet, which is on the way from India to China. There he had a vision of Buddha surrounded by beautiful girls, all drinking wine and cavorting.

They invited Vasishtha to join, but he refused. At that moment, however, a "voice from the sky" told him that this was the best way to worship Tara for immediate success.

Vasishtha thus took refuge in Vishnu-Buddha and asked for instruction. Vishnu-Buddha told him that this is a secret path, including unconventional things. By this path, said Vishnu-Buddha, one can live among the things of the world, good and bad, yet transcend them while in their very midst.

Vishnu-Buddha added that this worship is mental, not physical, in the sense that ordinary rituals are not needed and conventional restrictions are not imposed. There are no special times or places for worship. What one should do at all times, said Vishnu-Buddha, is cultivate a friendly attitude toward women, and actively venerate and adore them.

The legendary connection between Left-Hand Tantrism and China is of particular interest because sacred sex as a religious ritual was indeed practiced in Chinese Taoist communities centuries before the emergence of Tantra in India and Tibet. It would appear that Tantric culture was emerging in Bengal and India shortly before or around the same time as the founding of the nation of Tibet.

India and Bengal powerfully influenced nascent Tibetan Buddhist culture, and some forms of Tantrism evidently shared certain affinities with native Tibetan Bon religion. Bon may also have, like Indian Tantrism, received some Taoist influence from ancient China, with which proto-Tibetan tribes were in contact for many centuries before the foundation of the modern Tibetan nation. Under these conditions, it is natural that early Tibetan Buddhist civilization would be thoroughly infused with Tantrism.

There is no universally accepted opinion as to whether Tantra originated within Hindu or Buddhist traditions, but there were surely connections between the Hindu and Buddhist Tantric movements. The understanding and aim of Tantric practices in Hindu and Buddhist contexts may differ, but so do the appreciation and application of Tantric rites within the broad spectrum of Hindu beliefs. As in other aspects of Goddess religion, it is essentially in the higher ranges of metaphysical perception and spiritual experience that Tantric forms of Hinduism and Buddhism are most alike.

For the moment taking the legend of Vasishtha and Vishnu-Buddha at face value as a representation of the teaching, several observations may be made.

An important point that stands out in the story is the assertion that the Left-Hand rite, involving inebriation and sexual intercourse, is purely mental. It is well known that there are both Hindu and Buddhist Tantrics who take this literally and perform only what is known as interior practice. In this context, sexual intercourse is understood to refer to the kundalini or vital energy rising up the spine to penetrate into the brain chakra, the highest nerve center, or in visionary terms the psychospiritual center visualized in the head. This produces an ecstatic experience that might be described as a brain orgasm, followed by a sweet relaxation figuratively called the elixir of immortality.

Those Tantric devotees of so-called external practice actually used intoxicants and ritual intercourse with specially selected females. Nevertheless, it could conceivably be said that this form of religious practice is also purely mental, in the sense that the mental aspect of the rite is absolutely essential. In the case of exterior practice too, as with interior practice, the practitioner aims to arouse kundalini and induce it to rise up the spine into the brain. As the kundalini passes through several chakra nerve centers along the spine, it produces a variety of sensations before finally culminating in the brain orgasm.

From a modern point of view, this manner of experiencing sexual intercourse, whether symbolic or literal, may be described in terms of two effects.

First, the muscular contractions appropriate to the imagery and feeling of culling sexual energy and drawing it up the spine are precisely those that serve to control the male orgasm and promote the female (vaginal) orgasm. This has the effect of prolonged pleasure for both partners, enabling the couple to extend the ordinary joy of sexual union to a total spiritual communion in mutual ecstasy.

Second, the sensations created by the feeling and imagery of energy passing up through the spine enliven the sensuality of the whole body. The sensitivity of ordinary erogenous zones thereby becomes more subtle and refined, while the feeling in other areas is also heightened and transformed, so that the whole body becomes an erogenous zone. This experience also increases control of the male orgasm—since the erotic feeling is not concentrated in the sexual organ alone—while enhancing the female orgasm, connecting the whole body with the combined sensation of clitoral climax and vaginal convulsion.

Another essential point made in the story of the original dissemination of Tantra by Vishnu-Buddha is that the goal of the secret practice is to be able to transcend the world while in its very midst. In Hindu terms, this is the Tantric goal of *jivanmukti*—living liberation, or liberation while still alive.

There may be two ways of viewing this quest in the context of sexual spiritual practice. One is the idea that Left-Hand Tantrics were attempting to experience the most intensely captivating of earthly pleasures while maintaining a mood of serene devotional contemplation of divine realities. The theory underlying this view is that if the practitioners could transcend passion at its very peak, then ordinary temptations and seductions of the world would lose hold of their minds.

Another way of interpreting sexual yoga in search of living liberation is through the equation of *mahasukha*, or great bliss, with nirvana, or extinction. The theory underlying this idea, a Buddhist view shared with higher Hinduism, including higher Tantra, is that the great bliss effaces random thoughts from the mind, opening a window of opportunity for higher perception. The great bliss is equated with nirvana insofar as nirvana in the sense of extinction implies cessation of random thought, which is used as a tool to sever worldly bondage.

In the context of Hinduism, these views of sexual spiritual practice may be illustrated in terms of a traditional outline of seven modes of *sadhana*, or spiritual practice. In ascending order of sophistication, these seven modes are called the Vedic, Vishnu-oriented, Shiva-oriented, Right-Hand, Left-Hand, Complete, and Kaula or Family Paths. Some people spend their whole lives fulfilling one mode of practice, while others may progress from one to another as successive stages.

The first type of practice involves the routine performance of Vedic ritual. The second requires the abandonment of blind faith and the acquisition of conscious faith in salvation through Brahman, expressed in devotion to Vishnu, the preserving or maintaining aspect of divinity.

The third mode of practice represents entry into the way of knowledge, employing devotion and faith to seek power (*shakti*). Shiva stands for both destructive and creative forces of divinity; the mating of Shiva and Shakti is the source of the universe and the primary model of completeness.

The fourth mode of practice, the Right-Hand Path, involves meditation on three powers of Brahman, the creative aspect of divinity: action, will, and knowledge. The practitioners in this stage of development try to attune the self to devotion to these three divine powers, personified as Brahma, Vishnu, and Maheshvara ("Great God").

The fifth mode of practice, the Left-Hand Path, is described as going from activity (*pravritti*) to cessation of desire (*nivritti*), thereby severing the bonds of animal existence. This would confirm the Vishnu-Buddha teaching that the secret sexual rites of China Tara are for transcending the world.

The Left-Hand ritual makes reference to the Five M's—*madya, matsya, mamsa, mudra,* and *maithuna,* or wine, fish, meat, grain, and sexual intercourse, respectively. Esoteric interpretations of these have already been mentioned; here the focus is on literal actualities. The Five M's are also called the Five Realities.

The two kinds of Left-Hand practice are the *madhyama,* or middling, and the *uttama,* or supreme. The middling kind uses all five realities in its rites, while the supreme kind uses only *madya, mudra,* and *maithuna.* The word *mudra* has different interpretations in this context; it is often taken to mean a kind of parched grain, but some also take it to refer to ritual gestures, as in other ceremonial contexts. Both readings may apply, as the *uttama* or supreme form of the Left-Hand rite may suggest in the mutual support of the three ceremonial elements. It is true that certain acts of *maithuna* or sacred sex are ritualized in such a way as to heighten the pleasure of the woman and the self-control of the man. It is also true that taking parched grain with wine helps to regulate the absorption of alcohol into the system, and traditional Tantric texts say that the practitioners should not lose self-mastery to wine, just as they should not lose self-mastery to sexual ecstasy. Thus *mudra* may have both meanings of grain and gesture, as supports to the other ceremonial elements *madya* and *maithuna,* wine and lovemaking.

It has been suggested that *mudra* may have been a parched grain possibly containing some sort of drug, but this may be an unnecessary interpolation. The *Yoni-tantra* frankly mentions the used of the drug *vijaya,* which is a feminine form of the word for "victory" or "triumph." In Hindu mythology, Vijaya is the name of a friend of the goddess Durga, the Inaccessible One. In pharmocology, *vijaya* is *cannabis Indica,* a variety of marijuana. The resin of the female *vijaya* flower, like the moisture of a sexually aroused woman's yoni, was sometimes used, according to Tantric literature, for attaining a trance to facilitate meditation on the Goddess. This intoxicating resin could be dissolved in wine, whereby its effects could be controlled more precisely than if it were eaten in grain, the action of the drug being more immediately noticeable and the dosage more easily measured.

The sixth mode of practice, the Complete Path, represents the completion of shivahood, or human communion with the divine. This area of experimentation gave rise to many exercises in abstraction and introspection.

The name of the seventh mode, the Kaula or Family Path, has a special meaning in this context, generally referring to the Shaktas, or divine power-oriented mystics of the Left-Hand Path. Here Kaula practice means the attainment of living liberation and realization of the supreme soul through pure knowledge of the divine.

This system of classification shows how sacred sexuality was placed in a context of total spiritual development. The secret rites were embarked upon, in this scheme, only after the attainment of self-mastery and purification of the mind and senses through devotional and contemplative exercises. The effects of the rites on the psyche, in turn, were employed in the service of the intensive elevation of consciousness and ultimate liberation.

While it is true that specific variations of Tantric Hindu sexual rites offer promises of magical powers and worldly success of all kinds, and thus do not necessarily focus overtly on spiritual knowledge or enlightenment, it may also happen that the more extravagant promises of the rites were expedient means of inducing people to experience their instincts in ways that might conduct them unawares to higher knowledge of their own desires. This higher perspective might enable people to fulfill their desires by helping them to focus on useful objectives and obtain lucid perceptions of practical means to their ends.

Seemingly hyperbolic promises may have been more than an appeal to primitive superstition or material incapacity. They may have been a deliberately contrived way of counteracting natural human sluggishness and indolence by means of natural human desire and greed; or they may have been a way of using concrete interests to focus the mind on otherwise ungraspable abstract quests. This would be one example of the Tantric technique of "using a thorn to extract a thorn," as it is said in Buddhist Tantrism.

In actuality, the existing texts of Hindu Tantrism display such a wide range of precept and practice that generalizations are always conditional, exceptions seeming to appear to every rule. These differences evidently stem from the individual origin of each tantra in the teachings of an adept, a lineage, or a cult. There being no central authority or hereditary archpriesthood of Tantrism, it is natural that Tantric literature should display considerable individualism and diversity. The popular pursuit of mystical power and knowledge, nevertheless, probably resulted in the interaction and blending of variant formulas. For this reason different tantras may resemble each other, while one and the same tantra may contain disparate and even discordant elements within itself.

Examples of different interpretations of the elements of Left-Hand Tantric ritual have already been noted. There are also differences in the rules and routines of the rites. Within the framework of the literal interpretation of *maithuna* or sacred sexual union, there are considerable differences in understanding of the protocols of partnership.

One of the types of rules of the Tantric *yoni-puja* or worship of the feminine sex concerns the categories of women suitable for partnership in this rite. A well-known definition is the *nava-kanya* or Nine Girls. The often nonliteral nature of Tantric terminology is evident even in this simple term, where the word *kanya*, which normally means "girl" or an unmarried young woman, actually may refer to a mature woman or even a married woman. Depending on the source, the acceptable age range of the girls is between twelve and sixty or between thirteen and twenty-five.

The Nine Girls are called the dancer/actress, the skull wearer, the accessible woman, the washerwoman, the shaver or hairdresser, the Brahmin girl, the Shudra girl, the cowherd girl, and the garland maker's daughter. These seem to have both literal and figurative meanings.

Several of the girls are represented as members of lower classes, such as the washerwoman, the hairdresser, and the Shudra girl. The Shudras were the fourth caste, the servile class, systematically excluded from the rites of the orthodox Vedic religion of India. In Tantric rites, Shudras were not only allowed to participate, they could even become gurus.

The garland makers or florists of the type named in the list of Nine Girls were also of low estate in terms of Vedic society. They are formally called a mixed caste, but this term was often given to aboriginal tribes of the mountains or forests by Vedic scholars intending to incorporate them into the fringe of the dominant social order. It is thought by many observers that Goddess religion and Tantra may have roots in such ancient aboriginal cultures, many of which were matriarchal, matrilineal, or matrilocal.

Two of the Girls, the dancer-actress and the accessible woman, are categorized as prostitutes by orthodox conventions. A dancer-actress may only have been an artist, but the accessible woman is called a prostitute in non-Tantric usage. In Tantric terms, "accessible woman" is a technical expression denoting suitability for the rite; there are several subdivisions of accessible women, but none of them are prostitutes. It ought to be remembered, nonetheless, that in Indian terms prostitution does not necessarily imply promiscuity.

The type of girl known as the skull wearer refers to a member of a cult of naked or rag-clad ascetics known for such extreme practices as frequenting cemeteries, wearing garlands of human bones, carrying blood-stained human heads, and drinking wine from skulls. They used to eat leftovers of dog food and ashes, and were also reputed to eat human flesh. In spite of their asceticism, these cultists did not believe in seeking a liberation in which there was no pleasure; they concentrated their meditation on the idea of the supreme power resident in the female generative organ, and the men and women of the cult practiced free sexual relations with each other.

Some of the Nine Girls are also defined more figuratively in some sources. For example, the dancer-actress is defined as a beautiful woman of any of the four castes who starts to dance when she beholds the ritual articles. A skull wearer is defined as a beautiful woman of any of the four castes. An accessible woman is a beautiful woman of any of the four castes who desires sexual union when she beholds the ritual articles.

The accessible woman may also be of several types. A "secret accessible woman" is one who was born in a Tantric family, is not bashful, and has a passionate relation with a husband of animal nature. A "major accessible woman" is one who becomes naked of her own accord. A "family accessible woman" is one born in a householder's family. An "accessible woman of great compassion" is one who marries a man of humane or heroic nature and willingly follows the path of detachment from desire. A "regal accessible woman" is one who is free and independent like a king. A "divine accessible woman" is one who was born to a woman impregnated in a Tantric rite.

Tantric texts differ widely on the permissibility of performing *yoni-puja*, or worship of the female sex, with another's wife. Some texts permit it, but others forbid the man from even thinking about another's wife. At least one text permits intercourse with another's wife as long as there is no emission of semen. Some texts also permit sexual intercourse with one's sister or other female relatives. Some texts inveigh against a woman performing the rite with a man other than her husband, or with multiple partners. An accessible woman who resorts to more than one practitioner is said to be of the animal type; it is said that *siddhi*, or spiritual power, will be damaged if such a woman is chosen for a Tantric rite.

It is difficult to assess the various social and psychological implications of these different precepts and practices without knowing the particular local conditions under which they were carried out. From the *Kama-sutra*, the classic treatment of sex life in old India, it is clear that there were very different sexual customs in various regions of the subcontinent, among people of different ethnic origins, and among the distinct classes and castes of Indian society. Conforming to local customs is recommended, not only in Tantric tradition, but also in the *Kama-sutra* itself.

One element of Tantric yoni worship that does seem to be universal and invariable is the requirement that the woman be willing. No coercion, persuasion, or enticement is allowed. This essential factor seems to stem from the very nature of the religious practice itself, based as it is on the worship of the Goddess in the body of a living woman.

Another rule of Tantric Goddess worship is that a mother yoni can only be worshiped without sexual intercourse. A woman who has given birth is not a partner in ritual sexual union. The reasons for this taboo may have been partly biological or energetic, and partly social and psychological. In any case, it is clear that this restriction would greatly limit the scope of adulterous relations even when esoterically permitted in this form of worship, because most women would customarily conceive and begin bearing children soon after marriage.

The age range of the Girl who is to be the Shakti, or feminine power, begins with biological womanhood, the onset of menstruation. Although twelve or thirteen seems very young by most modern standards, in ancient societies the beginning of the monthly period normally signaled readiness for marriage and motherhood. There is no practice of sexual intercourse with children in authentic Tantra, in spite of reports of such activities in the present day. The *Yoni-tantra* even says explicitly that the woman's yoni must be hairy. While the importance of the hair is partly aesthetic and symbolic, representing the triangle Goddess yantra and being an object of playful dalliance, it also naturally shows that the so-called Girls were not children.

It may be true, as has been suggested, that there are places where sexual intercourse with children is practiced under the rubric of Tantra, proposing the notion that Tantrism is by its very nature all about breaking taboos and overcoming inhibitions—a popular but questionable conception. If it is so, this would be a modern perversion, a type of forced prostitution, concocted for pedophiles of the type reported to travel for this very purpose to certain Eastern countries with desperately impoverished sectors of their populations vulnerable to exploitation.

There is not to our knowledge any evidence for sex with children in authentic Tantric rites of any stripe. It is true that little girls were dressed up as the Goddess for ritual worship, but this is part of a different rite, known as *kumari-puja* or virgin veneration. In the rites of virgin veneration, no sexual activity or erotic ideas are involved, even when the virgin is in her teens.

Another sign of the religious criterion of biological womanhood for selection as a Shakti in Tantric sexual rites is the emphasis placed on the menstrual flow. While blood of any kind is normally a taboo in orthodox Brahminic Vedic religion, for Goddess worshipers menstrual blood, fondly called the "flower" (*pushpa*) of the yoni, was a sign and symbol of the universal Shakti, the power or energy of creation. The Tantric devotee who makes love with his Shakti during her menstrual period is particularly blessed, and is promised great rewards. One who entertains any prejudice against a menstruating yoni, in contrast, is destined for hell.

As we will see later on, Taoists also had great respect for menstrual blood, associating it with generative energy. In view of this association, some Taoist hygienists were known to prize menstrual blood for medicinal or tonic purposes, although it is not openly stated whether it was their custom to drink it directly from their female assistants.

Buddhist mendicants violated the orthodox taboos about menstruation in a somewhat less dramatic manner, favoring discarded sanitary napkins for the material used in making their mendicant robes. Unlike some of the extremist cults in old India, the ancient Buddhists were not interested in shocking society at large so much as in disciplining and humbling themselves. Mendicants who left ordinary life would gather used menstrual rags, launder them, sew them into patchwork robes, and dye them a uniform saffron.

Like other regulations in Tantric sex rites, the special recommendation of the menstrual period is not absolute. Its significance is not necessarily all symbolic either, but may also have had an unstated birth-control function. The taboo on intercourse with mothers in the rites might be one obvious reason for use of some kind of birth control method. There might also have been social reasons, since the production of children as a result of ritual unions might have created problems concerning the secrecy of the cults and the effects of the rites on families and society at large.

There were probably other methods of birth control besides rhythm, and prohibitions against the termination of pregnancies would suggest that they did occur. The *Yoni-tantra* seems to allude to the use of a barrier-type device of birth control, apparently made of a leaf or leaves of a plant that is evidently, at least according to Tantric medical treatises, without other pharmacological effects. The stated existence of a category of "divine accessible woman" conceived in a Tantric ceremony, nonetheless, forces us to conclude that children were sometimes born of these rites.

Sometimes Tantric works designate special venues for ritual lovemaking in the dark of the night of the new moon. The main theme of these special venues seems to be desolation, for they include an abandoned house, a lonely roadside through a wasteland or wilderness, and a cemetery or charnel ground, a place where the bodies of the dead are burned or left to decompose. There is even a rite involving the use of a corpse as a mattress on which to make love. Sexual union in such desolate places is supposed to confer exceptional benefits.

Alien as these practices may seem to modern Westerners, they are in a way reminiscent of a semi-esoteric Western custom, the Irish wake, only recently attenuated from earlier forms nearly as outrageous to outside observers as Hindu charnel ground meditations. A real old-time Irish wake includes not only keening but also carousing. The mourners eat and drink, and also offer food and drink to the dead, even sitting the corpse up and acting out the giving of a drink. (The word *whiskey* comes from Irish *uisce beatha*, "water of life.") What is more, young men and women attending a wake may slip outside to make love in the bushes, thus affirming life, indeed celebrating life, in the very presence of death.

These more "pagan" Irish practices were condemned by the Catholic and Protestant churches as a matter of course, just as the Tantric practices of the Left Hand were condemned by the orthodox Brahmins and Right-Hand Tantrics in India. Leaving aside the condemnations for the moment, juxtaposition of these similar Irish and Indian practices themselves may shed some light on the psychological and philosophical implications of both.

In the context of Indian Tantra, it is written that death is transcended through the rite of *maithuna*, or sexual union. The old Irish practice of carousing and making love at the scene of a wake may be expressing the very same religious conception and similarly reinforcing the idea with ecstatic experience. Either rite may appear barbaric when taken out of context, as both often seem to be.

Nonetheless, seen in terms of the totality of their endeavor, even if the Tantric and pagan methodologies differ from those of Brahminism or Christianity, their fundamental idea of life triumphing over death is not necessarily different. Tantric and pagan practices may be concrete, but their philosophical basis is not opposed to the aim of any other organized religions preaching attainment of eternal life through particular rites and mores.

The concept of sexual enjoyment as a religious sacrament may not be understood or tolerated in those parts of the world dominated by Christian ideology, where sexuality has commonly been considered dirty by both its denouncers and its devotees, and women in particular have traditionally been demonized for their sexuality. It must be remembered that the phenomenon of sexual enjoyment itself differs when practiced and experienced through the perceptions of sacred and secular understandings.

Just because Tantric worshipers did not observe the same rites and mores as orthodox Brahmins, that in itself does not mean they had no morals or were bent on social ruin. The Tantric Goddess worshipers had their own codes of ethics, which, if more relaxed than Brahminic codes in some respects, were nevertheless more rigorous in certain ways than the actual practices of upper- and middle-class Hindus as reflected in the *Kama-sutra*.

The permissibility of adulterous relations within a Tantric cult is one of the reasons for which the religion is commonly condemned as a front for libertinism. The *Kama-sutra* deals with the subject of adultery at considerable length, explaining the different forms in which it commonly occurred in fourth-century India. Although it was technically illegal and not approved by the author of the *Kama-sutra*, adultery is described in this classic as a fact of life. The various adulterous circumstances and situations illustrated in the *Kama-sutra*, furthermore, are often connected with venal motives far removed from any spiritual sentiments or any special respect for women. Could it be hypothesized, from this perspective, that the sex rites of some Tantric cults may have originally been devised in part not to promote adultery but to contain it and transmute it?

Considering the subject of adultery per se in the *Kama-sutra*, it is only fair to keep in mind that this particular classic designates *gandharva* marriage—love marriage—as the best of the various modes according to which marriages customarily were formed in India. The love marriage, which we therefore know is not a modern invention, was by no means the only or the most common way in which women were married. In legal texts it is in fact disapproved for Brahmins. Women were totally subordinated to men under orthodox Hindu law, thus exposing wives in coercive types of marriages to the risk of considerable ill use. From this point of view, the possibility of sanctified sexual relationships in Tantric Goddess worship outside of coercive and abusive legal relations may have been a mercy for many women.

Other factors would have to be taken into account to fully understand the effect of adultery within the secretive rites of Left-Hand Tantra. One element would be the degree to which secrecy was actually maintained; a question that also touches on the fates of the children born of secret ceremonies. Another would be the differences in the moral orders of the participants in the rites. As mentioned earlier, the various castes and classes of old Indian society had different cultural standards, and what might have been taboo for one may have been permissible for another.

The sexual customs of aboriginal tribes, for example, including those integrated into the margin of society as the lowest untouchables, were often freer or more feminist than those of the orthodox upper-class Brahmins. There were also self-outcasted people such as the Kapalikas (or skull-bearers) and others who made themselves untouchable deliberately, openly renounced and violated typical norms of civilization, and wallowed in extremes of life and death; for them there were no taboos on ritual sex of the Left-Hand Tantra. There were also independent women, known as *svairini*, with very free attitudes toward sexuality.

The hardships of the lives of those untouchables traditionally assigned to such revolting occupations as the disposal of the dead—hardships including the constant psychological duress of being despised and shunned by the rest of society, and despair induced by the cultural preclusion of social mobility—may have produced an excess of alcoholism among them. Tantric cults may have been a place where spouses of alcoholics could experience the connubial sacrament free from danger of violence, and even a place where alcoholics themselves could learn to moderate their habits while reorienting their mentalities.

From a perusal of the *Kama-sutra*, which is something like an anthropological survey of customs of the many regions of the Indian subcontinent in the fourth century, it would appear that meat, fish, and wine, forbidden to Brahmins except as secret Tantric sacraments, were not particularly shunned by middle-class Indians. In the *Kama-sutra*'s picture of the love-making habits of householders, as part of the pleasure of their mutual enjoyment both man and wife are depicted as attending meticulously to their grooming, including adornment and perfuming, and also enjoying rich food, wine or liquor, and *bhang*, a cannabis drink with which the Tantric *vijaya* is identified.

A Tantric rite is not necessarily so far removed from this picture, the optional special venues aside, except that Tantric love play is more devotional and reverent toward the woman. From this point of view it might be theorized that some Tantric cults may have been a way for the rest of society to enjoy, in a ritually moderated and mentally disciplined manner, what the wealthy middle and martial classes were consuming as their right.

In comparison with the love play described in the *Kama-sutra*, furthermore, aimed as the classic is at marital bliss of body and mind, it would appear that Tantric love play was also more physically tender to the woman than orthodox Hindu habit. While it is only fair to say, for example, that heterosexual rough play illustrated in the *Kama-sutra* is on the whole mutual and for the most part consensual, sexual Goddess worship such as outlined in the Yoni-tantra is by definition invariably consensual and involves no roughness whatsoever on the part of either male or female celebrant.

The norms of the Kama-sutra and those of the Yoni-tantra differ considerably as regards attention to the yoni, the woman's most sacred place. This would probably be considered natural, in view of the fact that devotion to the yoni is for celebrants a form of Goddess worship. Although it does not recommend everything it notes in its survey, the Kama-sutra describes some rough treatment of the yoni on the part of both heterosexual and lesbian lovers. Furthermore, in spite of its reputation for eroticism, the Kama-sutra speaks of the practice of cunnilingus without enthusiasm, not recommending it but allowing as a man might lick a woman's vulva, crotch, and armpits in an excess of ardor. This is evidently a Brahminic taboo, something that the classic generally notes but does not insist upon in the heat of the moment. The Kama-sutra's mixture of orthodox Brahminic propriety with frank discussion of variant practices and human nature may give some clue as to how Tantra could have eventually become so popular in India.

In contrast, the Yoni-tantra speaks of many tender and affectionate and arousing devotions to the yoni: anointing the yoni with perfume, gently tugging at the hair around the yoni, a hundred and eight or a thousand "fragrant kisses" of the yoni, murmuring a myriad mantras mouth to yoni, caressing and fondling every part of the yoni, all the while visualizing goddesses dwelling in and all around the triangle of the yoni.

In spite of the controversies surrounding the allegations of taboo practices in Left-Hand Tantra, the fact remains that the rite of yoni devotion can be performed by a man in his own home with his own wife. As mentioned earlier, the precepts indirectly mitigating adulterous relations were also supplemented in some later tantras by yet more stringent regulations. Certain authors claim that Tantric rites degenerated into wild orgies; if this is true, it may have been a reason for reforms seen in later texts. There are, in any case, many warnings about venal and exploitative gurus in Tantric literature—as indeed in other mystical traditions where the guru plays an important role—and the power of sexuality to muddle minds is well known in the lore of Goddess religion, as exemplified by the madness said to be induced by the Goddess as Tripura-Sundari, Beauty of the Three Strongholds. It is for this reason that men of so-called animal nature (*pashu-bhava*) are not supposed to practice sexual union in Tantric rites; they are supposed to worship women like children adoring a goddess.

It may be precisely because of their recognition of the powerful hold of sexuality on the human mind that the Tantric sages believed in the need to uplift and transform this instinctive urge into a religious and spiritual experience. It may be, furthermore, that the physical and emotional lovemaking in the Left-Hand Tantric rite was intended in part to solidify and vivify the final part of Vishnu-Buddha's teaching on Goddess worship, namely, kindness to all women.

Numerous Tantric texts emphasize this most general precept of Goddess worship, friendliness, goodwill, and reverence for all women. Some make particular mention of the rule that a man should never shout at a woman or beat a woman, even with a flower, even when she has done something wrong. Considering the legal and social weakness of the position of women under orthodox Hindu law, this feature of Tantric Goddess religion may have been considered a threat to society by those who believed that order depended on the subjugation of the female, even if by threat or by force. Its external influence may have created some relief for women at all levels of society. If the inspirational love of a woman, whether inspired by childlike devotion or by intimate communion, was indeed thus extended to all womankind through adoration of the essence of womanhood, the positive effects on the psyche of the men involved may have been calculated by the gurus to remedy a structural flaw in society.

To think of Goddess adoration in love of women in terms of breaking taboos may induce us to question the functional meanings of the taboos and thus better understand the realities of the social order. Yet it is not really adequate to describe any constructive effects of that worship on the psychological and social habits of the people it influences, except perhaps a sense of release from overwrought inhibitions.

In modern societies both East and West where there is, sadly, unending report of sexual abuse, spousal abuse, sexual harassment, rape, and even murder of women, it may not be irrational to cultivate an ideology of friendliness and nonviolence toward all women. This is surely an aspect of the Tantric philosophy of Goddess worship that is relevant to the present day, and as such ought not be obscured by overemphasis on more exotic or sensational facets of Tantric esoterism.

There may also be a relevant message from the secret domain of Tantra, nevertheless, if it can be understood within the context of consensual sexual relations as they are practiced today. Emphasis is on the consensual nature of the act here, because that is fundamental to Tantric communion, based on respect for the woman. This stipulation is a legal norm today in reference to the use of physical force or threat such as blackmail, but the Tantric precept also precludes any kind of inveiglement or seduction, even cajolery, and thus more stringently guards the self-determination of the woman.

From this perspective, if nothing else Goddess worship may inspire a reexamination of the treatment of women in society, including social structures such as marriage and family. Goddess worship may also inspire a reexamination of sexuality in a new light, from the point of view of the spirit of communion. Are we uniting with each other or using each other? Are we apart even when together or together even when apart? Do we enter into the most intimate personal relations inspired by self-gratification or self-transcendence? How do we experience experience? Do we embrace out of love for our own sensations, or out of love for the divine image and the divine light in the beloved?

3

Goddess of Rebellion

O NE OF THE MOST POPULAR VISIONS of the Goddess, and one of
the most controversial, is as Kali. The worship of Kali has been
traditionally associated with women and people of the servile and untouchable classes, who were excluded from orthodox Vedic rites. The
powerful draw of Kali worship for the margins of society, for the disenfranchised, the degraded, and the outcaste, eventually led to characteriza-
tion of Kali as the patroness of criminality and rebellion.

Among the most loyal worshipers of Kali in premodern India were
notorious organizations of hereditary criminals. Perhaps the most despised of these were the Megh-phunnists, who used to hang parents and
steal their children for sale into slavery and prostitution. More respected
in society were the Pindaris, powerful gangs of freebooters living by
highway robbery. Another class of professional robbers devoted to Kali
were the Dacoits, who used stealth as well as force and sometimes worked
as hired assassins. Most sinister of all criminal Kali worshipers, however,
in the opinion of many writers, were the secretive Thugs, who strangled
travelers as ritual human sacrifices to Kali, robbing the corpses and dispos-
ing of the remains so expertly that their activities went undetected and
unsuspected by society at large for hundreds of years.

To understand these paradoxes of human behavior, in which violence, depredation, and destruction of life are sanctified, we need to re-

flect on the psychological implications of the Goddess's duality and the ways in which she is envisioned.

The name of the goddess Kali literally means "time." Kali also means "black." As time is a measurement of being, Kali is in this sense identified with Bhavani, the Goddess as Being. As blackness signifies absolute transcendence beyond all qualities, Kali is also identified with Durga, the Inaccessible One. The benign and terrifying aspects of Kali are thus metaphysically typified by these alternative names for the goddess.

Kali is envisioned both as the progenetrix of the elemental universe and as the elemental universe itself. The congealing of the elements produces the universe; the dissolution of the elements destroys the universe. Time is movement; movement enlivens. Time is also transitoriness; transitoriness kills. The vision of lives as waves of the course of time flowing to annihilation may have spawned the predilection for seeing Kali in her terrifying, overwhelming aspect. This predilection, in turn, may have spawned the habit of religiously propitiating or placating her by sacrifice, of animals and even humans.

As the Absolute transcending time and transitoriness, Kali is the One Who Devours Time. In this aspect she is sought for highest knowledge, often through the most fearsome ordeals. Sometimes, it seems, devotees of the lower orders of Kali worshipers following a criminal path would undergo a change of heart and take to the path of spiritual knowledge. In a well-documented example, an experienced Thug once became so disturbed at the sight of a promising young candidate losing his mind during the initiation process that he himself abandoned Thuggee and entered a temple to become a renunciant.

The Ten Mahavidyas

Kali sometimes figures as one of the Ten Mahavidyas, which means Ten Great Knowledges, or Ten Great Mantras, represented as goddesses. Kali is often depicted as the chief goddess of the whole group; she is also envisioned as the Matrix, Mother, or Maker of the Mahavidyas.

Like representations of the Mother Goddess in general, and like Kali in particular, each of these Ten Mahavidyas has both benign and terrifying aspects. Nevertheless, for devotional purposes certain of these ten goddesses or Goddess emanations are typically associated more with one aspect than another.

Adividya

Kali as the first of the Mahavidyas is called the Adividya, or Primordial Vidya. The other nine Mahavidyas can thus in some sense be viewed as emanations of Kali, or as different aspects or manifestations of Kali. The many suggestive compound names for Kali dramatically reflect the chiaroscuro of human hopes and fears: Great Kali, Kali of the Cremation Ground, Secret Kali, Good Kali, Mendicant Widow Kali, Sorceress Kali, and Kali of the Art of Love.

Great Kali might be worshiped for knowledge, Good Kali for boons, healing, and protection. Kali of the Cremation Ground might be propitiated by seekers of power and success in horrifying rites using corpses. Secret Kali and Sorceress Kali might be worshiped for occult powers, magical attainments, and enchantment. Mendicant Widow Kali might be propitiated for transcendence of the world, or for paralysis of enemies. Kali of the Art of Love might be worshiped by the lovelorn, by jealous or insecure husbands or wives, or by courtesans and prostitutes, for attracting and captivating the object of their desires.

Tara

The second Mahavidya of Great Knowledge, or major manifestation of the goddess Kali, is called Tara, the Savioress. The vision of Tara is thought to have been imported into Hinduism from Buddhism, where she plays a major role in esoteric Tantrism. In the Hindu mythology of Tara, she is instrumental in the importation of Left-Hand Tantra, then known only to the god Vishnu in the form of Buddha, from China into India. Historically speaking, Chinese Taoists were in fact practicing rites like the Hindu and Buddhist Left-Hand Tantra several centuries before the rise of Tantra in India, Kashmir, and Bengal; this Hindu myth thus may have some historical truth to it.

In Hinduism, Tara is said to have as many as twenty-one forms. Twenty-one is the total number of aspects of *shunyata* or "emptiness" elucidated in Buddhist literature as absolute truth, according to Zen reckoning. This correspondence is analogous to the normal Buddhist identification of this goddess as Shunyata and as Prajnaparamita or transcendental intuition. The Hindu conception of the appearance of Tara in twenty-one forms would seem to strengthen the case for a Buddhist origin of Tara.

Like other Hindu-Buddhist visions of the Goddess, Tara has both gentle and terrible manifestations. There is Ugra-Tara, the Awesome Savioress or Terrifying Savioress, as well as Tara as Divine Mother and Queen of the Universe. Tara is herself also called Awesome Kali, Great Kali, and Good Kali. She is also known as Rain Goddess (again like Danu of the Celts), Nurse of the World, Earth, and Emanatrix of Everything. From these images it appears that the gentle faces of Tara outnumber her horrific ones, overwhelming temporal material death with eternal spiritual life, as it were, in her role as savioress. According to the testimonies of the Thugs, people of any class, caste, or religious persuasion would appeal to Kali as savioress in times of great distress, such as famines and plagues.

Tripura-Sundari

The third Mahavidya is Tripura-Sundari, whose name means Beauteous One of the Three Strongholds. Like Kali and Tara, She is also sometimes identified as an Adimahavidya, that is, a primordial Mahavidya or goddess of universal knowledge.

Several names identify Tripura-Sundari as the spirit of erotic desire, sexuality, emotion, enchantment, pleasure, and giver of youth. She is rarely adored in the "gross" sthula or anthropomorphic form. This apparent paradox—that she is identified with beauty yet her beauty is seldom envisioned—would seem to argue that the sacramental aspect of Goddess religion is not mere sensuality.

The magnetism of the Goddess as desire and emotion is explicitly connected with mental destabilization and madness, which may overcome those who overindulge in emotional excess. At a certain temple in Banaras, for example, she is worshiped as Queen of Kings; there, it is said, no ordinary person can withstand an overnight stay without losing mental equilibrium. Even the priests supposedly do not last long in service at that temple. Legendary or factual, such stories may be evidence that the gurus of Goddess worship were aware of the dangers and drawbacks of practices involving the heightening of emotional pitch, much as they seemed to acknowledge their potential potency for those who survived without losing their wits.

The triangle, a symbol of the yoni, or private part of the woman, is the representation of Tripura-Sundari adored by the Left-Hand Tantrics.

Accordingly, the Three Strongholds of which she is the Beauteous One may be understood in terms of the many fundamental triads of the Hindu worldview.

One such triad is the trinity of Brahma, Vishnu, and Shiva, personifications of creation, maintenance, and destruction. This set of functions attributed to the supreme triune deity, whether called Goddess or God, is common to many schools of thought and many varieties of divine imagery. The criminal Kali worshipers would seem to have emphasized the destructive aspect of the trinity in their customs, yet even hereditary criminals also had, in their own ways, concepts and habits corresponding to creation and conservation.

Another basic triad is that of Measurer, Measurement, and Measured, or Subject, Cognition, and Object. In mystical terms, this represents identification of the Goddess with the innermost mind, the cognitive structure, and the objective world. This sort of metaphysical interpretation is characteristic of schools marked by the confluence of Hindu and Buddhist spirituality. Many of these schools with Hindu fronts were outlaw from an orthodox point of view, in the sense that, like Buddhism, they rejected caste and ritualism.

Another triad is the Three Bindus or Three Drops, the red (egg/female), the white (semen/male), and the mixed (union/fertilization). This imagery may have been a common resort for an assortment of devotees including Tantrics, concubines, courtesans, and barren wives.

The Three Strongholds also refer to the sun, moon, and fire. These can be taken mythologically or theologically to stand for the Three Eyes of Divinity; or mystically to represent the knowledge of three levels of truth—relative, absolute, and in between. The sun, moon, and fire were also elements in ritual ordeals, as well as tamer ceremonies celebrating these three signs of divinity.

The Three Strongholds also symbolize the power of will, the power of knowledge, and the power of action. This way of perceiving and harmonizing with divine energy is common to numerous mystical schools, especially those emphasizing yoga. The practitioner views the world in terms of divine will, knowledge, and action, then attempts to harmonize mind and body with that perception of this triune flow of divine energy.

The Three Strongholds also represent the three manifestations of the Goddess. First is the *sthula* or gross manifestation, corresponding to the

45

anthropomorphic image of the Goddess. Second is the *sukshma* or subtle manifestation, corresponding to the mantra of the Goddess. And third is the *para* or supreme manifestation, formless in itself but latent in the chakra or yantra, the abstract geometrical form of the Goddess. The ultimate secret of the Tantrics was to unite these three manifestations in one integral experience. This meant unifying body and mind to create an integrated energy circuit, to be used as an instrument for direct perception of divine consciousness latent in the primal forces of awareness and life.

The use of triads to construct worldview categories is not peculiar to Kali worship or to Hinduism, but is extremely widespread. It is also commonly employed in Chinese Taoism, a parallel set of traditions that probably had more contact with Indian religions than is generally recognized today. The triadic device was also characteristic of the didactic methods of Druideacht or Druidry, the Celtic cognate of Hinduism, wherein the resemblance is hereditary. Some scholars even believe that the emphasis on the Trinity in Christianity was actually an early Celtic influence that entered the church from the British Isles.

Bhuvaneshvari

Like Tripura-Sundari, the fourth Mahavidya, named Bhuvaneshvari, Queen of the World, is also identified with the earth. Identified likewise with the five elements and with nature, She is also called Form of Everything, Omnipresent Form, All-Pervading Form, All-Containing Form, and Vast Illusion. In this sense she is both binder and liberator, both illusion and knowledge. She can be entreated for constructive and conservational purposes, in conformity with the divine acts of creation and maintenance; or she can be implored for refuge and deliverance from the destructive forces of matter.

The Goddess as Bhuvaneshvari is especially envisioned as the mother of the trinity of Brahma, Vishnu, and Shiva, the root cause of creation, maintenance, and destruction. In her gross representation she carries a goad and a noose, which may stand for compulsion and obsession. In the various nuances of compulsion and obsession, furthermore, the meanings of creation, maintenance, and destruction may all be found.

We are compelled to act by the force of life itself, and we are bound to depend on our environment for support. From this point of view, the goad and the noose could stand for creation and maintenance of this temporal life. We need motivation, indeed are supplied with a primitive form of it by nature in our instincts; and we need sustained attention, without which we could not learn or carry out tasks essential to the survival of our species.

On the other hand, when we come to act by the compulsion of habit rather than by the compulsion of necessity or the compulsion of reality, then this life becomes moribund, uncreative. When attention to practicalities becomes obsession with the things of the world through which this life is a journey, we dwell on things instead of taking them for markers and means of the way, never getting to the destination. In these senses, the goad and the noose also stand for death, when compulsion and obsession subject the spirit to the forces of impermanence by tying it too tightly to the physical body and to things of the temporal world. The imagery of the Queen of the World therefore shapes the way experience of the world influences the destiny of the spirit.

Chinnamasta

The fifth Mahavidya, named Chinnamasta, or Decapitated, also represents the ambiguity of existence. She stands essentially naked on top of Rati and Kamadeva, or Pleasure and the God of Love, in sexual embrace. Chinnamasta wears a garland of skulls, which may stand for transcendence of human thoughts or ideas; and a snake necklace, which apparently symbolizes kundalini, the "serpent power" that is supposed to elevate consciousness when awakened from its dormant state.

Chinnamasta gets her name Decapitated from the image of having cut off her own head. In her right hand she holds a billhook; in her left she holds her severed head. She has cut off her head to feed her devotees Varnini and Dakini with her blood; this may represent the cycle of creation and destruction.

Varnini ("Woman of Caste") symbolizes the quality of *rajas* or fiery passion; Dakini ("Rebel Woman") symbolizes the quality of *tamas* or earthy instinct. Chinnamasta's feeding of the two devotees may represent the sacrifice of the quality of *sattva* or etheric spirituality to the qualities of passion and instinct. The goddess's own severed head also drinks the blood, perhaps emblematic of sustaining spirituality to balance passion and instinct.

Chinnamasta's blood gushes from her neck in three streams to pour into the mouths of her devotees and her own head. In yogic interpretations, this may symbolize the rising of the kundalini power up the three main channels of the psychic body, known as the channels of animation, firing, and divinity.

In terms of natural philosophy, Chinnamasta's self-decapitation may represent the self-sacrifice of the earth, or creation, for the emotional and material support of creatures. Just as the goddess's head also drinks her blood, so is earth's fertility renewed by death, much as a tree is fertilized by the decay of its own fallen leaves.

Bhairavi

The sixth Mahavidya, named Bhairavi, Terrible One, is another vision of the Goddess as the creative force in its awesomeness. Bhairavi is identified with Brahma, the god of creation, and with the abode of speech, which is envisioned as the creative force in Hindu cosmology. Bhairavi is also identified with the nature of consciousness, and through this manifestation she grants yogic powers of overcoming lust, greed, delusion, intoxication, jealousy, and anger.

Bhairavi is also identified as half of Shiva, the god of creation and destruction, in the so-called *ardhanari* or "half woman" form representing the process of creation as the union of male and female. In this role, Bhairavi is envisioned as empowering Shiva to create the world. She is also identified with kundalini, which may be thought to be connected with generative vitality.

In terms of her fierce aspect, Bhairavi is identified with Mahapralaya, Cosmic Dissolution, and referred to as Kalaratri, Black Night, envisioned as the destructive power of Kali. Bhairavi is also called Ghora-Tara, or Terrible Tara. The word *ghora* means "venerable," "awesome," and "sublime" as well as "terrible" or "horrible." In reference to pains and diseases (which are associated with Kali's fierce aspect), *ghora* means "violent" or "vehement." Bhairavi's name Candi also means "fierce," "violent," and "cruel"; it includes associations of heat, ardor, passion, and anger.

This sort of vision of the Goddess may be considered appropriate for certain harmful Tantric rites called the Six Actions: killing, causing paralysis, ruination by causing people to leave their occupations, gaining control over others, dividing people by creating enmities among them, and abatement or neutralization of opponents. These would not necessarily be practiced by hereditary criminals, although some nonmagical forms of them, such as murder by strangulation and paralysis by drugs, were indeed practiced by Kali-worshiping Thugs and poisoners. Otherwise, it is thought that such antisocial practices were generally the resort of people who had been dispossessed, outcaste, and oppressed, and who had no legal, military, or otherwise socially approved means of redress.

Other names of Bhairavi represent benign or attractive visions of the goddess. She is called Giver of Success; Sum of All Perfections; Destroyer of All Fears; Consciousness, Intelligence, Soul, or Spirit; Queen of the World; Queen of Passion; Cornucopia Goddess; Supreme Queen; Mother of the World; Nurse of the World; Cause of Creation and Destruction.

Bhairavi is associated with semen and with the production of semen. She is also said to "dwell in the yoni," and to be "fond of semen and blood." As in other manifestations relating to sexuality, therefore, the goddess does not represent female sexuality alone, but sexuality itself. For this reason Bhairavi is commonly the name given to a woman worshiped in a Left-Hand Tantric sexual rite, and the male worshiper is called her Bhairava.

Dhumavati

The vision of the Goddess as sexual energy disappears in the image of the seventh Mahavidya, called Dhumavati, the Smoky One. Dhumavati is represented as a widow, old, ugly, and merciless. She is associated with death, pain, poverty, hunger, thirst, wilderness, desert, and mendicancy. Because of this focus on death, Dhumavati is avoided by married people. She is associated with dissolution and encourages indifference to the world. She may, nevertheless, grant boons, including siddhis or supernormal powers. The granting of boons and powers might be contingent upon indifference to the world, based on the idea that the ordinary concerns and desires of the world distract or screen the inner mind from the exploitation of the fuller range of its capacities, to be found beyond the boundaries of preoccupation.

Vagalamukhi

The eighth Mahavidya, Vagalamukhi or Bagalamukhi, Face to the Side, is also associated with magical or supernormal powers. In particular, she is believed to confer powers to smite enemies with muteness and paralysis, and to destroy intellects and impoverish people. People unable to talk would lose human contact and social presence, while people struck with paralysis would be unable to work as well as unable to fight. Those whose minds had been destroyed would be disabled in both private and public life.

The vengeance of the helpless might have been one reason for this aspect of Goddess consciousness, but considering the worldwide practice of prayer for deliverance from destruction and victory in conflict, it seems almost anyone might resort to divine assistance in great distress. Vagala-mukhi is traditionally worshiped to gain control of enemies, to paralyze others, to attract others, to kill others, to counteract planetary influences, to acquire wealth, and to win lawsuits. Whether or not criminality would be involved in any of these quests might depend on the point of view as well as the precise particulars of a given situation.

Matangi

Another of the Mahavidyas especially propitiated for psychic powers is the ninth, Matangi, or Intoxicated Limbs. While she is identified with prakriti, or nature, in practice Matangi is worshiped for attracting others, for dominating others, and for making one's word come true. Matangi is also worshiped for acquisition of wealth, for poetic talent, for victory over enemies, for divinatory knowledge, and for protection against kings and evil spirits.

Matangi is portrayed as a woman of an aboriginal tribe considered outcaste and untouchable by mainstream Hindu orthodoxy. According to legend, in a former life Matangi was Shiva's sister. Matangi objected to Shiva's habits of frequenting cremation grounds, taking intoxicants, and associating with ghosts and goblins. So adamant was Matangi in her objections to Shiva's extraconventional customs that Parvati (Mountain Goddess), Shiva's wife, cursed Matangi to be reborn in an untouchable community.

In one myth, Shiva's wife Parvati even disguises herself as Candalini, a woman of an untouchable hunting tribe, in order to seduce Shiva.

Matangi is also connected with outcaste untouchables in the form of the goddess called Ucchishta-candalini. The word ucchishta designates one who still has remains of food in the mouth or on the hands, has not washed mouth and hands, and is therefore ritually impure. It also means "that which is spat out," or "leavings" or "bits of food," such as the leftovers of a sacrifice. Therefore Matangi is the outcaste goddess of the unclean, the untouchable goddess of the dregs.

The original concept of pollution and untouchability seems to have derived from waste management issues. These vary by occupation, and customary avoidances may have stemmed from hygienic issues. Those people professionally engaged in waste management were considered polluted and untouchable precisely because of their habitual contact with waste of one kind or another, from animal or human remains to the sweepings of the streets.

Society may have fallen into the habit of identifying the people with the profession, but even if they were despised and marginalized the untouchables were indispensable to society. The mixing of Brahmins of the upper class with untouchables in the world of Tantric cults may have been a way to reawaken the Brahmins' consciousness of the common humanity of the persons and divine origin of the souls of the untouchables, meanwhile recognizing that the untouchable professions were essential to society and that the outcaste people were also integral members of society as a whole.

Reviewing scripts of the many Tantric *shava-sadhanas* or devotional ordeals involving the use of corpses, for example, one might be led to think that, supernatural aspirations aside, these practices may have been a way for people from comfortable and genteel circumstances to experience the everyday nightmares of the life of a Chandala or charnel ground worker. Whether or not this is so, history confirms that Kali worship and outcaste humanity did move Hindus of conscience to rethink the caste system. Modern movements toward reintegration of Indian society, including Gandhi's concern for the plight of the untouchables, are also waves of an ancient stream that surfaces from its underground depths at various places in the current of history.

This nonrecognition of hereditary caste, a counterbalance to the hardening of the Hindu caste system, dates back to such non-Vedic religious communities as the Buddhists. Later it was imported (or reimported) into some neo-Hindu movements of the Middle Ages, including Tantrism and certain other forms of Goddess worship. As in its other spheres of operation, Left-Hand Tantra was a particularly direct and powerful concretization of the caste-transcending movement.

Kamala

The tenth Mahavidya is called Kamala. This name is an epithet of Lakshmi or Shri, who is identified with fortune, beauty, glory, royal authority, nourishment, and security.

Lakshmi is often portrayed as the wife of Vishnu, God as preserver, who is associated with kingship and social order. She is also called Mother of the World, Progenetrix of All Gods, Universal Power, Life Energy, and Universal Illusion. Thus, like other Mahavidyas, particularly the Primal Mahavidya Kali, Kamala is identified with creation, with the cause of creation, and with supreme spiritual bliss.

There are various alternate names and lists of Mahavidyas, individually and collectively representing the bright and dark sides of reality. In one system, the variant names of the Mahavidyas are collected into two groups, one called the Shrikula, or family of Lakshmi, and the other called the Kalikula, or family of Kali. Shri Lakshmi is the bright side of the Goddess; Kali is the dark side. In the total perspective of Indian religion these are opposite, but not opposed; contrastive, but not contradictory.

Criminal Kali Worship

One of the seemingly paradoxical consequences of this inclusive embrace of extremes in the vision of Goddess religion was that even those practices of Goddess worshipers conventionally condemned as transgressive, reprehensible, or criminal were never wiped out by orthodox Brahminic inquisitions. The other side of this coin is that even the professional criminal elements devoted to Kali had no intention and made no attempt to derange the fabric of society. Quite to the contrary, hereditary criminal classes customarily contributed generously to the upkeep of the authorities, both religious and secular. Thus they were not persecuted until the British campaigns against them in the nineteenth century. Even then, most native authorities and even many British or British East India Company authorities refused to interfere with criminal Kali worshipers.

By the time criminal Kali worshipers such as the Pindaris, Dacoits, and Thugs were called upon by force to explain themselves to others, the average followers of these cults apparently thought their predatory practices were simply their jobs, to borrow words from the testimonies of captive Thugs. In its own way, this manner of thought was in accord with the same sort of later Hindu fatalism inculcated by orthodox religious authority to foster resignation to an intrinsically inequitable social structure.

British officers were amazed, for example, to witness religious processions in which bands of Pindaris, highway robbers who lived in border wastelands, marched along with the rest of the faithful in regal pride and dignity, showing no sign of shame or guilt on account of their criminal profession. Later they learned that the Pindaris called their pursuit "Royal Work" or "Imperial Business" and paid the conventional authorities handsome sums from their loot.

Some observers might see tolerance of the Pindari gangs as a type of primitive customs or import-export taxation system; others might see the Pindaris as remnant bands of unconquered warriors in a continent with a past and present of competing warrior kingdoms. In their own eyes, the Pindaris were doing what rulers normally do; their payoffs to the recognized authorities were to them a form of tribute or diplomatic courtesy customary among rulers. Pindaris could, of course, probably fight off the militias of many a local authority; paying off, however, would probably be more economical in the long run.

Thomas Paine, one of the intellectual founding fathers of America, wrote of European history that rulership came from bullyhood, and that the rulers were simply the biggest bullies. The Pindaris seem to have thought along the same lines, at least to this extent. Unlike Paine, however, who believed in individual freedom from oppressive government, the Pindaris supported any government that would let them exist and operate.

The Dacoits, another class of professional robbers, also worshiped Kali and supported the government and the temples. The real name of the Dacoits, who were made famous in the West by Rudyard Kipling, was Dakat, which literally means "from Dak." This alludes to Dak, a demonic familiar of Kali who works as her emissary or assistant, her Grim Reaper. In a parallel way, Dakats also worked as professional assassins for government authorities as well as robbers on their own account.

Sometimes a Dakat would not kill a king directly but would enter his bedroom by stealth, slipping past all manner of security, and leave a mark of entry, such as a tassel cut from a curtain, as a signal that the king could be reached at any time. This could literally worry the king to death, or provoke a fatal disruption of trust within his inner organization, leading to his assassination by one of his own men. Either eventuality would completely cover the tracks of the contractor who had sent the Dakat, thus preserving the perception of goodwill on the part of the neighboring kingdom that now might "reluctantly" step in to sort out the situation.

In these ways, as devotees and servants of Kali, the Dakats were professionally focused on her functions of deprivation and death dealing, and on the power of illusion. They were not opposed to social order itself, but they understood deprivation, death dealing, and illusion as parts of the totality of social order. Like everyone else in the Hindu world from the priest to the cemetery scavenger, the Dakat apparently thought he was just doing his dharma and his karma, his duty and his job.

The Thugs also demonstrated complete resignation to embracing both social and antisocial outlooks through the medium of the doctrine of illusion, but in a very different manner from the Pindaris and Dacoits. One indication that criminal cults did not believe in immorality per se, even if their moral systems were unorthodox, is that their members would take vigorous exception to each others' practices. As in other areas of Indian religion from the realm of asceticism to the worship of enjoyment, there was no monolithic unity among the criminal classes of Kali worshipers. Even though they were criminals by conventional standards, they considered themselves specialists in certain rites and had no belief that anything is permissible.

Thugs looked down on Dacoits and Pindaris, for example, because they would invade people's homes, something strictly taboo among Thugs. The violence of the Pindaris and Dacoits was also repugnant to Thugs, who tried to kill their sacrificial victims without bloodshed, taking them not by force but by inveiglement, overcoming them by complete surprise without causing pain or fear. Indiscriminate killing was also disdained by Thugs, who were religiously forbidden from killing women, priests, handicapped people, many of the lower classes, and certain other categories of people. On the other hand, Pindaris and Dacoits despised the practice of Thugs, because as robbers they themselves claimed to kill only those who resisted when they raided, whereas Thugs killed as a matter of ritual prescription.

Sometimes Thugs even killed Dakats, if the omens were favorable, for a Dakat could not recognize a disguised member of the secret fraternity of Thuggee even though both groups were Kali worshipers. This may have been one source of antagonism, but there is no sign of any concerted effort by one group to wipe out the other. The Thugs believed so strongly in their taboos and omens that when the British authorities finally prosecuted Thuggee and virtually stamped it out in the nineteenth century, without exception the captive Thugs believed that the exposure and downfall of their sect was a result of their violation of their own taboos and omens.

British attempts to convince them otherwise had no psychological effect whatsoever on Thugs, much to the wonderment of the authorities, who therefore decided to exile or imprison for life those Thugs and their children who were not executed. This extreme measure was adopted to prevent survivors from procreating so that they could not pass the secrets of their cult on to offspring, as had been their custom for many generations.

In their private lives, Thugs were the most scrupulous of people in regard to the duties of caste and conventional social life. It was on their religious pilgrimages that they carried out their ghastly rites, never within their own regions. Their ability to kill in cold blood was produced by their process of initiation, using the mechanism of mind splitting.

The cult mythology contains clear indication of the concept of overpopulation. In this context, the practice of Thuggee ritual murder is represented as a culling operation on behalf of their mistress, Kali. Thugs believed that their murders were divinely sanctioned when carried out according to their sacred taboos and omens, and that they were in fact dispatching their victims straight to heaven.

The officially stated British colonial policy in India was not to interfere with native culture or religion, but Thuggee was considered completely beyond the pale and in the end was made an exception to this rule. The irony of this position was that the chief British inquisitor of Thuggee himself admitted in print that there was no nation or people that did not perpetrate violence under the veil of ideological rationalization, whether political or religious. It should also be remembered that Malthusianism originated in England at the height of the empire, and the British imperial system still stands accused of having engineered major famines in Bengal and Ireland, both of which were considered overpopulated in the view of English economists.

If we add to the list of mass murders and other iniquities perpetrated under the banners of religious and political ideologies, including inquisitions, crusades, pogroms, genocides, purges, ethnic cleansings, and party power struggles, we might find that the Thugs, whom virtually no one will not condemn with horror and repugnance, were veritable altar boys in comparison to the agents of violence and destruction unleashed in the name of mainstream religions and societies.

This observation is not meant to vindicate Thuggee, of course, but to call self-righteous conduct into question wherever it occurs, whether in marginal criminal cults or in mainstream religious, political, or economic warfare and oppression. This self-questioning might be a useful and significant consequence of objective studies of rebellious Goddess worship.

Studies of these cults may also help us to understand criminal cults and gangs in modern societies. Research may be somewhat influenced or inhibited by the fact that the psychological and organizational methods of criminal associations can often be similar or identical to those employed by mainstream political and religious institutions. Nevertheless, both criminological and sociological advances might be made by a thorough understanding of highly successful cults that prefer their own laws to those of society at large.

In terms of criminal Kali worship, the murderous Japanese cult of AUM Shinri-kyo is a recent example of a paradox that shocked many observers after exposure of the cult's experiments with biological and chemical weapons. The leader allegedly studied esoteric teachings in India, and later proved to be a master deceiver and inveigler, whose disciples supposedly committed murder at his command. His connections in India have been questioned in view of possible links to remnants of Thuggee.

It was supposed by Colonel William Sleeman, the chief inquisitor of the Thugs, that he had succeeded in wiping out the cult by the end of the 1830s. In the time of his grandson Henry Sleeman's stint in India, however, in the 1890s, migrant laborers were returning from the Mauritius— where exiled Thugs and their families had been transported—with the habit of poisoning and robbing people. It certainly would appear that the legacy of Thuggee had not died out altogether.

What does seem to have been cut off entirely by the British suppression was the religious side of Thuggee, the esoteric system of taboos and omens, ceremonies and procedures, that circumscribed the ritual human sacrifices of the Thugs. What seems to have been somehow perpetuated was the technique whereby people could be trained to kill without psychological disturbance to themselves. This was not fundamentally peculiar to Thugs, although there must have been variants among the different practitioners of ritual murder since ancient times.

It is possible that the guru of the murderous Japanese cult of AUM Shinri-kyo learned this technique in India, where it is alleged to have been practiced on some of the "spiritual tourists" from the West who flooded India during the 1970s.

This may be one explanation for the otherwise paradoxical willingness of college-educated young men and women of respectable families in peaceful Japan to kill innocent people at the guru's behest. It may also explain the suggestion of interest in AUM Shinri-kyo on the part of militaristic fascist remnants in Japan, who would not only be likely to be interested in the Dakat-like capacities of its followers for assassination and murder but would also be interested in the special initiatory and training techniques for their own purposes. It is no secret that both Japanese fascists and German Nazis sought the aid of esoteric teachings in attempts to increase their mental powers and influence their people; and so have the communists in Russia, where AUM Shinri-kyo recently flourished in the confusion following the dismantling of the Soviet Union.

Understanding the full range of such teachings impartially, recognizing both light and shadow, may thus have many meanings and applications for the modern day, well beyond academic or popular theology. Indeed, this understanding may be as important for the security of nations against psychologically sophisticated criminals and interlopers as it is for the security of individuals and families against the seductions of predatory gurus and cults. Secular authorities who pursue ambitions by military means practice human sacrifice under the banner of national and popular interests. Predatory religious cults practice a type of human sacrifice in convincing people that they are being saved by devoting their minds and bodies to the amusement and pleasure of the guru and his coterie. In either case there is no possibility of real freedom, either political or spiritual, without understanding how the mechanisms of illusion and delusion work in both realms.

In the final analysis, Goddess worship may produce its effects by graceful expansion of consciousness through absorption in beauty and light, or by dramatic opening of awareness through challenging confrontation with the forces of darkness, destruction, and dementia. In either mode, the power and energy of Goddess worship clearly retain a lively capacity to extend and sharpen our perceptions and thereby broaden and deepen the perspective within which we understand ourselves, our societies, and our world.

Goddess worship still exists in India, and it is gaining greater attention in the modern West, where its lessons for humankind may be crucial to global survival within a century of the year 2000. In the following chapters we shall see how this feminine spirituality is also evoked and expressed in other traditions.

4

The Yin Factor

THE NAME TAOISM, like Hinduism, is an expression of convenience used to refer to a remarkably wide variety of social, cultural, scientific, religious, and spiritual pursuits. As in the case of Hinduism, the diversity of Taoism may be seen in any given era as well as over the course of its long history. Simply expressed, the basis of Taoism may be thought of as the primary body of knowledge underlying original Chinese culture. Its legends and traditions reach back to prehistory, preserving within themselves memories of an earlier matriarchal tradition preceding the historical emergence of patriarchal Chinese civilization.

The history of women and womanhood in China is an intimate part of one of the world's oldest stories. Even though patriarchy eventually supplanted matriarchy in mainstream Chinese society, revamping myth and history in the process, echoes of ancient matriarchal society were never entirely effaced. The *Book of Lord Shang*, a document of the first millennium BCE, writes of ancient society in which "people knew only their mothers, not their fathers." This means, of course, that the family and social structure was matriarchal, matrilineal, and matrilocal. The parenthood even of the revered founders of the patriarchal dynasties of early Chinese history is known only through their mothers.

Numerous women of those remote times are named in Chinese myth and history. Later literature produced in patriarchal times portrays the ancient male sages and culture heroes whose biological fathers were unknown as having been born of human women through miraculous conception. This mythological rationalization of unknown fatherhood is in itself a residual mark of the matriarchal and matrilocal custom of high antiquity.

In old proto-Chinese matriarchy at its peak, eight thousand to six thousand years ago, males married into the families of females and had no rights with respect to the children, who "belonged solely to the maternal relations." Females were polyandrous but had a principal husband among their men, while males were polygamous but likewise had a principal wife among their women. We do not know how the children felt about this, but they apparently continued to imitate their parents for thousands of years. Changes, nevertheless, did eventually take place. Marriage patterns shifted from endogamy to exogamy, or in-group to out-group marriage, accompanied by a more gradual shift toward a mixture of polygamy and monogamy.

Coming closer to historical times, in the early days of Chinese monogamy it was apparently customary for mates to continue living separately in the company of their own kin, with marital relations carried on in the form of visitation, the husband "visiting" the wife in her abode. Subsequently there was a move toward cohabitation, which tended to gravitate around the males as they accumulated wealth and grew in power and influence. Although marriages were apparently often unstable, the concepts of "parents" as "father and mother" gradually developed and ultimately became regularized.

In ancient hunting and gathering society, the gathering activity of the females was a steadier and more reliable source of food than the hunting of the males with their still primitive weaponry. Through their acquired familiarity with edible flora, furthermore, the females became the true mothers of agriculture itself. The development of herbal medicine in China also probably derived much from the activities of women engaged in gathering.

Elementary agricultural tools have been excavated from the tombs of females who lived seven thousand years ago, before the appearance of any such artifacts in the tombs of males. Remains of millet and vegetable seeds testify to early cultivation, and paddy rice, a crop of considerable sophistication, appears in prehistoric China between two thousand and three thousand years earlier than in the ancient Indus Valley civilization of pre-Aryan India.

Women also played a crucial role in the development of animal husbandry and domestication, as girls and women would raise animal young captured live by the hunters. Silk production, for which China has been justly famous since time immemorial, is openly recognized as a major contribution of Chinese women to the world.

Women are also believed to have invented and elaborated pottery, having discovered the clay firing process in the course of cooking foodstuffs. Females were in fact undoubtedly instrumental in the domestication of fire itself, and this is surely reflected in ancient mythology's representation of the Fire Spirit as female.

Spinning, weaving, and sewing were also early feminine inventions, as evidenced by elementary looms and bone needles unearthed in very ancient sites. A remarkable variety of decorative accessories using semiprecious stones and even ivory has also been discovered in archaeological finds.

The shifting of proto-Chinese societies from matriarchy into patriarchy seems to have taken place approximately five thousand years ago. Earlier, even mated men and women had lived separately and were also buried separately after death. Cohabitation and monogamy apparently came into fashion with patriarchy, as evidenced by the first graves containing couples, in which the male occupies the central position facing up, while the female is interred on her side facing the male. Private property, wealth, and poverty also seem to have emerged with the elaboration of patriarchal sociopolitical forms.

Prehistory closes with the prevailing of patriarchy over matriarchy, but Chinese myth and legend retain an ancient reverence and respect for the female, especially within Taoist traditions. One of the great female leaders of ancient times, for example, whose name means Feminine Harmony, is portrayed as the very creatrix of humanity: when heaven and earth first parted, according to the myth, she fashioned humans out of yellow earth.

Another popular legend has Feminine Harmony bracing up a falling sky, or patching a broken sky in the distant past. Because "sky" is a classical symbol for the male, this particular myth may symbolize the need for partnership to achieve wholeness. It may, however, also represent a faint echo of the origins of matriarchy itself as the dominant social structure of high antiquity.

Feminine Harmony is sometimes portrayed as the sister of the sage who supposedly first articulated the concepts of yin and yang and invented the original version of the classic I Ching or Book of Changes. That ancient sage's name means Hidden Breath, suggestive of creative energy or potentiality. Like other culture heroes of Chinese legend, Hidden Breath was married to a culture heroine, much in the same way that gods and goddesses are normally married in Hindu mythology. The fact that Hidden Breath and Feminine Harmony are also envisioned as brother and sister, like Osiris and Isis in Egyptian myth, may suggest that the ancient mythmakers were emphasizing a need for harmony between men and women in general, on a nonsexual social level and not just the level of conjugal relations.

Because society was anciently envisioned as a family, the mythological brother-sister pairing of a culture hero and heroine may reflect a time, whether prehistoric or imaginary, when neither gender systematically dominated the other, and sexuality did not necessarily dominate the social relations of men and women.

Perhaps nowhere are the pristine concepts of fundamental parity and complementarity of female and male more clearly expressed in Chinese tradition than in the aforementioned I Ching, supposed to have been originally devised by the sage Hidden Breath.

According to traditional legend, the ancient sage examined the natural, human, and celestial realms, then devised two basic symbols for classifying phenomena: a solid line for the yang principle and a broken line for the yin principle. These two basic elements were then combined and recombined in a variety of ways to describe all sorts of relationships and configurations of natural, social, and psychological forces.

The physical form of basic yin-yang symbols as broken and solid lines may have originated in sexual or procreation-related imagery, as so many icons of very ancient times suggest. The solid line for yang may have derived from an image of a man's erection, while the broken line for yin may have derived from an image of a woman's cleft.

It is essential to bear in mind, nevertheless, that yin-yang classifications are not limited to sexual associations by any means, being systematically extended far beyond the domain of gender polarity. It is, however, true that female and male images may be used in a literary or poetic manner to stand for yin and yang even in contexts where sexuality or gender are completely irrelevant to the real point of reference. Confusion of symbol with sense in this connection already concerned some savants centuries ago, and it remains a problem to this day in some quarters.

In the construction of the symbolic system of the I Ching, the broken and solid lines are first combined into eight sets of three lines each ("trigrams"); these eight trigrams are then permuted into sixty-four sets of six lines each ("hexagrams"). Every hexagram has a thematic name, indicating a particular context within which the component parts and their relationships are interpreted. This system, building from the simplest concepts up to the most complex, can and has been used in many different ways. The I Ching can be applied to seventy-two different spheres of life, and there are literally thousands of commentaries on the classic in the Chinese language.

As the title Book of Changes suggests, the essential principles of the I Ching are change, transformation, and evolution. The fundamental energetic modes of yin and yang are therefore not viewed as absolute and static but seen as relative conditions, constantly in a process of interaction and interpenetration. This provides for a great many subtleties of meaning and nuance, allowing for a wide latitude of analogical application.

Because the trigrams consist of three lines, there is no possibility of an equal number of yin and yang lines in any trigram. One trigram is all yang, one is all yin; the rest are mixtures. The all-yang trigram is called the Sky, the Creative, or the Father; the all-yin trigram is the Earth, the Receptive, or the Mother. As a mated pair, the Father and Mother form the constant axis of the system. The shifting proportions of yin and yang forming the six "offspring" trigrams represent the momentum of flux within elemental forces of nature produced by the interactions of Creative Father Sky and Receptive Mother Earth.

According to tradition, there have been three versions of the I Ching in the course of history. The first version is attributed to Hidden Breath, as already mentioned; the second is attributed to a mythical figure whose name symbolically reads Ruler of the Center; and the third and current version is attributed to historical leaders whose names symbolically read King of Culture and Duke of Universal Fairness.

For the purposes of appreciating the role of the yin factor in Taoist culture as we see it in the ancient I Ching, the second version of the classic deserves special attention even though it is no longer extant.

This second recension of the most ancient of books has historically always been considered lost, but it is traditionally mentioned and given the name *"Return to Storage" Book of Change*. There are different lines of formal opinion on the authorship, but the classical line of thought on this subject most relevant to the yin factor is that the *"Return to Storage" Book of Change* was composed by Huang Ti, a legendary figure whose name is commonly translated in patriarchal tradition as the Yellow Emperor.

According to ancient Chinese color symbolism, yellow is associated with the center (as, for example, the center of the four directions) and with earth. Earth, as already noted, is the Mother symbol of the I Ching. The word for "emperor" used here anciently meant "deity." So the name Huang Ti could be taken to mean the ruler or deity of the center, or of the earth. There is no inherent gender in this Chinese character either, so Huang Ti could actually mean Earth Goddess.

Modern research into very ancient strata of Chinese, pre-Chinese, and proto-Chinese civilizations has uncovered another fact that may strengthen this reading of Huang Ti's name. It appears that Huang Ti was actually once considered female and called the Consort of God. If the sky was God, then the earth would be Goddess, in this primitive naturalistic conception of high antiquity; or it could be said that if God were connected with the sky in some way, then Goddess would be connected with the earth.

The identification of Huang Ti with Earth Goddess, and the association of Huang Ti with the *"Return to Storage" Book of Change*, are tied together by one last relic of information about the ancient classic. Whereas the order of contents of the I Ching as known today, in its third recension, begins with the pure yang hexagram Sky, the earlier version thought to have been compiled by Huang Ti began with the pure yin hexagram Earth. This may confirm that Huang Ti was originally the Earth Goddess, and that this version of the I Ching was formulated in prehistoric times when the ancestors of the Chinese people still lived in matriarchal societies.

The symbolism of the mother hexagram Earth derives from its composition of all yin lines. Yin may have "good" or "bad" associations—

flexibility would be considered good or "true" yin, for example, while pliability would be the bad or "false" version of this yin quality. Nevertheless, as a whole, Earth is normally employed to symbolize aspects of good or true yin qualities.

The word *yin* originally meant "shade," in contrast to *yang*, meaning "sunlight." By extension, yin came to represent darkness and coolness, both literal and figurative. Yin also means "hidden," "recondite," "unseen"; therefore it came to represent secrecy, mystery, and abstraction. In social terms yin signifies deference and courtesy. In psychological terms it is used to symbolize docility, humility, openness, receptivity, detachment, restraint, and self-mastery. In metaphysical terms it stands for emptiness, transcendence, and spirituality. In meditation yin represents stillness, consciousness, or insight.

All of these meanings represent important developmental factors in Taoist education and training. Because all people have both yin and yang in them, there is no necessary or exclusive gender specificity in this context; both yin and yang factors, in mutual harmony, are essential for wholeness and health in every individual.

In empirical terms it is not entirely arbitrary, nonetheless, to symbolize the yin factor by feminine images, because females do seem to have superior facility in development of yin qualities. Social structure and conditioning may have eventually encouraged this, even exaggerated it, but underlying biological factors may be at the basis of some of the feminine yin skills.

In particular, the demands of childbearing clearly favor the yin factors of stillness, calmness, endurance, and self-mastery, while the process of nursing requires intuitive sensitivity, attentiveness, and receptivity to the needs of the infant. As we will soon see, these naturalistic connections were in fact made by Taoists in their descriptions of their meditation processes.

In this way the Taoist "worship" of the "Earth Goddess" had at once a scientific and a religious basis, purposely connecting biological, social, and psychological mechanisms to spiritual evolution. Thus, in keeping alive the imagery and practices of total life integration, Taoism provided Chinese society with a scientific and cultural "upward spiral" to counterbalance the "downward spiral" of its political and military history.

The Mysterious Female

It is conventional to contrast the historical sensibilities of Indian and Chinese civilization by describing the Indian conception of time as fundamentally cyclical and the Chinese conception as fundamentally linear. This difference in outlook is generally thought to be connected with the relative abstractness of much Indian philosophy in contrast to the relative concreteness of Chinese philosophy. Like all stereotypes, however, this one also has its limitations, both in principle and in fact.

Chinese thinkers did evolve metaphysical conceptions, and eventually Taoism elaborated a world-cycle theory somewhat like that of the Hindus. This development seems to have been a result of Taoist contact with Buddhism, and it remained rather esoteric as ideas go. The cycles of cosmic events pictured in Indian thought, meanwhile, were so immensely long that for practical purposes the flow of time was as linear to the Indians as it was to the Chinese. There is thus less difference between Indian and Chinese modes of thought than is commonly supposed.

The pairing of gods and goddesses, culture heroes and heroines, and even metaphysical abstractions as spouses or siblings is a feature also common to Indian and Chinese mythology and religion. This factor is even more consistent and more pervasive than coincidences of historical consciousness. The coincidence of symbolism of the man-woman pair in Indian and Chinese religions does not appear to have had its origin in any process of cultural borrowing, nor does any such supposition seem necessary. Eventual contacts between the two civilizations, nonetheless, undoubtedly produced some degree of syncretic elaboration.

While the metaphysics of divine communion and the complementarity of yin and yang remained ever present in the abstract, the flow of events had a tendency to obscure the original ideals with invented expedients. This is evident in the terrestrial role of females in society and religion, where there are two major historical trends, undoubtedly intertwined, tending to compromise the primal unity of humanity along both vertical and horizontal lines.

These trends may be seen in the course of both Indian and Chinese histories: the rise of dominant military-industrial elites and the erosion of the status and rights of women. The two phenomena seem to go hand in hand, not only in India and China but in many other parts of the world

66

as well. Because of the remarkable antiquity and keen historical sense of Chinese tradition, however, a model of the shift from matriarchal to patriarchal organization and the rise of technocratic militarism can be observed with particular clarity in the Chinese context and historical mode of perception.

Patriarchy as a "legal" custom was officially established in China by the first patrilineal heir of the first historical dynasty, King Ch'i of Hsia. King Ch'i reigned over four thousand years ago, according to tradition, from 2197 to 2188 BCE.

Earlier, Ch'i's father and mother had worked together to form a confederation of tribes, which they divided into the Nine States of classical Chinese lore. As male-dominated as Chinese society and politics came to be, this pattern of man and wife collaborating in governing the nation was to resurface later in China, even during historical times when the formal order was patriarchal and the de jure ruler was the male. The persistence of this practice was particularly evident in those cases where an empress or empress dowager openly took over after the death of the emperor.

Who was this Emperor Ch'i, who started the practice of patriarchy in China some four thousand years ago? Ch'i was the son of the great King Yu, one of the outstanding heroes of Chinese legendary history. King Yu had been master of waterworks under an earlier chieftain, distinguishing himself in public service at the time of a great flood of antiquity. Although he naturally did not work alone, Chinese myth represents Yu as the queller of the flood. He was also, according to legend, the first man to raise his own son.

The massive flood control project took twelve years. Yu took his son Ch'i to live with him, instead of leaving him with his mother's clan according to existing practice. It was no doubt necessary to organize the menfolk for the emergency of the flood, so as to achieve greater cooperation among the males than matrilocal customs normally fostered. The great flood was thus perhaps the critical factor in the construction of what would become the basis of patriarchy in China.

Yu was appointed chieftain for his service in rescuing the heartland from the flood. According to tradition, Yu was the last monarch to succeed to kingship peacefully in nonbiological succession. He was the third and last of the so-called Three Kings—Yao, Shun, and Yu—revered by

Confucians and Taoists as sages of olden times. These three kings lived on the edge of myth and history; they were not fathers and sons, and they did not succeed one another either by inheritance or warfare.

The nonviolent, nonbiological succession of the Three Kings is represented as a true meritocracy, though its historical reality is likely grounded in the fact that they all lived in matriarchal times. The principle of capability being the foremost criterion of leadership, more important than biological succession and morally superior to usurpation, remained an ideal of true Confucian thinking throughout history, even though it was never again enacted on the imperial level.

Even though King Yu remained an ideal for philosophers of patriarchal times, legend shows that he himself still had the mentality of the type of society in which he had grown up. Rather than turn into a despotic "right man" familiar to later history, in the more egalitarian manner of ancient sages Yu collaborated with his wife in leadership. Together the couple worked to forge the alliances of an expanded supratribal organization, whose cooperative foundation may have been started during the period of the great flood. This was the ancient Hsia confederacy, whose historical existence Western scholars had been inclined to deny until recent archaeological evidence removed their doubts.

Tradition holds the great King Yu innocent of initiating hereditary succession and patriarchal rule. When King Yu had become old, his son Ch'i initiated a deliberated and determined patriarchy movement, seeking to bring the control of women, children, and property into the hands of men. Hereditary succession of kingship from father to son went hand in hand with the rest of patriarchal organization, demanding it and depending upon it for existence.

From this perspective, Ch'i's patriarchy movement appears to have been subordinate to his quest for inherited political power—indeed, subservient to that quest. This underlying motivation may be, in concrete historical terms, why patriarchy in China has come to be associated so closely with oppression that it is sometimes assumed the association is inherent. The story of Ch'i's bid for power explicitly exemplifies this pattern.

Assassinating his opponents, Ch'i strengthened his movement by taking over the rulership of the Hsia confederacy after the death of his father, Yu. By this act Ch'i made himself the first hereditary patrilineal chieftain in Chinese history. As dynastic chief, moreover, Ch'i appears to have initiated another long-standing custom among patriarchal Chinese rulers, namely, exorbitant self-indulgence at the expense of both home and country.

Based on what is now known of the relationship between social dominance and body chemistry in simians, it may be theorized that the astounding excesses reported of many monarchs might have been stimulated to some degree by the biochemical consequences of dominance. If such excess did not occur so much in matriarchal societies, it may have been because patriarchal systems organized hormone-elevating environments—such as populous seraglios—to a degree never before known to human society.

It probably would not be fair, nonetheless, to assume that extreme dominance was inherently patriarchal in origin, and that matriarchal leaders did not also have many people submissive to them, or many sexual partners. Of the great Himiko (or Pimiko), a third-century chieftain of Yamatai (in ancient Japan), it was said that she had no "husband," but most of the men in her kingdom were her lovers, whom she bewitched by her magic. A shamaness herself, Himiko was assisted in affairs of government by her brothers.

This description of Himiko sounds typical of what patriarchal historians thought of ancient matriarchies. Many of the numerous domains in ancient Japan are believed to have been ruled by shamanesses, who by both nature and profession probably had great personal vitality and high-serotonin brain chemistry.

Back in China four thousand years ago, at the dawn of the patriarchal era, although monogamy was orthodox by the time Ch'i established himself as hereditary overlord, the kings of all the petty states within the Hsia confederacy were polygamous in actual practice. If nothing else, the tactic of proffering beautiful maidens as political gifts and bribes meant that the head of the confederacy would have access to many concubines and lovers. The practice of slavery was also widespread, and countless females were taken into slavery through warfare and conquest.

The ancient confederacies of premodern China were never very stable for long, on account of rivalries for territory and influence virtually necessitated by the clan structure and the expansion of the upper classes. Many tribes were not members of the confederacies, and these seem to have been labeled "uncivilized" and considered fair game to any confederates seeking to expand. Thus there were many opportunities for the dominant males of the upper classes to "acquire" disproportionate numbers of females for their seraglios, households, workshops, and slave stables. Militarism thereby enabled patriarchy to grip Chinese society within a relatively short period of time.

Ch'i's son and successor T'ai-k'ang followed his father's example in self-indulgence. According to tradition, his principal wife eventually abandoned him, taking their five children with her. This was a direct challenge to the new order. Affairs of state were neglected, and the leadership of the confederacy was taken over by another notorious character, Hou I.

Hou I also took rulership in the new fashion, as a personal license to do what he wanted. His wife abandoned him too. Powerful as it became, patriarchy was still new, and the women of legend show independent will. Hou I is thought of in legend and history as a master archer from the east, and this image may strengthen the traditional association of patriarchy with militarism and tyranny. The woman who abandoned Hou I was the famous Ch'ang E, the Lady in the Moon. She is said to have gone to live in the palace of the moon to distance herself from Hou I. Today Ch'ang E is reckoned the first woman to actively and openly protest the practice of polygamy in China.

The Hsia dynasty officially ended with Chieh (ruled 1818–1766 BCE), the sixteenth-generation ruler whose licentiousness and cruelty made his name synonymous with corruption, evil, and tyranny in classical Chinese canons of leadership. Over a long reign, he exhausted resources and people by massive construction projects and aggressive military operations, while creating a "lake of wine and forest of flesh" for his own amusement. Chieh was finally overthrown by a rebellion led by the chieftain of the rising Shang tribe.

The Shang were already an ancient tribe when their leader Tang rallied other lords of the confederacy against Chieh of Hsia in 1766 BCE. The first ancestor of the Shang, according to later patriarchal history, was still one of those whose mother is known but not his father, as characteristic of the matriarchal era that supposedly ended centuries earlier in the Hsia dynasty. The culture of the Hsia was therefore probably not imposed systematically on all the states of the confederacy; and it might be said that the true historical ancestor of the Shang was a woman.

Having its roots in ancient matrilineal society, the Shang retained some residual influences of antiquity in the relatively high status of women in its culture. In some cases there were women in ministerial positions as well as sacerdotal functions, and women of the aristocracy were widely involved in politics and affairs of state.

This pattern may still be seen in the thirteenth century BCE, when King Wu Ting of Shang warred with neighboring tribes and revitalized the Shang rule. In this campaign one of his main field generals was none other than his wife, Fu Hao, herself a large property holder and the leader of a militia under her personal command. Perhaps the first female general in the "patriarchal" era of Chinese history, Queen Fu Hao greatly strengthened the supremacy of the Shang leadership through her many remarkable exploits.

Marriage under Shang norms was legally monogamous but actually polygamous among the ruling classes. The Shang economy, furthermore, was based on slave labor, and female slaves were also exploited for the sexual gratification of their owners. Incalculable numbers of bastard children born to slaves were already building the bases of a permanent underclass or stratum of poverty in China more than three thousand years ago. In fact, one of the words for "common people" originally meant "bastards."

The status of women nevertheless remained fairly high among the upper class societies of the Shang confederation. Grandmothers and mothers were accorded considerable honor and dignity. Quite a few ancient bone inscriptions record ceremonies and rites for specific mothers and grandmothers. Ceremonies and rites for male ancestors, on the other hand, became central to the Chinese imperial cultus of later times, when patriarchy and patrilineal descent had more completely overruled earlier matriarchal norms.

The Shang dynasty ended as had the Hsia, with the overthrow of a degenerate ruler whose excesses led to overwhelming opposition. In 1039 BCE King Wu of Chou, another tribe of ancient descent reaching back to the matriarchal era, led a rebellion against Hsia that resulted in the establishment of a new order. The figures of King Wu and his father

King Wen later became heroic icons to the Confucians, who largely looked to the culture of Chou for their ideals.

King Wen's mother, T'ai-jen, is famous as the first woman known in history to have practiced "fetal education," which involves regulating the influences on the fetus through the daily habits of the mother. To this practice is attributed the exceptional talent later demonstrated by King Wen. His leadership ability was such that he led the Chou state for fifty years, developing it to the point where Chou was able to assert superiority over Shang within another generation.

The Chou dynasty subdivided the old confederacy into at least seventy-one feudal states, granting fiefdoms to members of the royal family, successful ministers, relatives, and members of the old aristocracies. All land legally belonged to the ruler, and clan structure and lineage were strengthened in patriarchal patterns. Thus the status of women declined considerably in Chou dynasty China, and upper-class men became increasingly attracted to the idea of having many wives and many sons.

Polygamy and concubinage increased during the Chou dynasty, following on Shang precedents. Many concubines were taken from among enslaved females. These customs tended to strengthen the Chou ideology, which explicitly assigned political responsibility to men and domestic responsibility to women, as illustrated in the classic dictum "The female's proper position is inside, the male's proper position is outside."

Here can be seen the Chou dynasty roots of Confucian patriarchal dogma; the victorious Chou leadership officially blamed the downfall of Shang on the involvement of women in political life, and in effect banned women from public affairs.

While women still had a certain status and respect within the context of home and family, their political subordination contributed to the development of palace intrigue as a significant modality of political affairs as they were actually conducted. Hence the image of the "hidden woman" or "mysterious female" came to have ambivalent nuances even as it was structurally established as part of the edifice of Chinese society.

The Mysterious Female in the Chou Dynasty

The first phase of the Chou dynasty, known as Western Chou because of the location of its capital, came to an end in 771 BCE with the assassination of the twelfth-generation ruler. The later Chou, called Eastern Chou, is generally divided into the Spring and Autumn Era (770–476) and the infamous Era of the Warring States (475–221), when militarism triumphed, saturating the atmosphere with violence and bathing the land in blood.

The Spring and Autumn Era was marked by political conflict and court intrigue. According to historical records, during this period of three hundred years, thirty-six local rulers were assassinated, fifty-two petty states perished, and countless lords fled their territories. That averages no less than one top-level political assassination per decade, with independent states perishing at an average rate of about one every six years. And this was before the savagery of the Era of the Warring States. With this disintegration of order, the income, prestige, and authority of the Chou kings waned drastically.

The political disorder of the Spring and Autumn Era was also reflected in social disorder, with many men and women of the ruling classes becoming infamous for their self-indulgence, including unbridled sexual relations often extending even to relatives. Another reflection of the political and social conditions of the time was the establishment of a government "escort service" by the powerful state of Ch'i under the guidance of the socialist scholar Kuan Chung (730–645).

Staffed by enslaved women, this official escort service provided entertainment for guests of state. The old tactic of "scheming with beauties" (one of the so-called Thirty-six Strategies), that is, trying to influence people by sexual favors, was now systematically carried out by government without the political complications of marriage and concubinage. The further decline in the status of women, which this system reflected, was to continue apace as militaristic and socialistic ideas and practices came to dominate Chinese statecraft over the following centuries.

Nevertheless, a number of highly placed and personally powerful women of the upper class collaborated with their husbands to bring about material progress and sociocultural development in their individual states. Even those who participated vigorously and constructively in state affairs, however, were themselves targets—like all influential people—of self-seekers, interlopers, and spoilers. Therefore they were not always able to avoid the harsh brutalities of court intrigue.

Their lesser sociopolitical status, furthermore, could force women to deal with such intrigues from a standpoint of greater vulnerability and fewer tactical choices than males. These factors, along with the prevalent exploitation of women for political alliances and favors, led to a congealing of the idea of excluding women from public life altogether, as suggested in the Classic of Poetry, sacred to Confucianists, where it says, "Disorder descends not from Heaven, but is born of woman."

After the Spring and Autumn Era, the last semblances of the Chou confederation disintegrated into the Era of the Warring States. During this period most of the petty states were swallowed by seven major states, all of which were competing for supremacy. Numerous schools of political science arose, trying to sort out the confusion of the times and lend constructive or strategic direction to future social and political developments.

It was during this era that the followers of Confucius solidified their sense of identity as a school and formulated the bases of doctrinaire Confucianism. It was in this same time that the followers of Lao-tzu, legendary older contemporary of Confucius, parted ways with moralists and militarists alike to develop a distinct line of Taoism.

In this epoch of intense violence among males competing for absolute dominance, Taoism focused on preserving the ancient respect for the female in every sense, keeping the lore of high antiquity alive. Taoist thinkers emphasized the natural yin virtues of peacefulness and coolness to counterbalance the aggression of the times, applying their concepts of human development to the whole body of society.

Pacifistic Taoism embraced the yin factor in both public and private life. This is clearly seen in the ancient Te Tao Ching, an old version of the Taoist classic Tao Te Ching. The Te Tao Ching came from the so-called Huang Lao school, which was named after Huang Ti, the Earth Goddess who became Yellow Emperor, and Lao-tzu, the Old Master who was believed to have compiled the Te Tao Ching/Tao Te Ching. Based on the mutual reflection of the microcosm and macrocosm, this school of thought tried to formulate principles of governing the body, mind, earth, and nation in accord with the laws of nature.

Applying the yin factor to the chaotic political life of the Era of Warring States, the Taoist classic says, "A great nation flows downward; female to the world, it is a meeting place for the world. The female always overcomes the male by stillness. When being still, it is appropriate to be lower. Therefore, a great nation takes a small state by lowering itself to the small state; a small state takes from a great nation by lowering itself to a great nation."

As Taoists understood it, the "yielding" quality of the yin factor does not imply incapacity or disability; neither does it imply an attitude of supine resignation or abject servility. Rather, it is more a means of prevailing against all odds with a minimum of wear and tear; it is a way of getting through the gaps when surrounded by unyielding forces. The *Te Tao Ching* says, "Nothing in the world is more yielding than water, yet nothing can outstrip it in attacking the hard and the strong; that is because nothing can change it. Everyone in the world knows water can overcome what is hard, and yielding can overcome strength, yet no one can practice this."

Naturally, the yin factor does not exist in isolation but in either contrast or complementarity to the yang factor. The classical Taoist recourse to yin principles and practices in diplomatic and military spheres, as in the passages just cited, was a response to the dominance of aggression and force; this is called using stillness to overcome agitation, using coolness to overcome heat. As a general principle of balance, nonetheless, it was always considered normal and desirable to embody both yin and yang potentials within oneself, to be activated in proportion to the needs of the time.

Thus it is natural that even those Taoist classics from troubled times, while emphasizing the essential importance of the yin factor for peace and security, still balance it with the yang factor. The critical distinction of the yang factor in Taoism, however, is that it is refined and moderated by the yin factor. This balance is admirably illustrated in these famous lines of the classic *Te Tao Ching*: "Knowing the masculine, preserve the feminine; be receptive to the world, and consistent effectiveness remains, returning to innocence."

The yin principle of "being female to the world" is proposed for public political life, but it is also a metaphor for perceptive receptivity. The balancing principle of "knowing" or "governing" the "male" (yang) while "preserving" or "maintaining" the "female" (yin) can be applied in both public and private life, in both political and personal spheres of action, as a professional and social person. The imagery of the yin factor is then singled out again on a deeper level as a metaphor of the interior life of the spirit.

The mystical element in Taoism has sometimes been treated as separate from the social and political elements, but the common thread connecting all these aspects of life in Taoist praxis is the preservation of the yin factor. The very idea of producing a peaceful society is based on the possibility of producing a peaceful person, and the Taoist technology for this is based on the yin factor. "Purify the spirit," says the Te Tao Ching, "and you won't be morbid; this is called the opening of the mystic feminine. The mystic feminine is called the root of the universe; a subtle continuity, it is indeed there; apply it without stress."

Over the ages, Taoists maintained this subtle continuity of the mystic feminine with even more reverence and delicacy as the world went to hell around them, secretly soothing and stilling society's fevers with serenity of spirit.

5

Usurping the Yin

CONTRADICTIONS IN CHINESE SOCIETIES deepened through the first millennium before the Common Era. One manifestation of this phenomenon was the proliferation of remedial philosophies of all sorts. Some of these philosophies proposed moral reform, some offered escape, some outlined strategies of statecraft and social control. Everyone knew something had gone wrong, it seemed, but there were many different opinions about the causes and cures of perceived political ills.

The occulting of the feminine yin factor in the social and psychic life of the Chinese civilization as a whole continued in step with the growth of despotism and militarism. While "preserving the female" by maintaining the yin factor in the body of thought and custom, Taoism also practiced "knowing the male" in exposing the aberrant nature of despotic militaristic governments and offering alternative approaches to organization.

The spread of Confucian ideology, based on an idealization of the patriarchal Chou dynasty, fortified the philosophy of male domination and female subordination. Even though Confucianism was predominantly pacifist in theory, in actual practice it came to be mixed with a legalistic approach to government that commonly went hand in hand with militarism. Even though Confucianism was called the Soft Way, this name referred to moralism and ritualism and did not reflect the balance of the yin factor.

The Confucian classics on rites and manners played a significant role in the formation of court, clan, and family etiquette. Here the shackling of woman by customary and ritual constraints came to encompass her all around, foreshadowing two millennia of social suppression.

The classic *Record of Rites* says, "Wives have no personal money, no personal possessions, no personal articles. They may not privately borrow, or privately lend." The "Detailed Etiquette" chapter of the *Record of Rites* also gives precise directions for demure feminine comportment: "Listen to the soundless, look at the formless; do not climb up to high places, do not look down into deep places; do not scold arbitrarily, do not laugh arbitrarily." It also says, "Do not eavesdrop, do not raise your voice in responding, do not look at anything indecent, do not be lazy or careless."

The subordination of girls to fathers and brothers, wives to husbands, and widows to sons was now rigorously defined. The shackling of females in a deteriorated social rank was also manifested in the practice of female infanticide. It was, however, still possible for widows to remarry without opprobrium, a social freedom that was eventually denied by patriarchal Confucian society in later eras.

On the political front, the incessant conflicts of the Era of the Warring States ultimately culminated in the triumph of the Ch'in, formerly the most culturally backward of the seven major states. One of the ordinarily unspoken and unsuspected sources of Ch'in's strength was the status of women in that state, which remained higher than elsewhere. In 334 BCE the ruler of Ch'in outlawed the custom of human sacrifice on the occasion of the death and interment of powerful men.

Most of the victims of these ritual executions had been women—killed by the dozens, even the hundreds in some cases—so the abandonment of this barbaric custom meant that there were more women in Ch'in, relatively speaking, than in other states, especially in the establishments of the rich and powerful. These women, often originally "culled" from the population at large, contributed directly to the strength of the Ch'in state.

In addition to its army of male soldiers, Ch'in also organized an army of females, as well as an army of older or less able-bodied men and women together. In private life, furthermore, Ch'in women owned personal property, unlike women of other states. The legally recognized personal property of Ch'in women, moreover, included both what they brought from their own homes and what they acquired after marriage. Ch'in women also participated in community economic life to a greater extent than did women of other states, engaging in crafts and trade as well as traditional silk making and agriculture. Women of Ch'in could also divorce and remarry without that in itself affecting their status or prestige.

Eventually the growing state of Ch'in overcame all of its rivals to establish the first imperial system in Chinese history, replacing the ruins of the political infrastructure of the ancient confederacy of states with a new centralized bureaucracy. So crucial was this historical watershed to the development of later Chinese civilization that it is from Ch'in that Western languages get the name China. The ruler who finally achieved the unification of China in this way is thus called the First August Emperor of Ch'in.

In spite of the relatively favorable legal and economic situation of women, which enabled them to contribute to the flourishing of the state, the ultimate dominance of the patriarchal imperial structure asserted itself in no uncertain terms on the burial of the First Emperor of Ch'in, with the sacrificial murder of every palace lady who had not borne a child.

Since the First Emperor is supposed to have had ten thousand women in his establishment, there must have been quite a massacre on the occasion of his interment.

The women of Ch'in may have had more rights than women of other states, yet the exercise of those rights were not only subordinated to the interests of the state but even made tools of the state's economic and military development. Curiously, this situation may be closer to some modern ideas of women's liberation than might be expected of a sociopolitical phenomenon of two thousand years ago.

The drama of the Era of the Warring States, culminating in the establishment of the first Empire of China, produced a flurry of philosophical activity relating to human nature, society, and government. Local rulers tried to take advantage of activist scholars—and vice versa—with the result that a great deal of formal thought and schooling centered on social, political, and military concerns. The First Emperor was keen on exploiting any ideas that seemed to promise power or profit, and Taoism was no exception. The classics of military strategy by then in vogue were already tinged with Taoist influence, and various elements of Taoist health lore were apparently well known. The First Emperor took an interest in Taoism, but his mania for power led him into obsessions from which he never escaped. One of these obsessions was his use of women in his efforts to attain personal physical immortality.

A distinct difference between modern American thinking and Taoist tradition can be seen in this context. When a dominant male copulates with numerous females, his sexual activities are currently construed as "conquests" to boost his "ego." An alternative explanation is that the man is a gene carrier compulsively dispersing genetic material. Some might say he does so for pleasure, but "womanizing" is ordinarily thought of as obedience to other impulses than sheer desire for physical pleasure.

In the context of Taoist practice as interpreted by men in positions such as that of the emperor, men who are already powerful and dominant but still have an insatiable lust for power and dominion, sexual congress with multitudes of women is one manifestation of a bid for immortality. These men also normally took various drugs for this purpose and also practiced certain forms of seclusion and quietism in alternation with their activities as warlords and rulers of men.

Interpreting hyperbolic descriptions of ecstasy literally, these men believed they could use the sexual energy of females to "fortify yang" by "culling yin"—even to the point where they imagined they could not only cure their physical illness but become all-powerful and immortal by taking the energy of thousands of virgins. Being in positions where they could purchase girls, even kidnap them, men of great power had considerable latitude for experimentation in this regard. All the failures, furthermore, could be blamed on the toxic effects of the drugs they were also taking, thus reducing the chances that they would discover the shortcomings of their efforts on their own.

Many repudiations of secret sexual arts are to be found in later Taoist texts. In light of the First Emperor's example, Taoist condemnations of sexual alchemy might not necessarily be manifestations of Confucian influence, as some observers have supposed, nor yet of the political repression of Taoist cultism, as others have believed, but rather authentic Taoist repudiation of impostures and abominations deriving from misinterpretation and misuse of genuine Taoist sexual lore.

If Taoism was to maintain the balance of the yin factor, including reverence for female energy, it would be natural for the mainstream to denounce those exaggerations of sexual yoga that led to abuse of girls and women by men who tried to use female energy for personal power. Some schools appear to go so far as to renounce sexual practices entirely on account of the potential for abuse or the currency of conventional misunderstanding.

Some modern Western interpreters, taking the aberration for the norm, have used the term "sexual vampirism" to describe Taoist sexual yoga. This usage gives some idea of how common the counterfeit is, in comparison with the real thing. When we look at this type of practice in the context of history, we can see that the degradation of Taoist sexual lore, including the degradation of the female, goes hand in hand with the degradation of every other kind of Taoist lore, and with the general social degradation of women under acquisitive, despotic, and militaristic governments and systems.

It may not seem necessary, from a modern point of view, to differentiate between "ego-tripping" and bidding for permanent power, but from a Taoist point of view it would trivialize the energy of sexuality to relate it only to psychological factors. If we are thinking biologically today, we might consider hypersexuality in dominant males a result of their dominance, but Taoist psychophysiology would suggest to us that it can also contribute to their continuation of dominance. Whether in psychology or politics, elements of hypersexuality may require scientific examination before moral judgment. Scientific understanding of the natural bases of behavior might yield deeper perspectives on the practical implications of moral or social principles.

An ominous hint at the moral question may be glimpsed in the use of drugs to attain immortality, another practice common among the same class of men who used girls and women as "alchemical vessels" to energize themselves. It is sometimes assumed that many of these drugs were aphrodisiacs to help men copulate with many women, but other more secret formulas were supposed to alter body chemistry to make physical permanence possible.

Historical record tells us that some emperors of China died from the effects of such life-prolongation preparations. The fact that these deaths sometimes occurred within living memory of each other suggests that the belief in these alchemical elixirs, or the desire to believe in them, was very strong indeed. Many factors, furthermore, could be blamed for failure, including an emperor's own mistakes in the complicated process of ingestion.

Today we are inclined to think of those emperors as greedy, ignorant, and credulous, and of the wizards who gave them the drugs as charlatans of the first order. The reality of the matter, however, may be that these poisons were given to the emperors deliberately to assassinate them. The wizard-chemists may have been agents or hirelings of political planners. Perhaps they were men of conscience who believed that it was in the public interest to remove rulers who wanted to rule forever, if it could be done without mass violence or the inflammatory appearance of intrigue.

As an extra advantage, a termination of this kind could have the side effect of dampening the enthusiasm for Taoism of some power mongers, at least for a time, thus relieving Taoist practitioners of some of the danger of being found out, hauled into court, and expected to immortalize the main man. Over a period of centuries such famous fatalities could have been intended to have the effect of discrediting these biochemical experiments for many people. While material alchemy generally faded from popularity, however, sexual alchemy apparently retained its allure, in spite of authoritative warnings about its abuses. Originally intended to enhance the health and well-being of men and women alike, Taoist sexology was gradually usurped by the dominant males of the upper classes and warped by ignorance and greed in the process of subordinating it to the interests of systematic despotism.

While seeming to liberate women from the feudal customs of older states, the First Emperor merely enlarged their prison and usurped their energies for the enrichment of his domain and the extension of his personal power and life span. Imprisoning the yin factor within its state structure by "employing" women in armies and factories for expansion of state power, by "enjoying" women in the imperial seraglio for extension of personal power, and by exploiting natural science for both state and personal power, the First Emperor of China set in motion certain strains of eccentricity that were to reverberate through history.

Womb of Wisdom

The Ch'in dynasty collapsed shortly after consolidating the first empire. The second emperor squandered the profits of the founder's system, and the people rebelled widely against the harshness of the laws and exactions of the central government. In 202 BCE a new dynasty, the Han, was established by a rebel leader named Liu Pang and his confederates.

After his assumption of the Dragon Throne, Liu Pang was greatly assisted in establishing a new government and polity by his wife, Empress Lu. According to historical documents, Empress Lu was a strong individual who helped the emperor pacify the country and clean out the officious, self-serving bureaucracy. In 188 BCE Empress Lu herself took over the reins of government in place of her late husband's successors, becoming the supreme ruler of Han China for eight years.

Women of great power like Empress Lu would subsequently emerge in Chinese history from time to time, no matter how suppressed or circumscribed the general role of women in society. This paradox of Chinese history exemplifies the resilience of the human spirit in face of inconceivable odds.

In the early decades of the Han dynasty, a Taoist political policy of noninterference enabled the populace, groaning under the militarism and bureaucratic legalism of Ch'in, to recover its basic health and productivity. After sixty to seventy years of respite and recovery, China under Han rule had attained an unprecedented level of prosperity.

The relative freedom and ease of the early Han dynasty came to an end with the rule of the powerful Wu Ti, the Martial Emperor (ruled 140 to 87 BCE). Strengthening the central government, Wu Ti abolished academic freedom and established the quasi-Confucian philosophy of Tung Chung-shu (179–104) as official orthodoxy.

This hybrid brand of Confucianism was little more than a politely disguised and fashionably rationalized version of an imperial cultus. The emperor demanded that all submit both outwardly and inwardly to this system, in the interests of national unity and social order. Included in the structure of this system were the so-called Three Regulators and Five Norms, which definitively subordinate wives to their husbands on the analogy of the subordination of subject to ruler. These principles became a permanent part of the sociopolitical infrastructure of imperial China.

After the Martial Emperor of Han authorized Confucianism and suppressed all other schools of thought, the regulation of women's lives became increasingly severe. Seven grounds of divorce were defined for men who wanted to reject their wives: infertility; promiscuity; disobedience to parents-in-law; complaining and talking back; stealing; jealousy; and malignant illness.

On the other hand, a new genre of literature, "stories of exemplary women," also began during the Han dynasty. This new literature presented morality tales about women exemplifying motherliness, wisdom, humaneness, intelligence, faithfulness, chastity, eloquence, treachery, and so on.

With the suppression of non-Confucian schools of thought by the Martial Emperor, the ancient spiritual tradition of Taoism, which was foremost in nurturing feminine spirituality, largely went underground. The harshness of the imperial machine without the comforting and cherishing effects of Taoism can be seen in the Martial Emperor's establishment of garrison brothels for the soldiers of his expansionist armies.

An extension of the ancient state diplomatic "escort service" brothels, the military brothels set up by the Martial Emperor were staffed by enslaved women. Many if not most of these women had been wives and daughters of men who were captured or killed by the imperial machine as convicts. The monetary profits realized by the official brothels were reinvested by the government, furthermore, in military expenditures. Prison profiteering, like forced prostitution, has a long, long history in China.

Han women were also commonly used by the imperial establishment as gift brides or concubines for chieftains of neighboring peoples for diplomatic purposes. Many Han maidens were wed, for example, to tribal leaders of the powerful Hsiung-nu, the original Huns, whose mounted warriors worried China for centuries.

A pattern of women and womanhood being made into tools of imperial gangsterism was thus permanently established in China along with other elements of persistent patterns of domination and bondage. This did not happen all at once, but through centuries of domineering aggression and terror, in what amounts to gang warfare among the most powerful clans and cliques arising from tribes along the old Yellow River Basin.

China's Sorrow is a traditional epithet for the Yellow River, on account of the floods that take so many lives when the river overflows its banks from time to time. The anguish of the women and the men victimized by these power struggles, from the conscripts and convicts and their enslaved wives and children to the millions who starved while emperors and generals feasted, would be enough to flood China's Sorrow with a river of tears for centuries on end.

The internal patterns of Chinese society and polity remained fundamentally fixed over four centuries of Han rule. After the breakup of the Han, similar patterns were repeated. Men of lesser powers strove to emulate the wealth and prestige formerly held more exclusively by men of greater powers. Increasing competition brought increasing disintegration, until the ancient heartland of China, as well as much of the northern and western territories acquired under Han imperialism, wound up in the hands of smaller but more vigorously united pastoral peoples of the Central Asian steppes. The new kings included descendants of the Huns, China's ancient nemesis.

Mixture with these peoples, and political subordination to them, brought some elements of change into Chinese habits and mores. Over the centuries, the Central and North Asian peoples who ruled parts of China also absorbed Chinese political culture and habit. Tribal leaders, after all, had to rely on native Chinese infrastructure to rule over vast subject territories. Chinese civilization was aware of itself, moreover, as having already absorbed other peoples and cultures in the remote past as part of its own evolution.

Centuries of division followed the Han dynasty. China was united in 589 CE under the Sui dynasty, which soon collapsed under mismanagement. The basic unification, however, was maintained and built upon by the succeeding T'ang dynasty, which was established in 618 and lasted for nearly three hundred years, until 905.

While the long and convoluted history of China is thus marked by a succession of imperial dynasties, each with its own political and cultural identity, it was in this T'ang dynasty that the apogee of Chinese civilization, the golden age of China's culture, was ultimately attained in the estimation of many scholars, historians, and critics.

Although it was a patriarchal society, women in T'ang China were considerably freer than in later times. After the death of the third emperor of the T'ang dynasty, his widow deposed his two successors—his brother and his nephew—and personally took over the throne herself. She even founded her own dynasty, naming it Chou, and assumed the title of emperor.

This woman proved to be one of the ablest rulers in Chinese history.

85

She is known for cleaning up the central bureaucracy, increasing the effective element of meritocracy in the government examination system, and patronizing cultural development along diverse avenues. She was a particularly generous patron of Buddhism, funding the invitation of foreign scholars and the translation of sacred texts from Sanskrit into Chinese.

During the T'ang dynasty, women could divorce on their own initiative, divorcees and widows could freely remarry, and married women could have paramours. Although excluded from the civil service system, many women were educated and literate. The crippling custom of foot binding, for many the arch symbol of suppression of women, had not yet been invented in the T'ang dynasty.

Taoist writings of later times say that the "real people," or Taoist adepts of the highest orders, generally concealed themselves from public notice for a thousand years, from the early Han dynasty through the T'ang dynasty. This millennium of Taoist history seems somewhat arid in comparison with what preceded and succeeded it, but this appearance is superficial in some respects. In more positive terms, this thousand years of hiding was like a period of gestation in the great body of the mystic female of Taoism, preparing for a rebirth soon to follow.

This very imagery of gestation, in fact, would itself surface in the yin-yang vocabulary of the developing traditions of Taoist alchemy, which ultimately emerged from the shadow of obscurity to become the dominant symbolic format of Taoist practice.

Curiously, the Taoist renewal following the T'ang dynasty would have to repeat the ancient formula of spiraling upward as society spiraled downward. As the dynasties following the T'ang become increasingly militarized, the rights and privileges of women eroded. The liberal ways of the T'ang dynasty were denounced as infections of "barbaric" Turkic mores, and divorce and remarriage became taboo for women. This was all part of a reactionary Chinese cultural movement rejecting Central Asian elements of its diverse, syncretic heritage as imperial China's diplomatic relations with Central Asian neighbors worsened.

In the midst of this deterioration of the status of women associated with deflection of Chinese cultural consciousness into xenophobic political aims, Taoism maintained the yin factor in its symbolism, its morality, and its methods. Taoist sexology, however, became very secretive as the government promoted more rigid sexual mores among the Chinese gentry after the end of the T'ang dynasty.

This was a marked change in the historical expression of the yin factor in Taoist China. Ancient texts had depicted Taoist adepts as married folk living in the midst of the people. Magicians of the Han dynasty were well known to use the energies of sex and drugs in their quest for health and longevity. The priests and priestesses of the Taoist cloisters that grew up after the Han dynasty and flourished through the T'ang dynasty were also free to marry and cohabit as part of their religious regime, but the T'ang government encouraged a movement toward monastic celibacy in Taoism. Nevertheless, two of the greatest poets in Chinese history, distinguished even in the context of the immensely rich culture of the T'ang dynasty, were in fact Taoist nuns expert in the "chamber arts."

As the meditative format of spiritual alchemy developed within Taoism, sexual symbolism emerged as a standard mode of expression within this tradition. This process may be considered natural, in view of the fact that Taoists generally married and considered nature their ultimate guide. So powerful was the impact of this dramatic symbolism, moreover, that sexuality remained a primary metaphor in later Taoism even after abandonment of sexual yoga and normalization of celibacy in some sects.

The imagery of sexual intercourse is used on several levels in Taoist alchemy, representing the mating of yin and yang energies in the total experience of life. While there are numerous variants of this system, in simple terms there are three "weddings" in the alchemical process. These are called the wedding of heaven and earth, the wedding of fire and water, and the wedding of wood and metal. The yang "bridegrooms" are heaven, water, and metal; the yin "brides" are earth, fire, and wood. The marriages of the couples represent the restoration of natural human integrity; their connubial bliss symbolizes the exhilaration and well-being of really feeling alive.

The first couple, heaven and earth, stand for firmness and flexibility, two complementary qualities that must be balanced in the individual personality. Heaven and earth also stand for mind and body, which are to be unified in the alchemical process. In meditation, earth stands for a condition of thorough calmness and inner silence, while heaven stands for unadulterated natural energy. The belief is that when the mind and body are brought to a climax of stillness, an infusion of pure positive energy

87

occurs naturally, revivifying the whole being. This is the "impregnation" of earth by heaven on their wedding night.

The second couple, fire and water, represent consciousness and intuition. Consciousness tends to be mercurial and flighty, so it is "married" to deep intuition in order to stabilize it. Intuition tends to be vague and ungraspable, so it is "married" to conscious awareness in order to make it clear and accessible. In modern terms, this marriage of fire and water might be likened to a joining of the right and left sides of the brain.

Among male Taoist practitioners, the mating of fire and water was also used to represent the psychophysical posture of focusing the attention (fire) in the lower abdomen or genital area (water). This was an initial step of an energy circulation exercise designed to obtain a calming effect on the mind while producing an energizing effect on the body. Women practitioners also used this exercise, except that in the initial stage they were taught to focus attention on the valley between the breasts instead of the lower abdomen. In women, this part of the exercise is sometimes called "turning blood into milk."

It is said that the difference between the practice for males and females is based on purely physiological factors, and that it is perilously unhealthy for women to make a habit of keeping the body still and concentrating the mind in the lower abdomen. This caveat does not apply to the practice of Taoist arts of movement, wherein energy is naturally dispersed through the body by physical activity. It is the stagnant pooling of energy in the womb in stillness that is said to produce negative side effects, supposedly even cancer.

The third "couple" in the marriages of yin and yang, wood and metal, stands for essence and sense. Essence, which is categorized as yin and "fluid," refers to the ethereal essence of awareness. Sense, which is categorized as yang and "solid," refers to intuitive knowledge. The third marriage represents the ability to consciously sense the essence of awareness, in order to free the mind to operate subtly without fixations. This is supposed to produce a condition of inner clarity combined with external alertness.

The offspring of the esoteric marriage of yin and yang is called the sacred embryo. From this point the symbolism of the developmental process is modeled on gestation, birth, nursing, and nurturing. It would seem that this convention is not simply a matter of traditional Taoist reverence for nature and female biology, nor merely a conveniently vivid mode of literary expression. Some observers have written that most Taoist literature was written for men, but even if this is so, the primary reason could be that it was precisely because men were in greater need of developing the "soft" yin qualities symbolized by pregnancy, nursing, and nurturing to balance the exaggerations of "hard" yang qualities fostered in males by the social and political norms of their society.

Taoists thought females to be naturally more proficient than men in yin qualities. This feminine capacity may have been attributed to the biological and psychological bases of motherhood. In the course of time, certain yin qualities were selectively fostered by the increasing personal and social repression of females in Chinese society.

Taoist manuals expressly for women do not use the imagery of pregnancy, childbirth, and nursing. The yin image of the "womb breath," however, which is common in later Taoist literature, is to be found in works for women and men alike.

The practice of the "womb breath," "embryonic breath," or "fetal breath" appears in many Taoist texts. There is even a standard work devoted entirely to the subject, the *Womb Breath Classic*. As with many other elements of Taoism, there are numerous obscurities, opinions, and controversies about what "womb breathing" (or "fetal breathing") really means, but it is referred to so commonly in Taoist meditation manuals that no treatment of Taoist meditation can ignore it.

The general image is of the "respiration" of a fetus in the womb in concert with the mother, through the umbilical cord rather than through the nose and mouth. The simplest definitions treat this as a metaphorical expression of a meditative state in which the breathing has become so calm and quiet that it is externally unnoticeable and is not felt passing through the nostrils, yet is inwardly manifest as energy imbued with awareness.

This state of coordinated mental and physical calm is approached by way of the common Taoist practice of abdominal breathing (rather than chest breathing) with the attention settled in the lower abdomen. This body-mind posture mimics, in a male body-mind, the image of a pregnant woman, the abdomen rounded and protruding, attention absorbed within. It is sometimes even referred to as "a man becoming pregnant."

The imagery invoked here is not only physical and not only mental, but implies the unification of body and mind. The related *Treatise on the Womb Breath* says, "Spirit and energy join and preserve the internal breath." In this formula, "spirit" conventionally means awareness, while "energy" refers to the breath. Thus keeping the attention on the breathing is called the joining or mating of spirit and energy. As attention is the conscious engagement of mind, while breathing is what supports the body, keeping the attention on the breathing is used as a means of unifying mind and body. This is also called the mating of sky and earth.

The meditative process called "gestation" or "incubation" begins after the "spiritual embryo" has "congealed" and its "womb breathing" has been stabilized. The gestation process is called "ten months" of incubation, based on the conventional reckoning of an average human pregnancy at about ten lunar months.

Again, like many other elements of Taoism, interpretations of this procedure differed in practice. There were evidently those who took this term literally to mean a specific period of calendar time during which one was to continue the exercise. Others understood it figuratively to mean however long it took an individual to reach the stage of mental development metaphorically represented by a mature fetus ready to be born.

In Taoist iconography, the completion of the "ten-month work" of gestation has been portrayed in the form of a "pregnant" man pulling open his duly distended belly to reveal a small replica of himself sitting within. This is the inner spiritual embryo "warmly nurtured" to the point where it can be externalized. The subsequent externalization, called "emerging from the womb," is portrayed as the internal spiritual infant being "born" by emerging into open space through the aperture at the top of the man's head.

Here again some take this more literally, others more figuratively. More literal interpreters take this "birth" to refer to the ability to "project the spirit" outside the body. This is a capacity attributed to mystics of a certain degree in other traditions as well.

Certain Taoist texts outline month-by-month descriptions of the development of the fetus as models for meditation on the inner world of the human microcosm, its investiture with spiritual guardians, and its outer correspondences with the elements, rhythms, and bodies of the spiritual, energetic, and material universe at large. The *Scripture on Inner*

Gazing gives the following contemplative images of conception, gestation, and birth:

> Heaven and earth combine vitalities, yin and yang evolve, and human beings receive that life.
>
> In the first month it is an embryo, sperm and ovum having congealed.
>
> In the second month it is a fetus, the form of the body beginning to take shape.
>
> In the third month, the yang spirit constitutes the triple higher anima, animating the fetus with movement.
>
> In the fourth month the yin soul constitutes the sevenfold lower anima, stabilizing the body by calmness.
>
> In the fifth month the five elements are apportioned to the five inner organs, stabilizing the spirit.
>
> In the sixth month the six pitches stabilize the six viscera.
>
> In the seventh month the seven vitalities open the apertures to let light pass.
>
> In the eighth month the spirits of the eight celestial bodies are present.
>
> In the ninth month the chamber is arrayed to stabilize the vitality.
>
> In the tenth month energy is full and all forms are complete: elemental harmony provides nourishment continuously; the god of Overall Unity inhabits the brain, coordinating all the spirits; the manger of fate and life resides in the heart, taking in life-giving energy; the "Peach Pit" god of the spleen dwells in the umbilical region, maintaining the root of vitality. The "Unflowering" god inhabits the left side, controlling the triple higher anima; the "Pure Basis" god inhabits the right side, controlling the sevenfold lower anima. Thus the whole body is full of spirits.

Another intriguing system or version of this type of meditation is found in the *Scripture on Causation*:

> People first receive their bodies from nothingness: turning yellow into white, solidifying energy and congealing vitality, receiving from heaven in accord with earth, combining and transmuting yin and yang.

The first month, it is an embryo; the energy of the highest heaven descends, pervading the body.

The second month, it is a fetus; the energy of the heaven of infinite life descends, pervading the body.

The third month, the higher anima is present; the energy of the heaven of timely portion descends, pervading the body.

The fourth month, the lower anima develops; the energy of the heaven of tranquillity descends, pervading the body.

The fifth month, the five organs are developed; the energy of the heaven of nonexcessive enjoyment descends, pervading the body.

The sixth month, the six viscera are completed; the energy of the heaven of the sound of evolution descends, pervading the body.

The seventh month, the apertures are cleared; the energy of the heaven of the assistants of the god of creation descends, pervading the body.

The eighth month, all features are there; the energy of the heaven of clarity and light descends, pervading the body.

The ninth month, the spirits come down; the energy of the heaven of nonattachment descends, pervading the body.

There are eighteen thousand celestial spirits and eighteen thousand body spirits, together totaling thirty-six thousand. When the spirits and energies are all fully present, the birth takes place in the tenth month.

There are also meditation programs that use the symbolism of gestation but not the detailed visualizations of month-to-month development, focusing on the breathing without other imagery. Here the ten-month period is reckoned to contain thirty thousand micro-years. Each breath is counted as a micro-year, based on the analogy of the process of breathing with the rising and setting of the sun, the waxing and waning of the moon, and the alternation of the four seasons. Unbroken attention to the breathing throughout the whole process is therefore believed to have an effect on the development of consciousness equivalent to thirty thousand years of life experience.

The intensity of awareness this produces is held by some to be the real meaning of the spiritual immortality for which Taoists sometimes said they were aiming. The infinite extension of life, in this view, is metaphorical; extension is actually a representation of intensification. This representation is not merely symbolic, furthermore, because it approximates the actual subjective experience or sensation of this intensification of consciousness, in which it first seems that time stands still, as a moment seems an eternity and eternity is seen in a moment.

The gestation theme of Taoist meditation may have been a by-product of fetal education. Fetal education was practiced in China for more than a thousand years before the emergence of Taoist texts using the imagery of pregnancy as a format for exercises in inner contemplation. No doubt this was a natural development, in view of the Taoist interest in the correspondence of the physical and the mental dimensions of existence.

While later Taoist texts indicate a most intense occupation with development of the psychospiritual embryo, concern with development of the psychophysical embryo naturally remained an intrinsic part of Taoist traditional teaching for parenting. From the perspective of total human development, of course, both of these types of cultivation are closely related to one another.

In meditative psychospiritual gestation, consciousness is shifted from active outward orientation to tranquil inward orientation; in psychophysical fetal education, consciousness of the external world is selectively refined to regulate the influence of the mother's outward consciousness on her inner world, because her inner world is the external world of the fetus inside her.

According to a Taoist text on pregnancy, in the three days after conception the embryo is unstable. During this period it is recommended that the mother-to-be try to see pictures of rhinoceroses, elephants, and other fierce animals, as well as pearls, jades, and jewels. She should also try to see good and wise people, cultivated people, and virtuous religious people.

It is noteworthy that both gentle "yin" and strong "yang" impressions are recommended in fetal education, in a controlled and balanced discipline. This is also true of further general recommendations for pregnancy, which include watching performances of classical music, religious ceremonies, and military parades.

The text goes on to recommend using the finest incenses and reciting classical poetry, histories, and instructional stories of past and present. The mother-to-be's room should be uncluttered and quiet. She should play the lute to tune her mood, making her emotions gentle. She should also moderate indulgence in desires and purify her mind.

If a mother-to-be will do these things, it is said, her children will be good, long-lived, loyal, filial, humane, intelligent, and healthy.

It is evident that much of the content of "fetal education" is essentially the same as what is normally recommended not only for good upbringing but for general cultivation of wholesome habits throughout a lifetime, irrespective of gender. This may be simple common sense, but the emphasis on beginning the process of upbringing and lifestyle formation in pregnancy also lends weight to the notion that there is something of unique importance in the process of gestation, for both mother and child.

Pregnancy is not only a process of constructing the biological and psychic foundation of the life of the child but also a time of spiritual renewal for the mother. In the process is formulated the character of the relationships between mother and child, and thus between child and world. So critical is this primary formative process to the whole experience of life that it was perhaps only natural for Taoists to attempt to devise an analogous developmental program for the enhancement of this subtle interior consciousness in males as well.

6

Women of the Way

MANY RECORDS, REPORTS, AND RUMORS of female wizards, illuminates, and immortals are to be found in the annals of Taoist lore. Some of the figures in this fascinating literature are mythological or prehistoric, but most of the famous women of Taoism were historical people; accordingly, their stories reflect the world they lived in as well as their own personalities and peculiarities.

Like any traditional literature containing an element of mystery and marvel, stories of Taoist adepts often seem to be a blend of fact, fiction, and fantasy, handicapping attempts to evaluate them objectively. Many variant themes were developed, furthermore, in the process of utilizing traditional mythological motifs to explain or discourse upon ongoing social developments, sometimes making it impossible to prefer one version over another. Certain perceptible patterns may nonetheless provide clues to interior meanings when placed in the overall context in which these stories of wizards and immortals were constructed. Even if we do not take such lore as literal truth, we can still profit from understanding a phenomenon such as Taoist immortalism in terms of its function as a possible response to social conditions that inherently curtailed self-expression for the majority of individuals.

Self-expression of females was suppressed with increasing severity as Chinese history wore on under the twin yokes of imperial and regional militarism and bureaucracy. Power struggles among imperial in-laws, court eunuchs, and scholar-officials often tied up whatever power of effective central government had not already been usurped by generals turned warlords. There were educated women, but females were officially excluded from civil service; many of the ablest men of learning also came to boycott the system because the education for passing civil service examinations tended, or was intended, to castrate the scholars intellectually and spiritually.

For these reasons, and perhaps also because of the economic conditions consequent upon corruption in government, at various times in history the ranks of Taoist orders and circles swelled with both men and women. It is not possible even to estimate how many women escaped society into Taoist communities over the ages, but literary imagery and historical record both tell us that the number of Taoist nuns or priestesses was far larger than the number of known "immortal women" or adepts, perhaps by many orders of magnitude.

According to traditional sayings, at any given time there may be no more than one or two finders for ten thousand seekers. That, of course, is one reason why believers over the ages have been so eager to get to see those they believe to be true adepts, or even to find some notice of their actions or words. So scanty are these notices, even so, that great attention may be devoted to their minutiae, in hopes of divining some secret of the immortals, perhaps concealed in an image or a formula.

In the worldview of Taoist immortalism, in addition to the exoteric government of the world there is also an esoteric inner government, staffed by immortals. Western scholars have sometimes thought this Taoist idea of a celestial government to be an outgrowth or reflection of secular Chinese thinking, or bureaucratic Confucian thinking. Taoist classics suggest that the idea of the esoteric celestial government was not an imitation of the terrestrial government, but rather the terrestrial government was originally an attempted imitation of the esoteric government.

One factor that distinguished the spiritual Taoist inner celestial government from the nominally Confucian outer terrestrial government was that women were officially included in the celestial government, but not in the terrestrial government. This fact alone might be enough to suggest that the Taoist concept of an invisible hierarchy of immortals was not just an imitation or extension of the secular Chinese cult of the bureaucracy.

There may well always be those who believe that the idea of a spiritual government is superstition or fantasy, and certain aspects of the belief are by their very nature not subject to proof on demand by customary means. While it would be folly to make unfounded assumptions regarding the plausibility of supernatural intervention in the world of ordinary affairs, it may be possible to observe some of the historical, social, and psychological contexts and effects of belief in such intervention.

Like Hinduism, Taoism contains both monotheistic and polytheistic conceptions, with deities both single and in pairs. In the hierarchy of the spiritual immortals, this is reflected in the appearance of various lords who reign supreme in a particular context as well as the concept of the Absolute One, which may be envisioned as a metaphysical supreme being energizing all beings, including the deities, spirits, immortals, and realized people. On the level of anthropomorphic personification, the male contingent of the Taoist spiritual government has various emperors, lords, or kings whose domains and reigns may be envisioned as hierarchical levels of organization or as something analogous to the dynasties of the terrestrial government. The celestial rulers all have wives, naturally, who also normally work for the spiritual government, whether in office or as special envoys.

In contrast, a distinguishing feature of the ladies' branch of the titular spiritual government is that the paramount leadership remains the same throughout all time, personified by the Golden Mother. Also called the Queen Mother of the West, or the Golden Mother of the Tortoise Pedestal, she is the eternal queen mother of all Taoists.

Extremely old images of the Golden Mother portray a wild sorceress in command of demons; later her image became more civilized, and she ultimately became ensconced as the permanent queen of the secret world of Taoist spiritual immortalists. She was believed to reside in the K'un-lun Mountains, a formidable range dividing the regions of Tibet and Sinkiang in what is today western China.

According to legend, the Golden Mother was the teacher of the Mystic Woman of the Ninth Heaven, one of the teachers of Huang Ti, the ancient Earth Goddess who was transmogrified into the Yellow Emperor. This Mystic Woman supposedly taught Huang Ti magical methods of warfare, by which a famous insurrection was quelled. The Golden Mother herself is supposed to have transmitted a book on summoning ghosts and spirits to the great King Yu, who quelled the flood.

The Golden Mother was portrayed as unmarried, with numerous young male lovers and more than twenty children. Apparently not all of her offspring became immortals, even in the accommodating annals of myth. For some reason the fourth, thirteenth, and twentieth daughters are considered immortals, as well as one other who is named but not numbered. It is said that the Golden Mother practiced esoteric sexual yoga, which was considered by many to be a normal part of immortalism and would account for her perpetual youth. Even though traditionally associated with such an eminent figure, nevertheless, this aspect of the religion was kept secret, it is said, because it cannot be made into a general social norm.

It would be a simple matter to relegate the Golden Mother to mythical imagination, but recent archaeological finds in western China may suggest otherwise. Mummified remains of "Caucasian" people with fair hair have been unearthed in the Taklamakan Desert, just north of the K'un-lun Range where the Golden Mother was supposed to live. Could it be that the epithet "golden" originally referred to blond hair, and that Chinese myths of mysterious people in the K'un-lun area really derived from ancient contact with Aryan tribes? If so, who were they?

Perhaps the most plausible answer is that these ancient Aryans buried under Asian soil were probably Scythian. The wide-ranging Scythian peoples are believed to have originated at the feet of the Altai Mountains approximately four thousand years ago. The "white" mummies of China are judged to be up to four thousand years old, and they were found in the region between the Altai and the K'un-lun mountain ranges, where ancient Scythians would be at that time.

According to later descriptions, there were in fact blond and red-haired Scythians, speaking a language resembling Iranian but also customarily integrating other peoples into their system. By the time the Scythians emerged into history as a cultural identity they were already a mixed race. Fair-haired people in Afghanistan and Pakistan sometimes said to be descendants of Alexander's armies may really be descendants of Scythians who settled in those regions centuries before the time of Alexander the Great.

Supposing then that the Golden Mother of Chinese mythology may have originally been modeled on impressions of a Scythian shamaness-queen, is there a similar figure from Scythian mythology that would appear to confirm this historical identification?

The problem here is that there are no Scythian literary remains. Or are there?

Traditional Irish historians claim Celts to be descendants of Scyths. Celtic culture, according to its own lore, descended from Scythian culture. Thus there is a traditional basis for claiming a historical context for understanding analogies between Chinese Taoist mythology and Celtic Druidic mythology.

Pursuing these assumptions, the identification of the Golden Mother as a Scythian in her role as a woman wizard and monarch may be strengthened by the fact that certain very ancient Celtic tribes were matriarchal. Both Picts and Gaels had women warriors, wizards, and chieftains. Even the greatest of Irish warriors, a redoubtable fighter since childhood and tutored by all the men of his tribe, had to go to the land of the Picts to study with a woman warrior of great magical powers to become the champion of Ireland.

Perhaps the Celtic figure closest to the Taoist Golden Mother, again making us suspect an ancient Scythian germ to the Golden Mother myth, is Queen Maeve (Medb), immortalized in the epic *Tain Bo Cualgne*. Maeve, who is blonde, is a rich and powerful queen. She is represented as queen of the western fifth of Ireland, so she is also Queen of the West, just as the Chinese Golden Mother is also called Queen Mother of the West.

Naturally, the implication here is that the figure of Maeve, like many other figures of Celtic myth, did not originate in Ireland but was projected there by the druids who were accompanying the Scytho-Celtic settlements of Ireland over three thousand years ago.

Maeve is also depicted as a shamaness capable of magical spells—her name means "intoxication." She is especially known for her ability to disable male warriors by casting a spell over them inducing the feeling of labor pains. This amusing image may be thought to represent so-called Irish humor, but its assumptions about human capacities are reminiscent of the Taoist concept of meditation as "a man becoming pregnant." Queen Maeve's capacity to thwart enemies by magical means may also remind us of methods taught to ancient Chinese sages and rulers by the Golden Mother and her disciple the Mystic Woman of the Ninth Heaven.

Another aspect of Maeve's image that is like the Taoist Golden Mother is having many lovers. She says of herself that she has "never been without one man in the shadow of another." From an anthropological point of view, this statement may hearken back to a matriarchal age. Symbolically, it is ordinarily taken to mean that the person of Maeve represents the high kingship of Ireland. Curiously, even in this abstract role Maeve still resembles the Golden Mother of Taoism as an eternal monarchy.

In Irish epic, as in Greek and Hindu stories of gods and goddesses, Queen Maeve also has a human and symbolic side that can be less appealing than the fully immortalized image of the Golden Mother of Taoism, but that can be explained by historical circumstances. By the time Taoism became widespread and defined its own language of myth, the Chinese had no trouble immortalizing the memory of the Queen Mother of the West because now another people, the Huns, occupied the western borderlands of China, erasing the living memory of the magical golden Scyths from the minds of the Chinese.

However unlikely an ancient connection or contact between early Scythian and Chinese cultures may seem from the point of view of modern myths about the supposed isolation of ancient peoples, the fact remains that this hypothesis enjoys the advantage of archaeological support—Scythian-style chariots, for example, have also been unearthed in China. This picture of ancient times, furthermore, makes it easier to explain the remarkable coincidences between Chinese Taoism and Celtic Druidism, including their common interests in natural science and mysticism, not to mention their feminism.

Even the Taoist idea of a government of immortals seated somewhere out West is paralleled by the Druidical legend of Tir na n-Og or Land of Youth, also traditionally envisioned as being somewhere west of the lands of the Celts, to which good people may go after death in this world, and from which great souls may return from time to time, to instruct and assist faltering humanity.

The idea of spirituality in government was not entirely lost on secular leaders in China, but Taoist texts over the ages present such vivid descriptions of decadence in latter-day political and social practices that it can hardly be supposed Taoists equated patronage of religious or intellectual Taoism with good government. Many of the great Taoist wizards were educated men who had retired from political and military affairs, while many of the immortal Taoist ladies were educated women of the upper classes or had been slaves or concubines of emperors and kings.

One of the earliest "historical" immortal women was a princess of the Shang dynasty, which lasted from the eighteenth to the twelfth century BCE. She is supposed to have subsisted on a certain kind of raspberry root, maintaining the appearance of a twenty-year-old maiden all her life. She is said to have come and gone "above and below"—commuting between the celestial realms and terrestrial reality—perhaps implying that she alternated between extraordinary and ordinary states, often reported of mystics.

This princess is supposed to have gone back and forth between the higher and lower realms this way for more than two hundred years. In the context of Taoist immortalism, this motif seems to illustrate the practice of alternate withdrawal and emergence. This is one mode of alternation of yin and yang. The yin phase of withdrawal is for the purposes of recuperation, reduction of stress, and storage of energy; the yang phase of emergence, or expression, is for the welfare of the world and the positive release of the soul from earthly gravity, sorrow, and death.

In withdrawal this immortalized princess is pictured as returning to the heavens above, while in emergence she leaves her royal palace to gather plants and sell them to help out the orphans, the sickly, the widows, and the paupers, for whom the earthly government provided no assistance.

Even if today we find a life span of more than two hundred years implausible, considering the length of duration of the Shang dynasty and the many offspring sired by its polygamous rulers, this woman may represent more than one independent young woman of conscience born to the ruling house of Shang over a period of centuries. Each reappearance of such a woman among the people, an angel of mercy in a cruel society based on slavery, may have readily been linked to stories they heard from their parents, until the image of an eternally youthful immortal princess who ministered to the needy became imprinted into legend.

A number of other ladies from imperial or noble houses also appear in the ranks of the immortals. One of them was a younger half-sister of Crown Prince Chin of the Chou dynasty, son of King Ling, who reigned from 571 to 545 BCE. She was princess of one of the feudal states in the Chou confederation but disliked the courtly life and went into the mountains to practice the "path of escape from the net" she learned from a Taoist. She spent thirty years in obscurity, eventually attained the Tao, and became immortalized.

Another immortalized woman claimed to have once been a palace lady of the First Emperor of China, founder of the Ch'in dynasty. When the emperor died, she fled the palace and went into the mountains to avoid being killed. As will be remembered, all the palace ladies who had not borne the emperor a child were ritually executed at that time. In the mountains the fugitive met a Taoist who taught her to eat pine needles until she no longer felt hunger or cold and her body was so light that she felt as if she were flying.

One of the imperial concubines of Emperor Wu of the Han dynasty (ruled 140–86 BCE) also came to be ranked among the immortals, even though she evidently died. It is said that she had quietistic inclinations from childhood, and at one point in her life she was sick in bed for six years. During this time her hands became permanently clenched. Emperor Wu "found" her while on tour and considered her very fine looking in spite of her clenched fists. Many people had tried to open her hands, to no avail; now the emperor himself tried, and her hands relaxed. They became lovers after that, and the lady was called Madame Fist.

Later this lady was promoted to a high rank among the imperial concubines and eventually became the mother of the next emperor, who reigned from 86 to 73 BCE. According to Taoist lore, she "understood the Huang Lao arts, and gave birth to Emperor Chao after fourteen months of pregnancy." This image of extended pregnancy might have some connection to the idea of intensive "fetal education" for an emperor-to-be; Taoist mythology holds that the old master Lao-tzu was in his mother's womb for eighty-one years. In any case, Emperor Wu noted the legend that the ancient sage king Yao was also born in the fourteenth month, and in honor of her and their son he named her residence House of the Mother of Yao.

Afterward this woman died without apparent reason. When she was entombed, her corpse was not cold and was fragrant. When her son assumed the throne, her tomb was moved. Now her casket was found to be empty, containing only her silk slippers.

These images are rather common elements of stories of immortals, which like other supernatural items might readily be relegated to sheer mythic imagination. On the other hand, it is possible that even seemingly extravagant stories may in fact contain some germs of truth somewhat more natural, if little less fantastic, than disappearances of "undead" corpses by some sort of mysterious spiritual sublimation.

There may be a fairly simple explanation in a case like this woman. She was a highly honored concubine mothering the crown prince of an enormous imperial establishment, in which many concubines were vying for the favor of the emperor under pressure from the families who gave or sold them into palace service. She herself was quiet and delicate by nature and had no ambitions. Under these conditions, it is not impossible to think that feigned death and secret flight would be the most graceful and indeed the safest exit from such a situation.

People of unusual knowledge or ability were sought by princes, kings, and emperors in those times, and opportunities undoubtedly arose for other people of the ruling houses to meet Taoists. It would not have been impossible for Taoist confederates to help an inmate of an imperial house abscond; even if it were necessary to stage a cataleptic artificial death by drugging or sublethal poisoning, Taoist pharmacists would not be unlikely to have the expertise to do so.

This latter explanation of the lady's mysterious "death" would seem to account for the corpse's remaining warm and fragrant, showing no signs of rigor mortis or decay. The convenience of covering the tracks of such an operation with the pleasant myth of immortalization may not have been serendipitous. The avoidance of political and social complications (and perhaps emotional complications as well) would be an obvious advantage of such a ruse in a context of rigid external control. If such ladies were spirited off to secret communities in the mountains where they could devote themselves to spiritual refinement, moreover, the myth of their assumption into the celestial realms was not such a far-fetched fiction, but more of an artistic expression of an esoteric rite of passage whose real nature, clandestine by necessity rather than choice, could not be revealed without endangering the freedom and safety of the individuals and communities involved.

Numerous other stories tell about women eventually disappearing after having separated themselves from marriage and home life to cultivate Taoist immortalist practices. These women came from all classes of society, from the aristocrats to the peasants. In some cases the in-laws were excessively harsh, or the woman concerned was frail, sickly, or otherwise unsuited to household life. In other instances the women had already borne children and in effect "retired" afterward.

Some women were allowed by their parents to forgo marriage for a devotional life; others who were already married arranged with their husbands to live separately to practice meditation. Some women had husbands who were also Taoists or aspirants to the Tao; the men either practiced in tandem with their wives or agreed to let their wives live apart for devotional purposes. Some women were not so fortunate and had to flee their husbands and in-laws.

Happily, it is recorded that some couples "flew to heaven" together, although this phenomenon is comparatively rare in the annals of the historically known immortalists. The rarity may be due to, or illustrative of, the acknowledged difference between men and women in Taoist practice. In one story where a couple made the ascent to heaven together, for example, the husband had to climb a tree to get a head start to compensate for his wife's superior levity.

Among the women who mysteriously disappeared or allegedly "flew to heaven in broad daylight" were some who claimed to be immortals in exile. Generally speaking, these women had been unusual from childhood and often refused marriage or separated from their husbands before leaving the world. According to the belief that they were immortals in exile for minor offenses in heaven, these women are portrayed as waiting out their "sentences" on earth, then "flying" back to the celestial realms once they have fully dissipated the "gravity" holding them to the mundane world.

One such immortal in exile was the young Huang Kuang-fu, daughter of a peasant who lived during the early Tang dynasty. She is supposed to have disappeared in the year 664. Even as a child she liked quietude and used to sit absolutely still, doing nothing at all. She supposedly lived on cedar needles and water. Her parents, perhaps thinking she was "touched," took pity on her and let her do as she wished.

When she came of marriageable age, she told her parents she was really an immortal of the Heaven of Lofty Purity; she had been exiled for a minor offense, but now her time was up. Before she disappeared, she repaid her debt to her earthly parents by warning them of an impending disaster and giving them some gold to relocate. An epidemic followed her disappearance, perhaps "proving" her supernatural status to the parents she left behind.

The information and logistics for such disappearances could probably have been supplied fairly easily by communities of Taoists, wherein both material and metaphysical wealth were concentrated. It would no doubt have been easier for unmarried peasant women to disappear, moreover, than it was for married women and royal concubines. The "immortal in exile" theme may have been convenient not only for covering up disappearances but also for explaining the unusual people or behaviors that somehow have to "disappear" in a manner that neither threatened conventional senses of normality nor demonized authentically extraordinary or eccentric individuals.

The image of subsisting on cedar needles, or pine nuts, or other severely restricted diets, is a common theme in stories of immortals. This type of fasting is only a fragmentary picture of Taoist practice, always preceded by mental and physical preparation and never done in isolation as it often appears in the fables; yet it seems to have been something that caught the imagination of Chinese writers since time immemorial. The common isolation of images of fasting may lead us to suspect that symbolic or social values may be involved in this emphasis, because they are incomplete and misleading in their literal forms.

Some of this diet lore seems to be extremely ancient and is no doubt an indication of a living residuum of the hunting and gathering lore of high antiquity. All traditional hunters, gatherers, mountain ascetics, and warriors knew that certain plants and minerals could keep them healthy and enable them to survive for a time in emergencies. When stories tell of women who ate sesame seeds or pine nuts for thirty years, from a conventional point of view that may represent part of a gradual program of adaptation to another way of life in the esoteric societies of the mountains.

Taoist texts say that physical training, or refinement of the body, is the first priority for women; this may be one reason for the frequent mention of fasting in stories of immortal women, although the same theme appears often enough in stories of immortalized men. Speaking in concrete and practical terms of society and its economic structure, the ability to abstain from cooked food would represent one aspect of freedom. This would apply to a single person of either gender, but it may have been that women had in fact less choice in the matter than did men, having by law no independent wealth and being more vulnerable to exploitation in the general labor market.

Stories of women who lived without eating or drinking, or subsisted on meager diets of fruit and water or nuts and water, often note that they got to be that way after ingesting some kind of special alchemical preparation, either in a waking state or in a dream, generally given to them by a wizard or a spiritual being. Some take these images to refer to the ingestion of chemicals supposed to alter the chemistry of the body in various ways to stabilize it and retard decay.

Traditional accounts of alchemical experiments make a point of warning that successful transmission and application of the methods required consummate mastery. It is no secret that people were known to sicken and die from poisoning after taking alchemical drugs, and later Taoist literature on spiritual alchemy contains as many warnings on the misuse of chemistry as it does on the misuse of sexuality. Nevertheless, just as there are still people who market aphrodisiacs in the name of Taoism, in modern times there are still those who, after long preparation of their physical systems, ingest toxic substances alleged to purify their bodies in some extreme manner.

Aside from the esoteric question of toxic alchemical pills whose use is intrinsically limited by the severity of the preparations and effects, some stories of immortals contain material suggesting an ordinary scientific basis for apparently unusual diets. Some of the "nonfood" substances certain immortalists are known to have ingested, which included various kinds of mica, might have originally have been taken as dietary supplements for essential trace minerals such as magnesium, sodium, and iron, all of which may have been deficient in the diets of poor people and ascetics. The needles of cedar and pine are rich in vitamin C, which being water soluble is easily lost, and may also be seasonally deficient in certain local diets.

The nuts of pine and cedar are rich in oil and provide a high ratio of calories to mass. Taoists felt that massive quantities of food burden the system and eventually cause illness; thus abstention from grain, the main mass of a normal Chinese diet, is one of the hallmark types of Taoist physical fast. Physical lightness without loss of strength is among the qualities pictured admiringly in Taoist stories, and even if the immortalists were only to be considered mountain recluses, the advantages of lightness to their lifestyle are obvious.

Many other such examples could be extracted from Taoist immortalist and alchemical lore, and this lore will undoubtedly continue to form part of the comparative study of medical and hygiene systems in the future. In the meantime, when we think of the nutritional plight of the poor, and of refugees fleeing from social oppression into wastelands and mountains, we suspect that this aspect of Taoism was of greater concrete significance than ordinarily meets the eye. This may be illustrated by a deceptively simple story from the fables of feminine immortals.

One of the most ancient of the historical immortalized women was simply called the Hairy Woman, because she supposedly had hair growing all over her body. She was seen in the mountains generation after generation by hunters and travelers, it is said, suggesting to the modern mind that she is a "type," a refugee woman, an escapee from overwrought "civilization" living in the mountains. Her, or their, hirsutism may have been a symptom of malnutrition.

That would not necessarily mean everyone who fled to the mountains suffered in this way. It may, however, suggest that those who wandered alone and were not taken in by secret communities, or were not taught how to live in the mountains, may have been numerous enough, given the known extent of warfare in ancient China, for a strange-looking malnourished "hairy woman" to be sighted in the mountains now and then over generations. Since nobody ever got to know her personally, in that cultural context anyone might as well think that all the stories one heard of the "hairy woman" were of the same individual.

Rumors and legends of unusual people living deep in the mountains remote from human society seem to go back as far as history itself in China. Perhaps this was connected with the sense that no earthly organization could ever be complete or perfect and there would always be those beyond its pale. The idea of entire communities hidden in the mountains may be as old as the earliest confederations of Chinese states, which never completely consolidated their rule or dominated all the tribes of the Yellow River basin. But the cornerstone of this idea in the permanent edifice of Taoist myth was undoubtedly cemented into place during the latter half of the third century BCE, when the feudal states were finally destroyed and the first empire was founded.

The first empire of China was founded on the principles of Legalism, a political and social philosophy based on wealth, power, and the rule of law. Countless people were killed, widowed, orphaned, and displaced by the wars prosecuted in the liquidation of the old states, the establishment of the empire, and the extension of its borders. Countless others were executed, imprisoned, enslaved, maimed, or exiled during the short-lived first imperial dynasty by despotic authorities enacting countless laws to enable the government to remove anyone at will on some legal pretext. Countless more died from exhaustion on corvée—forced labor—in the construction of the Great Wall and a grand canal linking the Yellow and Yangtze Rivers.

Along with the rich and powerful empire that emerged from this cataclysmic upheaval there was also born the immortal legend of Peach Blossom Spring, a never-never land where the people who fled the horrors of the first imperial dynasty of China established a wonderland of freedom and peace. This legend was not the sole property or interest of Taoist mystics, but became a symbol of a better world in the folklore of the masses as well as the poetry of the scholars.

Many incidents in the stories of the early lives of the Taoist immortals reflect some kind of contact with another dimension that may have been, at least in part, another form of society. According to Taoist classics, this other dimension of life, or other form of society, had its own government seated in remote and unknown places or higher states of being, but its citizenry could exist incognito in the midst of the ordinary world. Maintaining contact between these two dimensions was one of the functions of the spiritual government.

Taoist lodges and organizations eventually developed, perhaps in the attempt to actualize these ideas of social and political refinement. Although many women entered Taoist orders, relatively few of the immortal women were formally ordained as Taoist priestesses. Two major sects of early religious Taoism nonetheless derived from teachings of women wizards.

One of these was the School of Purity and Light, founded by Hsu Sun (239–374). This man was a great Confucian as well as a great Taoist, well known first as a public servant and later a religious teacher. His most important Taoist teacher was a mysterious wizard woman of unknown origin called Ch'en Mu. Ch'en Mu, on whose historical existence no source will cast a shadow of doubt, was one of those said to have been seen for generations.

This recurrent appearance may suggest that if Ch'en Mu was not literally immortal, she may have been a member, or a composite memory of successive members, of an esoteric lineage or association of Taoists. Such associations may have sent people out into the world from time to time to test the atmosphere for renewed projection of spiritual teachings. If this were so, it would not be impossible for stories of an unaging wizard woman to crystallize over generations.

Another sect arising about the same time as the School of Purity and Light likewise honored a historical immortal woman as its matriarch and root teacher. An influential movement referred to as the Stream of Higher Purity, this type of religious Taoism was based on the Scriptures of Higher Purity, which were to become canonized as one of the main bodies of Taoist scripture. The prototype Scripture of Higher Purity was supposedly transmitted to the Taoist adept Yang Hsi in the 360s by Madame Wei, one of the greatest of historical immortal women, who had ostensibly died thirty years earlier in 334 at the age of eighty-two.

Yang Hsi claimed to have been visited by at least half a dozen immortal women, the most clearly historical of whom was Madame Wei. Some sources say that the scripture was recorded or "transmitted" by automatic writing; others assume that Madame Wei had been Yang's teacher when he was much younger. Numerous other scriptures were composed with the phrase "superior purity" in their titles, modeled on the teaching Master Yang claimed to have received from the immortal Madame Wei. This class of writings became a major influence in the development of religious Taoism.

The historicity of Madame Wei seems to be well established, in spite of the supernatural embellishments. She is said to have been unusual from birth, an image neither uncommon nor universal in such stories, and took a liking to Taoism from childhood. She read such Taoist classics as the *Tao Te Ching*, the *Chuang-tzu*, and the *Huang Ting Ching* or *Book of the Central Court*. This last title, representing several works on meditation, is also mentioned in several other stories of immortalized women, some of whom are said to have recited these texts for up to thirty years as part of their practice.

According to tradition, Madame Wei wanted to live separately even before her marriage, but her parents would not allow this. She was married at the age of twenty-four—rather late, it would seem, for a woman of those times, perhaps indicating some resistance—and bore two children. Later she took to sleeping alone and practicing Taoist methods in private.

Madame Wei apparently attained to a high degree of spirituality, because she is one of those historically known and outwardly observed immortalized women who are particularly associated with supernatural connections. She was allegedly given an esoteric text by a celestial wizard—something that occasionally happened to a select few among the immortalized—and was also supposedly visited by the Golden Mother, a distinct honor even in the generous terms of legend and myth.

The fact that Madame Wei is believed to have transmitted the original Scripture of Higher Purity thirty years after her death may be taken to be a mark of her immortalized status, yet it may also suggest that the influence of Madame Wei may have been perpetuated by a private circle of disciples after her death. The founding of a school may be signaled by publication of a secret text and the development of an exterior devotional framework, but its spiritual inspiration naturally precedes these activities.

The seeming anachronisms of this and other stories like it in Taoist history may reflect a sense of an inner continuity that may be or become externally invisible at certain points. Because these points of outward invisibility are perceived as breaks or contradictions in historical continuity, illustrative folklore may "patch" them with representational thematic devices such as apparitions, visions, dreams, revelations, and so on. Something of this nature is conventionally done with ordinary "history" as well, because it is in reality impossible to reconstruct all the facts of any given situation.

With the development of organized Taoist sects, many women entered religious orders. Originally Taoist clergy normally might marry and cohabit as part of their regimen, but later married clergy were widely replaced by celibate clergy. This change was encouraged by selective patronage, undoubtedly prompted by government fears of tax-exempt religious communities with populations growing by natural reproduction. It is probably for this same reason that Tantric Buddhism vanished in China at the same time.

The remarkable T'ang dynasty (619–906) introduced a new wrinkle to Taoist activities when the ruling family declared itself to be biological descendants of Lao-tzu, the "author" of the classic Tao Te Ching and in some sense the "founder" of Taoism. A system of examination in Taoist classics was instituted for a time, and large numbers of men and women entered Taoist religious orders. Whereas the ranks of Taoism had previously swollen with refugees from chaos, now they were swollen with adherents of the established order.

Earlier associations of Taoism with escapism and later associations with state religion may both have had bearing on the relatively small number of known immortalized women who were themselves Taoist nuns or priestesses. Even of those few who entered religious orders, a remarkably large proportion were not originally ordained of their own aspiration but became nuns only after an emperor had heard of them and had them brought to the capital. The popularity of Taoism in the profane world had in effect made them prisoners of the esteem in which they were held.

There could be óther drawbacks to the life of a Taoist priestess, furthermore, even in the highest echelons of an external hierarchy. A revealing story illustrating this is told in the driest of terms about an immortalized woman who as a priestess with extraordinary abilities caught the attention of the emperor.

Summoned to the imperial palace, the woman at once "got pregnant." On the eve of parturition, a violent storm arose. When the thunder stopped in the middle of the night, the priestess "was no longer pregnant."

No comment is made in the traditional account, and probably no comment has ever been needed for anyone in that cultural context. In whose interest was the disappearance of the infant?

The emperor himself would probably prize a child by a wizard woman. Since the Chinese believed in eugenics and in fetal education, an emperor could be expected to value such a child by any cultural standard. The other concubines of the emperor, in contrast, and their families, would not be so likely to welcome a wizard woman's child to the ranks of princes or princesses. The wizard woman herself might expect an extended period of imprisonment and endangerment if she were to be the mother of a child of the emperor.

If a rival faction within the imperial establishment were suspected of foul play, it must be asked why the priestess was not eliminated and her pregnancy was allowed to progress to full term. One answer may be secrecy; the woman may have kept her condition secret, perhaps assisted by special knowledge.

If the woman herself were suspected of infanticide, perhaps supposing she could rationalize this as an act of mercy, the question would again have to be asked why the pregnancy went to full term and was not aborted.

Barring the possibility that the wizard woman's baby did indeed vanish into thin air during a storm on the eve of its birth, it might be imagined that the child was in fact "spirited away" by confederates. Little more can be realistically said, except that the story ends with this woman's own disappearance. This means she actually escaped from the palace, one way or another, and for all we know may have even rejoined her own child in some mountain refuge.

State sponsorship does not seem to have had a salutary effect on church Taoism, and by the end of the T'ang dynasty a new Taoist movement was germinating in the person of Lu Yen, an erstwhile Confucian scholar. Supposedly born in the year 798, Lu was to become one of the most famous immortals of Chinese folklore. From among his disciples arose the powerful School of Complete Reality, or School of Total Realization, which continues to exist up to the present day.

At least two immortalized women are associated with Lu Yen. One of them, called Wizard Woman He, encountered him when she was only twelve years old, having gotten separated from a party gathering medicinal herbs in the mountains one day. According to Taoist theory, adolescent virgins have the greatest facility for the mystic path. Later on Wizard Woman He was known for her prescience, like numerous other immortalized women, who could use their uncanny ability to foresee the outcomes of human activities and events. She was also one of those who apparently no longer felt hunger, and ultimately she physically disappeared. Some of Lu Yen's directions to Wizard Woman He are cited in Taoist literature.

Another immortalized woman associated with Lu Yen is listed in Taoist lore simply as Ms. Kuan. This woman was from a poor family and supposedly had aspired to "leave the dust" of the world since she was a child. Her mother betrothed her when she was fifteen, but she ran away in protest, going deep into the mountains. She had been in the mountains for a time, eating wild chestnuts to keep alive, when she met an old man she herself later identified as Lu Yen.

This took place, it should be pointed out, in the 1200s, when Lu Yen would be over four hundred years old. Such a "time warp" is not out of place in Taoist lore, however, especially the lore surrounding Lu Yen, who is still thought to exist in the present day.

According to her story, Ms. Kuan had her menses stopped by the wizard, in order to facilitate her entry into the path. This idea of deliberately stopping menstruation in female practitioners seems to be unique to Taoist immortalism and is referred to repeatedly in the writings of later followers of the Complete Reality School, which traces its spiritual pedigree from Lu Yen.

After stopping her menses, Lu Yen taught Ms. Kuan mystic doctrine. Then he gave her a small, shiny chestnut and told her she would no longer hunger after eating it. This too is a fairly common theme, perhaps symbolizing a special dietary or medical regimen that would recondition the metabolism to enable an individual to survive on gathering.

According to the story, it took Ms. Kuan quite a while to eat the chestnut. This seems to emphasize the point that long and demanding preparations are required for Taoist fasting programs such as abstention from cooked food or from grain.

When she had finished the chestnut, Ms. Kuan found the old wizard gone. This motif is frequently seen in Taoist lore; it seems to illustrate the magical character of the wizard, but more practically it portrays the concentration of the practitioner in the program of practice. When the process is perfected, the instructor's job is done, and the wizard is gone.

When Ms. Kuan returned home from the mountains, she no longer ate anything except fruit and water, and she never had her menstrual period. Her parents, no doubt perceiving the change in her, no longer insisted on her marrying. Evidently people heard about her, for she was summoned to the imperial court, where the emperor took a liking to her. He had her ordained as a priestess and conferred a formal title on her.

The spiritual descendants of Lu Yen were already flourishing long before the time of Ms. Kuan, providing a well-established cultural context for her story of having learned her arts from the immortal wizard when she was a runaway girl in the mountains. The nominal founder of the School of Complete Reality (or Total Realization), Wang Che (1112–70), also claimed to have met and studied with Lu Yen himself, as well as one of Lu's great disciples. The School of Complete Reality attracted many women, including one of the most famous immortals of all time, Sun Pu-erh, whose teaching is still current today.

Sun Pu-erh was married and bore three children before she became a Taoist adept. Her husband was a wealthy philanthropist and a disciple of Wang Che. Conflicts between the Jurchen and Chinese nations at that time created widespread disturbance, and the Complete Reality School gained many adherents through its relief work. Sun Pu-erh helped her husband in his philanthropic activities but was not inspired to follow the mystic side of Taoism until she personally witnessed Master Wang demonstrating extraordinary abilities while feigning the opposite, showing how a Taoist can be active in the world without being a prisoner of the world, hiding enlightenment under the appearance of folly in order to accomplish a higher purpose effectively unopposed.

When Sun Pu-erh herself became a student of Master Wang Che, she was already fifty-one years old and her children were grown. She had a cottage built where she could cultivate refinement in peace and solitude while remaining at home. Later on she went to the ancient capital of Loyang, where she pursued advanced studies with a woman wizard and also did missionary work teaching others. She passed on just six years after entering the path, having finished her practice and attained, it is believed, spiritual perfection.

Sun Pu-erh's legacy includes two mystical meditation texts alleged to have been transmitted to her from a spiritual source, and fourteen poems treasured ever since as classics of spiritual alchemy.

7

The Cult of Orgasmic Energy

S EXOLOGY IS ONE of the traditional branches of Taoist science, touch-
ing upon both physical and psychological aspects of sexuality. Although a wide range of opinions and concerns are to be found in Taoist
sexology, generally speaking these are related to four main issues: fertility, health, happiness, and longevity. In some Taoism, as in Hindu Tantra,
there is also a certain interest in magical or mystical effects associated
with sexual yoga.

Taoist sexology appears to be very ancient in origin. Even the extant
versions of some Chinese works are as much as five hundred years or
more older than the *Kama-sutra*. Some Taoist texts are supposed to be dialogues between Huang Ti (the Earth Goddess or the Yellow Emperor) and
her/his sex teachers. These teachers are women, who like many mythical
characters have names with two or more layers of meaning. They are the
Pale Woman and the Dark Woman, or the Elemental Woman and the
Mysterious Woman.

In patriarchal tradition, these women are supposed to have taught
Yellow Emperor how to make love without ejaculating, a central technique of Taoist sexual yoga. This enables a man to retain the potency to
satisfy one or more women fully while allowing sexual excitation to pervade the entire body, thus promoting a more complete experience for the
man as well.

According to legend, using this technique the Yellow Emperor deflowered over a thousand virgins in one night without ejaculating, thus attaining health and long life. Like many other popular but extravagant stories in Taoist lore, this one seems to contain certain essential elements of the branch of Taoist science it represents. Understanding the theory and practice of withholding ejaculation is critical to appreciation of such illustrative stories about Taoist sexology.

The idea of prolonged postponement of ejaculation during sexual intercourse may have initially arisen from concerns about diminished fertility in dominant polygamous males. Legend and history portray powerful men as acquiring seraglios of hundreds, even thousands of women, along with their acquisition of material and military might. The number of virgins deflowered by Huang Ti in the famous story may be a figurative representation of this custom. A natural result of sexual hyperactivity in males, however, is a chronic depletion of semen, resulting in reduced fertility. If a man's sexual partners number in the hundreds or thousands, furthermore, potency problems may well develop along with fertility problems.

The popularity of aphrodisiacs among rich men may testify to the common occurrence of potency and fertility problems in polygamous males. For men in positions of power, whose main connubial liaisons were also political relationships, the pressures to please their partners and to produce heirs were more than matters of personal pleasure. Over the ages such men may have injured their health as much by the use of aphrodisiacs as they did by the use of longevity drugs.

In view of the cost and possible dangers of aphrodisiacs, it may be that the characteristic Taoist sexual practice of withholding or postponing male ejaculation while promoting multiple female orgasm was originally devised or discovered as a reliable, nontoxic means of addressing potency and especially fertility issues in males. Other aspects of this practice, however, including more general physical effects as well as mental effects, seem to have been or become subjects of great interest to those who followed or borrowed from Taoism.

In addition to issues of reproduction and general physical health, one of the main concerns addressed by the development of sexology or "chamber arts" was marital conviviality. This was of particular importance in old societies where the majority of marriages were arranged. While the contemporary myth of romance as a modern phenomenon is plainly untrue, as can be seen from poetry and song over three thousand years old, on the whole spontaneous romance has never been an adequate means of mating the majority of the members of any society. Consequently, family or community arrangement of marriage has ordinarily been involved at some level all over the world throughout history. Particularly under such social conditions, the cohesive function of a mutual satisfying sexual relationship in marriage was such that it could not be left to individual curiosity and chance. This was a very practical reason, tradition avers, for the origin of sex manuals, erotic literature, and erotic art.

The texts of the earliest extant Chinese sex manuals are more than two thousand years old, couched in terms of dialogues between yet more ancient figures. These texts already present the idea of postponing ejaculation until the woman has climaxed as many as ten times, with the aim of reaching *shen ming*, which originally refers to the spirit, human or divine, and means "uncanny clarity," "spiritual luminosity," or "a sense of the miraculous."

In this early lore, both mental and physical aspects of sexual intimacy are deemed important, indeed inextricably related. Proper mood, prolonged foreplay, and conscious awareness of the woman's state of arousal all play a part in the art of lovemaking depicted in these works. The various nuances of a woman's sounds, scents, and motions are described in considerable detail, illustrating a loving attention to the woman and her responses.

The basic principles of technique outlined in this lore provide for stimulating pleasure throughout the woman's body, but their particular applications are all a matter of sensitive response to the specific signals of the woman's feelings and sensations, from the initial love play through the ultimate ecstasy.

While Taoist and pseudo-Taoist sex lore became increasing complicated as time went on, not all of this development seemed to follow a natural course. Among the less desirable innovations, for example, was the tendency to replace the pristine methods of ejaculation control, which enhance pleasure for both partners, with topical anesthetics and mechanical devices of dubious worth having potentially harmful side effects. This trend seems to go hand in hand with the increasing social suppression of women and the growing spiritual gender gap.

It is still possible to discern in Taoist lore, nevertheless, certain basic natural techniques of sexual enhancement that have withstood the test of time. In the original vocabulary of Taoist sexology, these are called "going in soft and coming out hard," "nine shallow and one deep," "stabilizing vitality with stillness," "closing the yang pass," and "recycling vitality to repair the brain."

Going in soft and coming out hard has two closely related levels of understanding. One is based on the rhythm of excitation in the male organ, referred to in Taoist lore as the golden stalk or jade rod. "Going in soft" means that the man penetrates the woman in the trough of his excitation wave and then withdraws at the peak of the wave. This may be made more effective by coordinating the breathing with the movement, either inhaling or exhaling mindfully on the penetration and on the withdrawal, using the interval between inhalation and exhalation to sense the timing of the excitation wave.

The second level of understanding, or way of practicing going in soft and coming out hard, is based on the tension and relaxation of the musculature that controls the flow. "Going in soft" means penetration with the muscles relaxed, "coming out hard" means tensing the muscles and then withdrawing. The tensing of the muscles causes the normal erection to swell and harden somewhat more, thus stimulating the woman internally, and also prevents ejaculation when held during the course of the withdrawal. Once the hypertensed "golden stalk" is withdrawn, the musculature is relaxed, and the cycle is restarted.

This method is also called "going in dead and coming out alive," which may suggest that the "long life" or "immortality" promised by such techniques might refer to unlimited potency as well as to actual extension of life span through enhanced health and happiness.

The technique of "nine shallow and one deep" also can be used to postpone ejaculation and prolong intercourse, but its most dramatic effect is the production of ecstasy in both partners.

This technique is simple yet effective. The tip of the man's "golden stalk," where his most acute sensations arise, is inserted into the entrance of the woman's "golden blossom," where her most acute sensations occur. Six to nine shallow strokes, exciting these most sensitive places, are followed by one to three deep penetrations, typically eliciting a contraction of the woman's "sheath" around the man's "rod." This brings the woman to a dual climax, while alternating and combining the man's sensations so as to enable him to experience an analogous two-tone ecstasy without loss of self-control.

This particular technique is so effective that to counter the admitted existence of unbalanced obsession the orthodox Taoist literature specifically denies that there is anything magical or supernatural about the method. In more naturalistic terms, the old story of the Yellow Emperor deflowering hundreds or thousands of virgins in one night may refer to the "nine shallow, one deep" method in respect to the female reaction as well as to male ejaculatory control. Even if a woman has given birth, the tightness in her golden flower created by contractions induced by this rhythmic alternation of depth reproduces the body tone of a young woman who has never given birth.

The practice of "stabilizing vitality by stillness" is also a natural and effective method of ejaculatory control and prolongation of sexual communion. In simple terms, this means resorting to stillness, both physical and mental, to sustain erotic excitation while preventing it from overheating or "boiling over" into ejaculation.

This stilling may be combined with "locking the yang pass," or contraction of the musculature as if to stop outflow. This is only "as if" to stop outflow because ejaculation itself is normally not actually stopped by this muscular contraction except in emergencies, as can be easily understood from the simple physical fact that voluntary muscular contraction cannot be held indefinitely. While the contraction does temporarily block or stop the passageway of the man's seed, the actual ejaculatory control is a result of repeated contraction and relaxation of the musculature, causing the orgasmic tide to recede each time before the wave "breaks." The beauty of this technique is that the alternation of contraction and relaxation causes the man's rod to throb inside the woman, giving her subtle pleasure while the man "stabilizes vitality by stillness," controlling his orgasm by temporarily ceasing movement and quieting down.

A more general meaning of "stabilizing vitality by stillness" refers to the factor of serenity in the meditative aspect of intimacy. Wild excitement, in the Taoist view, is a wasteful dispersion of energy. To experience the heights of erotic bliss while in a state of lucid calmness, in contrast, enables people to store the energy of sexuality and stabilize its beneficial effects on the body and mind.

The crudity of the aesthetic experience of wild excitement, furthermore, is believed to cloud the appreciation of finer senses. Addiction without satisfaction is the ultimate result of this desensitization process. The vulgarity of Western pornography may bear out this contention. The counterbalancing effect of spiritual serenity and calmness on sexual arousal, in Taoist terms, is not to dull or dilute the excitement but to refine it and produce an exquisite sensitivity to subtleties. This applies, naturally, to both partners in a couple.

The consummation of the Taoist sexual communion, "recycling vitality to repair the brain," refers to induction of the orgasmic energy up the spinal column into the head. In the man, this is initially an extension of preclimactic "locking the yang pass," while in the woman it is an extension of the contractions caused by the ecstasy of climax itself. The contraction of the musculature governing the organs is combined with kinesthetic imaging of orgasmic energy entering the coccyx and traveling up through the spine into the brain. The result is an energizing of the body and a clearing of the mind.

This "recycling" practice may be more important for males than females because of the physiological differences between the genders and their orgasms. Although there may be great personal variations, by nature a woman in ecstasy radiates vitality, whereas a man in ecstasy ejaculates vitality. The idea of "recycling" is to fill the whole being with that vitality; were it to be emitted prematurely without "recycling," the ecstasy would come to an end with that climax.

These simple techniques are conducive to an experience of sexuality that cannot be attained by artificial means. It is sometimes thought that Eastern sexology is based on exciting and exotic lovemaking positions and maneuvers, but this is an external view, for without the essentials even the most sophisticated erotic choreography cannot produce the "uncanny clarity" and "luminosity of spirit" of the Taoist art of love.

The pleasure and power of sexual communion naturally attracts people to teachings such as Taoism that seem to offer enhanced experience of this aspect of life. One consequence of this fact is that exploitation of this attraction has dogged the name of Taoism over the ages. Part of the problem, of course, lies in the historical deterioration of supposedly Taoist lore on this subject. If modern people are to derive realistic under-standing of human sexuality from Taoism, account of counterfeit currencies must also be taken.

Other aspects of Taoist teachings have degenerated—according, we hasten to add, to the opinions of their own authorities—so it should not be surprising that Taoist sexology would deteriorate over time. It would not be fair to suppose that everything going by the name of Taoism, past or present, whether in the realm of "chamber arts" or other esoteric practices, would actually pass traditional muster.

One area in which particular care may be appropriate is the supposed Taoist practice now referred to by some scholarly investigators as "sexual vampirism," by which one partner in a sexual liaison takes energy away from the other, or one person takes energy away from many people. Chinese lore has stories about women staying young by "taking" energy from many young men, and even more stories about men becoming young and powerful by "taking" energy from many young women. There is no need to assume, according to traditional authorities, that there was any spirituality in this activity, or that those who lived longer this way outnumbered those who crippled themselves trying. In old China, wealthy people could buy boys and girls to use at will, and rulers regu-larly acquired thousands of girls and women in the belief that this would enhance their power. Very few are believed to have succeeded, even so, while many are known to have been ruined and to have ruined others in the process.

The irony of history was that those rulers were partially correct in their belief, but still ignorant of what they were really doing and therefore shortsighted and ultimately tragically mistaken. They did, however, make and break empires, and the world still bears the burden of their prece-dents. Among the uglier relics of their race for power is a certain amount of supposedly Taoist sex lore in which one-sided "vampirism" is actually considered normative rather than unbalanced and aberrant.

Political exploitation of personal power most certainly has ancient roots in China, as in other empires, but the proliferation of "secret" sex formulas probably reached a peak in the Ming dynasty (1348–1644). At that time esoterism of all kinds abounded in an atmosphere of political paranoia, social repression, and cultural and moral decadence. Later Taoist literature consequently contains many repudiations of merely physical or energetic interpretations of sexological concepts and practices, warning against mistaking energization for spiritual attainment.

In terms of American English vernacular, this critical distinction might be illustrated with some accuracy by the difference in nuance between the expression "have sex" and the expression "make love." To relate esoteric Eastern lore to contemporary Western public conscience and cultural concerns, it may be useful to ponder the traditional conception of the peril of divorcing energy and spirit. This may be brought home today by reflecting on the psychological roots of these American idioms—"have sex" and "make love"—and the effects of their general usage on attitudes toward sexuality.

In the context of Taoist tradition, there is some commentary by women on the "divorce" of energy and spirit in sexuality. This is found in the works of Chinese Taoist priestesses who wrote of the essential element of love more than a thousand years ago. By the time the status of women in China had been reduced to that of chattel, and sexual alchemy was envisioned as a man using girls for his own enhancement, no real issue was made of love in manuals of "sexual vampirism."

Love had been written off by males, it would seem, as a sentimental indulgence. This was a convenient ruse for rich men who purchased their partners, because it placed no onus on them for personal development. Evidently men generally thought of sexual alchemy as a way to be healthy, live a long time, increase their fortune, and maybe even gain mysterious powers; the question of their worthiness for any of these things was too much of a challenge to make many of them pause for long. Thus the Taoist poetesses were obliged to articulate the importance of the catalytic element of spiritual love.

In a poem addressed "to a neighbor girl"—that is, to young womanhood in general—a Taoist priestess writes, "it is easier to find a priceless jewel than a man who has a heart," and encourages the young woman not to lower her standards, for "once you've seen a righteous man, why cry for a gadabout?"

A priestess famed for her beauty and accomplishment, pursued by many men, also speaks of the importance of inner worth in a lover, lamenting the general run of suitors as "evening sparrows twittering, uselessly circling the grove." While living in a time when she did not risk social disapproval by taking as many lovers as she wished, this priestess still advises women not to be too accessible—to "live in hiding, do not choose a place in easy reach." Her reserve is based on the character of the prospective partner, not on social opinion.

This priestess refused many suitors, dismissing them as "moths of the wilds flitting 'round the guttering lamp" and preferring solitude to solace after her true love was taken away from her by forces more powerful than they. The popular image of Taoist priestesses as courtesans, even mere prostitutes, created a special duress on them. This preconception put the onus on these "free" women to extol the ethereal element of spiritual love. One poem by this priestess echoes this higher human need, in what otherwise would seem mere aloofness:

How clamorous the crowds around
The rich and influential;
By myself, I sing alone
In the light of the moon.
What motivates the man to come
With poetry in mind?
Here he shows up at my door
With his elegant rhymes.
I chant among the jasmines
And hide in poverty:
Above the pines are mountains yet;
Don't seek me ardently!

Estrangement of the sexes in China increased after the T'ang dynasty, and so did celibate monasticism in religious Taoism. In later Chinese erotic literature, some of which is actually Taoist didactic lore, graphic parodies of decadence and degeneration in the sexual habits of the times highlight certain factors that reflect disregard for women. These factors notably include the systematic nonexistence of ordinary domestic companionship and the habitual negligence of foreplay in the course of sexual relations.

It is therefore perhaps most poignant that the "secret" of the sexual "elixir" sought over the ages is divulged in this very context. The secret, according to the voice behind the scenes in a Taoistic erotic novel, is that the magical elixir of youth cannot be taken, only given. This is illustrated

in the fact that the sexual activities of the men in the novel do not invigo-
rate them but rather exhaust them. The only exception to this effect is
when one woman willingly gives a lover that "special something" because she wants to give it to him in particular, in admiration of his human
character. Of all the men in the novel, this is the only one who becomes
youthful by making love.

While this "special something" is typically portrayed as material or
energetic in nature, even in this vignette, it is not necessary to take this
literally to see that the quintessential factor in its "release" is the will of
the woman. None of the elaborate psychological flattery and cajolery of
seducers so deftly parodied in this book, and none of the exotic physical
acrobatics so wryly described, are able to capture this "essential ingredi-
ent" in the absence of a woman's will to give it to him.

This does not equate a woman's physical submission to a man with
the woman's will to give that special something. Rather, the woman's
will is an outcome of admiration or love at once emotional and rational,
a threshold to the spiritual. Her sexual communion with him is an expression of her spirit, and she unites with him spiritually as well as physically.
This is true union of yin and yang in the sense that it unites mind and
body, and in the sense that it enhances both partners in the communion.

This esoteric Taoist belief in higher spiritual love was enshrined in
the image of intimate communion "without untying sashes or removing
robes." The most sublime mode of interpersonal intercourse, it is spiritual
communion, or oneness of spirit, unobstructed by time, space, or the
world. Thus, even as the morale of society deteriorated while its structures rigidified, the poetess-priestesses of the Tao were able to use the
language of love to immortalize the survival of the human spirit and the
recognition of kindred souls:

> Silent shines the moon on lovers
> Speechless as they part;
> Light is in the lunar orb,
> Feelings are in the heart.
> The longing of lovers separated
> Is like the light of the moon;
> It pierces the clouds
> And rides the waters
> To the beloved's room.

8

The Underground Path

I N THE CONTEXT of Hinduism, we have seen how Goddess religion
has been associated with disreputable practices and criminal organizations. This is sometimes attributed to the role of Goddess religions as
"alternatives" to mainstream Hinduism, which systematically subjugated
and suppressed society, especially the women and the lower classes. The
analogy of Taoism to Goddess religion as a non-mainstream "alternative"
tradition therefore raises the question of whether Taoism similarly contains antisocial elements.

The *Tao Te Ching* says, "The Tao is universal; it can go left or right."
Just as the goddess Kali, in her nature as the elemental universe, can be
viewed as giving life and as dealing death, so can the Tao, as natural law,
be perceived as creative and as destructive. Although moral conceptions
are drawn from the Tao, certain aspects of the Tao are amoral in themselves, and their practical value to humanity is conditional.

As with Kali worship, the outcome of following the Tao depends on
what aspect of the Tao is pursued and how it is applied. While there may
not be exact Taoist equivalents of Pindaris, Dacoits, and Thugs devoted to
robbery, assassination, and ritual murder, there has long been a "countercultural" aspect to Taoism that sometimes included violence. In the case
of Taoism, however, this was normally directed against oppressive gov-

ernments, whereas the criminal organizations of Goddess worshipers in India were supporters of their governments.

Taoist countercultural and revolutionary conceptions are not necessarily violent and indeed eschew aggression and force in principle. But even the constructive Taoist ideas of government tend to undermine the otherwise dominant political approaches to social order, based as they have long been on military force, police power, bribery, division, and indoctrination.

Taoism operated on several fronts in this regard.

As is well known, several of the classic Chinese manuals of strategy bear the stamp of Taoism, including such greats as The Art of War by Sun Wu, another Art of War by Sun Bin, and the most powerful and secretive Master of Demon Valley by Wang Li. These texts, emerging from the militarized context of the Era of Warring States, teach methods whereby the weaker could withstand and even defeat the stronger, while the most skillful of all could actually "win without fighting."

It might be said that seeds of the methods of guerrilla warfare, terrorism, and psychological warfare—substitution of quality for quantity in force—all could be found in these works, presented as alternatives to the far more destructive methods of military operation in current use. It can be difficult for sentimentalists to perceive this type of Taoist operation, however, without adequate opportunity to compare the effects of various types of warfare.

The potential power in Taoism was not ignored by the empire builders of China, as we have already seen. The First Emperor actually sent expeditions of youths out to sea looking for the fabled Isles of the Immortals, and he had incredible quantities of mercury produced in alchemical laboratories dedicated to the quest for the elixirs of eternity.

The First Emperor also kept ten thousand concubines for the "bedroom elixir" and is said to have had so much energy that every night before retiring he normally perused "one hundred pounds" of documents of the empire's proceedings. In the belief that personal inaccessibility was one of the avenues to longevity, the First Emperor also had an elaborate system of palaces built, interconnected in such a way that it was not known where he spent each night.

Extravagant as these pursuits may seem today, some may appear constructive in having added to the development of human knowledge in some sense. The question of the cost, however, and the possibilities of alternative methods, is another issue that ancient extravaganzas may raise in modern minds.

The first two sons groomed by the First Emperor to succeed him died in the course of their developmental tasks, and the actual successor was an inferior man who squandered the wealth of his father and was assassinated by a minister. The third emperor also soon perished, and the dynasty was shattered by military uprisings.

Ever since that time the rulers and would-be rulers of China have sought to employ Taoist methods to attain power. People of all other classes have also tried to apply Taoism to problems of personal power, including health, long life, and success in their worldly undertakings. Insofar as the power potential of Taoism was sought without the noncompetitive parts, however, power mongers sought to monopolize occult arts and use them to maneuver people secretly. In cases like this, whether the activity was called "left" or "right," or moral or immoral, depended on where one stood.

The interplay of light and shadow became very complex at times, when power struggles immediately involved the welfare of large masses of people over vast areas, with many regional interests involved. "Orthodox" governments and rebel organizations both resorted to Taoist methods, either side being more covert or more overt in this respect at various times in history.

Taoist texts under pseudonyms decry corrupt government from even before the Era of the Warring States, providing a semi-underground stream of political criticism. Popular organization on a large scale, as an alternative to the wasteful and negligent secular government, was undertaken by Taoist charmers in the early centuries of the Common Era. The organization of these charmers, who called themselves the Celestial Guides, started an insurrection that fatally undermined the corrupt Han dynasty in the second century CE.

The practices of these Celestial Guides have always included elements of the so-called Left Path, which are like Indian Left-Hand Tantra and are similarly considered reprehensible by many outsiders. Hindu legend, it will be remembered, links Tantra to China.

Taoist-inspired revolutionary groups emerged again during the occupation of China by the Chinggisid Mongols of the Yuan dynasty in the thirteenth and fourteenth centuries. The founder of the following Ming dynasty, which restored native Chinese rule, was himself originally an upstart from an underground revolutionary Buddhist group, and when he gained power he tried to have religious orders suppressed and controlled in order to prevent them from threatening his throne. This resulted in the outcasting of certain "left-hand" sects, which only tended to make them more secretive, more antisocial, and more sinister than ever. Over its long life span of more than three hundred years, the Ming dynasty was repeatedly disturbed by uprisings led by charismatic religious cultists of the very type it had all along sought to control.

Similar activity reemerged during the following Ch'ing dynasty, another alien regime, most conspicuously in the so-called Boxer Rebellion against foreign domination of China. The esoteric martial arts that had grown up through centuries of Ming dynasty cultism, so dramatized in popular literature then and now, ultimately proved no match for Western weaponry. Even so, some temporary psychological advantage was gained for the Boxers by the notorious difficulty of killing them when they were mystically entranced. In the end this may have added to the suggestion of the sinister that has historically shadowed esoteric Taoism.

The modern organizations known generically as Triads, usually considered part of a demimonde or underworld, are commonly supposed to be descended in the main from remnants of Ming and Ch'ing Taoist sects and cults fending for themselves in feudal times. Sun Yat Sen, one of the noted revolutionaries of the twentieth century, was allegedly a Triad member, and the original Chinese communist party is also supposed to have used connections with the Chinese underworld in the 1920s and 1930s.

For women, Taoist martial arts remained important as methods of "refining the body" for immortalist practices. As means of personal self-defense, furthermore, martial arts allowed women who mastered them greater freedom to travel without fear of being molested. One of the more secretive arts, by which it is deemed possible to stun, paralyze, and even kill with the fingertips, was particularly suited to the self-protection of women caught by would-be abusers at close quarters.

By this time in Chinese history, girls and women of upper-class and well-to-do families had their feet bound and could not run. Self-defense against molestation and rape was therefore a particular problem for them.

Another close-range martial art handy for such situations focused on the dislocation of joints, by which an attacker could be temporarily disabled without causing death or permanent harm. The expert dislocation of even one finger joint can halt the progress of a rape or a choking.

In short, the traditional Taoist philosophy of minimalism in warfare and empowerment of the weak is concretized in these powerful arts. When seen in the context of sexual harassment and domestic violence, they remain relevant and useful to the present day, regardless of the proliferation of modern weaponry.

More problematic, perhaps, than Chinese grassroots organization or self-defense may be the proliferation of cults based on experimentation, deception, or delusion. Taoist texts are quite candid about these phenomena over the ages, and reports or rumors of Taoist-labeled charlatanism continue to surface in China and elsewhere.

One of the most obvious forms of supposedly Taoist charlatanism is some type of prostitution scheme alleging to teach mystical sex. Another form of pandering consists of deluging supplicants greedy for excitement, power, and self-importance with all sorts of supposedly esoteric exercises consisting of primitive mind-altering techniques, sometimes including methods traditionally considered not only useless but harmful. This may be criminal, or experimental, or delusional; yet public demand for gratification may keep such activities in business indefinitely, regardless of who may disapprove.

There are questions about what mind-altering cult practices actually do to the overall mental balance of the people they affect, as well as issues of what other influences groups devoted to these practices may serve to channel, whether in ignorance, in disguise, or otherwise. This is an age-old concern within Taoist traditions themselves and would naturally form part of any normal evaluation of supposedly Taoist phenomena in modern times.

At present there are public standards for the practice of psychiatry and medicine, but the same stringency of public standards in the practice of spirituality, even in orthodox religions, does not formally exist. This lacuna may be attributed to the separation of church and state, but in the case of religions new to the West there is also the historically conditioned and surmountable element of innocent ignorance.

When we consider the question of the "underground" aspects of

Taoism, we soon realize that global conditions have moved this concern from a distant past to the here and now. If there is a legitimate role of historical inquiry in this regard, it should help the modern world, East and West alike, discern and select the best of its own experience and knowledge.

9

Goddess of Wisdom

B UDDHISM IS SOMETIMES CONSIDERED an offshoot of Hinduism, originating as it did within a Hindu milieu and sharing certain elements of the Hindu cultural background. Yet Buddhism was in some sense already a counterculture in the Hindu context, and it spread far beyond the range of Hindu civilization. Buddhists were originally one of several new religious movements referred to by Hindu orthodoxy as *nastika*, or deniers, meaning those who did not accept the authority of the Vedas, the fundamental scriptures of Hinduism.

Buddhism rejected several elements of Hinduism as it was understood in Buddha's time, including its theology, its hierophantic ritualism, its exclusion of women, and its system of social discrimination. In Buddha's view, "the gods" are still part of "the world," routine performances cannot liberate the soul, men and women both have the capacity for spiritual realization, and so do people of all walks of life and classes of society. Some of these views were later adopted by certain unorthodox neo-Hindu movements such as Tantrism, wherein caste and gender prejudices were relaxed.

The relationship of Buddhism to Hinduism is of particular significance in that it reflects the Buddhist relationship to the world and thus also mirrors the Buddhist relationship to gender difference and sexuality.

There are three phases of this pattern of Buddhist relationship, echoing the Buddhist pattern of three cycles of teaching.

The first phase of Buddhist teaching involves detachment for the sake of objectivity. Buddha initially withdrew from automatic acceptance of the premises of his cultural upbringing to reconsider the fundamental problems of life firsthand. At the same time, he withdrew from marriage, family, and society so that worldly concerns could not influence his search for absolute truth.

In the first phase of the life of a Buddhist, following this pattern, emphasis is on individual mastery of self. Involvement in the world is maintained at a minimal level during this initial clearing of the heart and cleaning of the mind. This is so-called Hinayana, Lesser Journey or Small Vehicle Buddhism. Those who were deeply mired in their lives might become mendicants at this stage to train themselves in nonattachment. The essential note in gender relations is nonsexual and transcendental.

Mendicancy itself had become part of the culture and society in Buddha's world, so the second stage of Buddhism taught detachment from detachment. This follow-up phase was the so-called Mahayana, Greater Journey or Great Vehicle Buddhism. On the open road of the Mahayana, the inwardly liberated and purified individual now reenters society, "neither grasping nor rejecting" the world.

Projected on a historical scale, the tolerant, accommodating, and adaptable attitude of the second phase of Buddhism naturally embraced the Hindu (and non-Hindu) milieu in India. As a consequence, various figures from these traditions, including goddesses, appear with greater prominence, frequency, and metaphorical potency in the scriptures of Mahayana Buddhism.

These goddesses are of many types, both Hindu and aboriginal in origin. In terms of essence, however, the Goddess is identified as the supreme principle of emptiness (shunyata) and the corresponding intuitive insight of transcendent wisdom (prajnaparamita). The Zen Buddhist classic called the Blue Cliff Record says, "Shunyata is the goddess of emptiness. Space is her body. She has no physical body to be conscious of contact. When the light of Buddha radiates, then she manifests her body." This radiance symbolizes formless insight into absolute emptiness, believed accessible to the universal "buddha-nature" of living consciousness.

At this stage, the essential tenor of gender relations is still based on spirituality, but the egalitarianism of spiritual liberation is now expressed in more social terms. Here the fundamental norms of sexuality are rooted in empathy and consideration.

The third phase or cycle of Buddhism, referred to as Vajrayana, or Thunderbolt Vehicle Buddhism, represents the Buddha as being reunited with his wife after having transcended the world and then returned to the world to channel wisdom through compassion. This stage represents the full development and maturation of the preceding cycle; the methodology of the Thunderbolt Vehicle is thus the freest and boldest in its employment of expedients beyond the boundaries of formal religion as ordinarily understood.

At the level of Thunderbolt Buddhism, sexual identity assumes symbolic significance, and sexual communion assumes sacramental status. Like Hindu Tantrism, the Tantrism of Thunderbolt Buddhism has both Left and Right branches; these differ in their interpretations and observances along much the same lines as Left- and Right-Hand Hindu Tantra differ. Controversies also surround rumors of deviance or corruption in Left-Hand Thunderbolt Buddhism, as in the cases of Left-Hand Hindu Tantrism and Left-Path Taoism. These controversies occur within Buddhism as well as in the context of comparative and competitive religion.

The basic differences in the three cycles of Buddhism can be illustrated in their relationship with the absolute Goddess, which is traditionally equated with *shunyata* and with *prajnaparamita*, the intuitive experience of Emptiness.

This metaphysical Buddhist version of the Goddess is comparable to the Hindu Black Kali as the transcendental absolute beyond all human conception. In Buddhist terms, emptiness does not mean absence, annihilation, or nonbeing, but rather nonabsoluteness. This nonabsoluteness may be perceived and contemplated in many ways, as expounded in scriptures. Among the most basic and most accessible of these is contemplation of the transience of things.

In the first cycle of Buddhism, emptiness is articulated pragmatically in observations of the conditional and impermanent nature of things. Objective emptiness is implicit in the act of transcending fixations on things of the world by contemplating these observations.

In the second cycle, emptiness and existence are considered inherently equivalent because nothing exists absolutely of itself. This realization, thoroughly absorbed, becomes the basis for transcending the world while in its very midst. Expressed in terms of attitude regarding the world and its experiences, the keynote orientation of this phase of understanding emptiness is "neither grasping nor rejecting."

In the third cycle of Buddhism, elucidation of emptiness becomes more sophisticated, while the expression of emptiness is more creative and magical. Because all things are considered "pure" in having no fixed nature, what had been viewed as the mundane world now itself becomes as if sacred by the radical transformation of orientation and perception inherent in realization of emptiness.

Theory and practice must support each other in Buddhist developmental procedures, and the pragmatic issues encountered in realizing "emptiness" were considerable. Hindu devotees of the Goddess as a representation of the absolute, such as Black Kali, might subject themselves to extreme ordeals to quell the mundane commotion in their minds, in order to concentrate on the transcendental absolute symbolized by the all-destroying goddess. Buddhist devotees cultivating realization of emptiness also attempted to use similar if somewhat less horrific ordeals, in order to "remove the world from their minds and their minds from the world."

Untoward side effects of the enthusiastic overindulgence in such practices included physical, mental, and moral breakdowns, even permanent dementia in some cases. These dangers led to the refinement of more subtle thought-transcending techniques and the development of a cautionary motif on the whole subject of emptiness and its realization in Buddhist lore. Because it relates to the totality of life experience, this motif is expressed in psychological, social, and spiritual terms.

The main misconceptions of emptiness classically noted are based on identification of emptiness with nothingness, annihilation, or absence. The various mental problems associated with concentration on such disorienting notions naturally depend on the degree and duration of concentration. In their pronounced forms these ailments are known to include dissociation, enfeeblement of mind, moral depravity, and depression. There is also a syndrome called "immersion" that is often mistaken for enlightenment because the mind seems clear and one feels good. This state is traditionally identified as a seductive delusion that can fatally impede the real spiritual progress of anyone who indulges in it.

In view of these historical experiences, some intellectual opposition to Buddhism in the East was stimulated by observation of accidents and failures. Buddhism is often derided in the literature of some other religions for being nihilistic or antisocial, and the "doctrine" of emptiness is commonly taken to task for this negative bias. Buddhist writers could show, however, that the classical literature already diagnosed errors and corruptions within Buddhism, even in the time of Buddha.

In spite of these age-old and oft-repeated criticisms of Buddhism, both external and internal, the orthodox elucidations of emptiness have never eliminated the appeal of pseudo-emptiness. This is because there will always be those who will seek and find moral and intellectual license therein, and there will be those who seek and find intoxication and oblivion therein. "Emptiness wrongly apprehended," wrote the eminent Buddhist philosopher-saint Nagarjuna, "is harmful to the weak minded, like a snake wrongly held or a formula wrongly applied." From this point of view, the Hindu vision of Kali as horrific and devastating may be seen to represent more than a human emotion such as fear of loss and death; it is also descriptive of what can happen to the psychic structure when the awareness of life and death is unbalanced.

Nagarjuna also wrote, "It has been declared by the Victors that emptiness is departure from all views; but it has also been said by the Sages that one who holds to emptiness as a view is incurable." In the broader perspective of Buddhism, therefore, existence and emptiness are fully integrated, so nirvana is not a realm apart but inner peace in everyday life. This is the living perception of the Goddess made manifest, as the Zen saying goes, by the light of Buddha.

Mother Maya

As we have already seen, the Hindu goddess Kali is sometimes personified as Maya, "Illusion," or Ma-Maya, "Mother Illusion." In Buddhist tradition we also encounter a metaphysical Maya, personified as the Mother of All Buddhas.

In the simplest terms, the Buddhist image of Maya as mother of Buddha represents the relativity of illusion and enlightenment. Enlightenment emerges from understanding illusion, so illusion is the mother of Buddha.

As an educational theme, this construct illustrates the principle that

Buddhist liberation is attained not by trying to escape illusions but rather by penetrating them with insight. The idea that illusion is the mother of all buddhas also helps keep in mind the Buddhist principle that enlightenment must be relevant to the world in some way, not as a static condition existing in itself apart from the ordinary facts of life.

Illusion is the creative face of emptiness. The metaphysic of emptiness elucidates the unreality of things as we conceive them; when realized as empty of absoluteness, the ethereal power underlying illusion is transmuted into knowledge, artistry, and magic.

The Buddhist understanding of emptiness and illusoriness not only serves to dissolve the fixations of thought habits but also thereby releases the mind's creative potential from the inhibitions produced by those fixations. This release may also be the underlying psychic mechanism of the types of Hindu Goddess worship undertaken for various kinds of empowerment and success.

In the context of Buddhist literature, the most magical and constructive portrait of Lady Maya as mother of buddhas is to be found in the *Avatamsaka-sutra* or *Flower Ornament Scripture*, where she is not only the transhistorical mother of all buddhas but also a living teacher and guide on the path. This dual personality is a reflection of the Buddhist idea of two bodies, concrete and abstract, through which the ordinary world and the realm of spiritual understanding are connected.

In this scripture a pilgrim finds Lady Maya sitting on a throne transcending everything in the world, beyond all states of being yet facing all creatures, appearing to them according to their mentalities and in their own likenesses. This represents her dual personality as an abstraction and an actuality, the mysterious power of illusion and its myriad reflections in a multitude of minds.

Maya's power, in this Buddhist context, is consciously directed toward enlightenment and liberation. This stands for using realization of emptiness to empower the free employment of expedient methods. In other words, methods of liberation are adapted to individual needs and capacities. Thus expedients are not confined to rigid systems but applied like medicines to specific ailments.

The purpose of Buddhist teaching is liberation, not indoctrination. Therefore this flexibility of approach, a practical necessity in actual situa-

tions, is also an essential principle of Buddhist teaching. That is the pragmatic meaning of the saying that "Maya is the Mother of All Buddhas."

The vision of Lady Maya in the *Flower Ornament Scripture* comprises many
complex images with multiple layers of meaning. As illusion, a personification of the capacity of consciousness to construe order from chaos,
she is "like a reflection, appearing according to the minds of all beings;
like magic, made of the magic of knowledge; like specks of light, sustained moment to moment by the thoughts of beings." Thus she is "like
a shadow, bound to all beings by commitment; dreamlike, appearing to
beings according to their mentalities."

The vision of Maya as Mother of Buddhas includes imagery of nurturing and protection, emblematic of compassion; her appearance was
"adapted to develop and guide all beings, descending into the presence
of all beings, involved in the affairs of all worlds, issuing from universal
compassion, engaged in the protection of the community of beings." The
pilgrim in the scripture, "emptied of notions of the forms of all beings,
penetrating the minds of other beings, saw Lady Maya in the minds of all
beings, her virtue sustaining all beings." He saw her "engaged in nondis-
criminatory charity, impartial toward all beings, having united all beings
in the fellowship of universal compassion."

In the context of Taoism we have seen how pregnancy was used to
represent the inner attentiveness of meditation. Scriptural images of Lady
Maya, Mother of Buddhas, also make reference to meditation, contemplation, and spiritual knowledge: "Her mind was expanded with a flood of
energy of all knowledge; she was tireless in clarifying all spheres of truth;
she was adept in meditation on the essence of things; she engaged in all
aspects of meditation without confusion and had perceived the unique
sphere of meditation of those who arrive at being-as-is; she focused on
various meditations to evaporate the ocean of afflictions of all beings."

According to Lady Maya's own account in the scriptural story, these
qualities and capacities of hers emerge from an enlightening liberation
called magical manifestation of knowledge of great vows. This is a perfect
description of her imaginal representation of a metaphysical realization.
"Magic" stands for what is apparent yet ultimately unreal, and thus is a
metaphor for emptiness as well as illusion; "manifestation" means that to
be empty or illusory does not imply absolute nonexistence. "Knowledge"

is the pragmatic realization of the identity of existence and emptiness; "great vows" are the creative applications of this knowledge.

When rigid fixations of view and constructs of thought are dissolved by understanding their subjective nature, it is then possible to focus that same capacity of mental construction with deliberate intent. The enlightened one who sees the reflections of illusion in the minds of others is thereby enabled to use those very reflections, and that very capacity of reflection, to contact the buddha-nature or awakened essence in everyone. In that sense as well it can be said that "Maya is the Mother of the Buddhas."

Spirits of Enlightenment

Because Buddhism basically has no theology or demonology, it is often supposed that the deities and spirits appearing in Buddhist scriptures are simply borrowings from the Hindu cultural milieu. There is also some question of Buddhist influence, as has already been seen, in the development of the personifications of the Hindu Goddess. Then again, many divinities or spirits appearing in some Buddhist scripture appear to have entered the Buddhist fold from aboriginal tribal religions rather than from orthodox Vedic Hinduism.

Ultimately, what seems to define "Buddhist" deities or spirits is not their supposed origin but their function. Some texts may make no mention of such beings, while others may portray them as present in the natural and psychic worlds. In the mythology of Buddhist scripture, goddesses and angels appear primarily not as bestowers of boons but as teachers, guides, or helpers on the spiritual path.

An interesting example of this function appears in the *Vimalakirti-nirdesha-sutra*, "The Scripture Spoken by Vimalakirti," a popular Buddhist scripture focusing on the transition between the first and second cycles of Buddhism, from the narrow path of Hinayana Buddhism to the broad way of Mahayana Buddhism.

Most of the lessons of this scripture are derived from the conversations of the buddha named Vimalakirti, or Pure Repute, an enlightened householder who chides Buddha's disciples out of rigid fixations on limited views and practices. One of the pithiest lessons, however, is given to a disciple of Buddha not by Vimalakirti but by a goddess who appears in his house. With a sense of humor that is deep but gentle, and ever so magical, the lesson of the goddess touches on misogyny and gender bias as deformations of the concept and practice of chastity and purity.

It may seem remarkable that a book over two thousand years old would address the problems of misogyny and gender bias, but the argument is based on a Buddhist understanding of reality, and the scriptural application to sex differences and discrimination is explicit and needs no modern retrofitting.

According to the story, there was a goddess in Vimalakirti's house, listening to the enlightened man converse with great Buddhist saints and major disciples of Buddha. She appeared before the "great men," as the scripture calls them, and in a traditional gesture of respect she showered them with flowers.

When the flowers showered over the great saints on the Greater Journey of the Mahayana, the petals slipped right off. When the flowers showered over the senior disciples on the Lesser Journey of the Hinayana, however, the petals stuck to them. The disciples used all their spiritual powers to get rid of the flowers, but they couldn't get them off.

This vignette illustrates an essential difference between the Lesser and Greater Vehicles of Buddhism. The greater ideal is to transcend the world in its very midst, neither obsessively attached to things of the world nor obsessively averse to things of the world. The lesser ideal of personal nirvana is taken up by those who cannot yet uphold the greater; they seek detachment precisely because of their attachment. This "attachment to detachment" is symbolized by the flower petals sticking to the disciples as they frantically try to brush them off.

It is appropriate that a goddess should deliver this lesson, in the sense that woman is what most attracts man in the world, and therefore the attraction of man for woman has long been used as a symbol of attachment to the world. On the other hand, woman can also be understood as a symbol of warmth and compassion, which characterize this Mahayana teaching of transcending tranquil nirvana to reenter the world after liberation.

The use of something beautiful such as flowers to represent phenomena in this story intimates that the benefit of transcending the world can be nullified by the loss resulting from exaggerating nonattachment into aversion.

139

The story continues with the goddess asking a disciple why he is trying to get rid of the flowers. He replies that he is trying to get rid of them because they "are not in conformity with religion." The goddess retorts, "Don't say that these flowers are irreligious. Why? These flowers have no false discrimination; it is you yourself who are producing discriminatory thoughts, that's all!"

The goddess then defines the religion by essence rather than profession: "If someone who leaves attachments on account of Buddha's teaching has any false discrimination, that is not in conformity with the religion; if one has no false discrimination, that is conformity with the religion." She drives her point home by referring to the example of the great saints: "Observe how the flowers do not stick to the bodhisattvas— that is because they have already stopped all discriminatory thinking."

Now the goddess presents an intriguing insight into the psychology of negativistic approaches to detachment: "You are like people who become possessed when they get fearful; disciples like you are fearful of life and death, so you are possessed by form, sound, scent, flavor, and feeling. Desires for those things, however, cannot do anything to those who are already detached from fearfulness."

Then the goddess summarizes the psychology of "protesting too much" evinced by soured penitents and ascetics: "It is simply because your compulsive habits have not been eliminated that the flowers stick to your bodies. The flowers will not stick to those whose compulsive habits are gone."

Now the disciple asks the goddess, "How long have you been in this room?" Has the reality she elucidates been there all along?

She replies, "I have been in this room as long as you have been liberated."

He asks, "Have you been here long?"

She counters, "How long have you been liberated?"

The disciple remains silent, giving no answer. The goddess asks him why he is silent in spite of his great wisdom. He replies, "Because liberation has no verbal explanation. Therefore I do not know what to say about this."

The goddess, however, does not accept one-sided transcendentalism or absolutism that does not accommodate the relative or account for it in some way. She responds with a representation of the subtle interpenetration of emptiness and existence that underlies the freedom and compassion of the Mahayana: "Verbal explanation and letters are all manifestations of liberation. Why? Liberation is not internal, not external, not in between; letters too are not internal, external, nor in between. So there is no talking about liberation apart from letters. Why? Because all things are manifestations of liberation."

The preceding scene with the flowers illustrated two attitudes toward the five senses; this reference to speech and writing illustrates two attitudes toward the intellect. Those who take nirvana to be dwelling in quiescence are not really detached; they are actually obsessed with that from which they are ostensibly trying to rid themselves. The resulting conflict results in bigoted attitudes. By trying to dwell in quietude, moreover, the nihilistic "nirvanaholics" lose opportunities for constructive development and employment of their senses and intelligence. In Buddhist terms, this indicates lack of effective compassion.

The disciple in the story, a homeless mendicant, is taken aback by the goddess's statement that "all things are manifestations of liberation." He retorts, "But isn't detachment from desire, anger, and folly what constitutes liberation?" The goddess further shocks him by asserting, "It is only for conceited people that the Buddha says that detachment from desire, anger, and folly is liberation. For those who have no conceit, Buddha says that the very essence of desire, anger, and folly is liberation."

This lesson of the goddess is essential Mahayana Buddhism, based on insight into the principle of emptiness or nonabsoluteness of temporal phenomena. It is not that emotions and impulses themselves have any ineluctable power to bind and delude, but the exaggerated self-importance of the conceited, who take themselves and their feelings too seriously, imbues subjective states with the mesmeric force to trap consciousness into compulsive reactions to the world.

After some further discussion, the disciple at length comes up with a question that illustrates his failure to understand, asking the goddess, "Why don't you transform that female body?" Just as he had exaggerated the status of phenomena and therefore concentrated his effort on detachment from everything, now the disciple exaggerates emptiness and imagines it to mean that things can be made to vanish or change at will. If she has realized freedom, he therefore reasons, why does the goddess not liberate herself from the handicap of the inferior status of a female? Again the disciple demonstrates the rigidity of his thinking, not only about people and things, but even about emptiness.

Seeing that the disciple cannot make the intuitive leap, the goddess tries to lead him out of his conceptual fixation by reason. "For the last twelve years," she replies to his challenge, "I have searched for the marks of femaleness but ultimately cannot find any; so what should I transform?" She points out, in the language of contemplation, that gender-specific characteristics are secondary, and that social definitions of femininity and female roles are temporal conventions, not eternal absolutes.

Now the goddess pursues the theme of conventionality and unreality, pressing the disciple further: "Suppose a magician produces a phantom woman, and someone asks the woman why she does not change her female body—would this be a reasonable question?"

The disciple admits, "No, it would not. A phantom has no fixed form—what would one change?"

The goddess then drives home her point: "So it is with all phenomena; they have no fixed forms. So how can you ask why I don't change this female body?" If the definition is but a temporal convention, what liberation is there in exchanging it for another temporal convention, even were it possible?

Unwilling to leave the lesson on an intellectual level, the goddess proceeds to demonstrate experientially. Using magical powers, she transforms the disciple's body into a form like hers, while transforming her body into a form that looks like his. He can see himself in her, and she can see herself in him; an empathic link is formed, making deep communication possible.

The transfigured goddess now asks the transfigured disciple, "Why don't you change that female body?"

The disciple, in the form of a goddess, replies, "I don't know what has changed, but I've turned into a woman!"

The goddess says, "If you could change that female body, then all females could change theirs too. Just as you are not a woman and yet appear embodied as a female, so it is with all women; even though they appear embodied as women, they are not 'female.' For this reason Buddha says that the elements of existence are neither male nor female."

Ability to relate to other people simply as human beings, without the burden of social or sexual discrimination, is an essential foundation of the

Mahayana Buddhist ethic. Just as "emptiness" does not erase existence, furthermore, the ability to relate to other people as "neither male nor female" does not erase or deny gender or sexuality but rather empowers people to see through the obsessions with these secondary characteristics that blind us to our common humanity.

A whole host of goddesses appear as guides and protectors of the teaching in the *Flower Ornament Scripture*, already mentioned as the source of the most developed images of Maya as Mother of Buddhas. These teachers are encountered by a pilgrim in the dramatic final book of this monumental sutra.

The first goddess of the series is an earth goddess named Sthavara, which means "still" or "stable." This is an image of concentration, or mental stabilization, and the capacities of the goddess emphasize the function of concentration as a foundation of mental development and a means of gaining access to latent potentialities. Magically transforming the appearance of the earth, she shows the pilgrim the spiritual treasures he has produced through his good works, now appearing as deposits of jewels. "Take of them," the goddess tells the pilgrim, "and do whatever should be done."

The earth goddess then goes on to explain to the pilgrim that she has attained an enlightening liberation called "unassailable asylum of knowledge" and has protected and accompanied the buddha Vairocana, "The Illuminator," ever since his first inspiration. This protective function reflects a traditional Buddhist understanding of concentration, or mental stabilization, as functionally complementary to insight and knowledge. Sometimes concentration is likened to the glass cover of a lamp, protecting the flame of insight from the wind of distraction, so that the light can shine steadily. Here concentration as an "asylum of knowledge" is represented as a place of storage, or safekeeping, of the higher capacities of consciousness, just as the earth is a mine of all treasures.

After the earth goddess of stability has taught the pilgrim her knowledge, she sends him on to another goddess, this time a night goddess, whose name is Vasanti, "Lady of Spring." Outside of Buddhist tradition, this is a name given to various plants and to forest goddesses as well, for it is a direct derivative of the word for "spring" and has a generic sense of belonging to spring.

Naturally, Lady of Spring is remarkably beautiful. She is adorned with

143

all sorts of ornaments, robed in red, and crowned with the moon, her body manifesting reflections of the stars and the constellations. In the pores of her skin the pilgrim can see visions of the people she has rescued, delivered, taught, and guided, as well as all the ways in which she did these things. The pilgrim also can hear the teachings she has used to develop people, as well as the various timings, adaptations, and applications of the teachings.

Transported by this enlightening sight, the pilgrim addresses the night goddess with his plea for instruction and guidance on the way to all-knowledge.

The night goddess answers, "I have attained an enlightening liberation, a means of guiding people by the light of truth, which dispels darkness for everyone. I am kind to the evil-minded, compassionate to evildoers, pleased with those who do good, impartial toward the good and the bad. I aspire to purify the polluted, guide the misguided, inspire higher aspirations in the low-minded, increase the energy of those with inferior faculties, free those attached to the mundane whirl from its repetitious circles, and set those seeking individual salvation onto the path of all-knowledge."

The goddess then proceeds to describe many ways in which she helps people who run into difficulties in the dark of night. The lost, the beleaguered, the imperiled, the troubled—all of them she helps, by various means. The direction of the sun, moon, and stars is her guidance; the caves in the mountains, the fruits of the wilds, the water of the streams are her assistance to travelers. The songs of the birds, the luster of medicinal plants, and the glow of mountain spirits are examples of her beneficence.

The list goes on and on, gradually refining the image of the night goddess, from the beauties and blessings of the natural world, through consolation of economic, social, and psychological ills, ultimately to reach the realm of spiritual liberation and enlightenment. This revelation of the night goddess Lady of Spring is one of the most highly articulated of the lessons of the pilgrim in the scripture, and she is just the first of a series of eight night goddesses. Like the other guides, after instructing the pilgrim this night goddess sends him on to another teacher.

Lady of Spring directs the pilgrim to another night goddess, who she says inspired her and encouraged her on the path of enlightenment. The name of this night goddess is Samanta-gambhira-shri-vimala-prabha, which means "Universal Profound Radiant Undefiled Light." Her name is emblematic of transcendental insight, a fundamental "identity" of the Goddess in Buddhism.

In this story, the enlightening liberation realized by this night goddess is called "the bliss of tranquil meditation boldly going everywhere." Meditation is traditionally thought of as a means of awakening insight, hence the connection between her name and her state. The sense of "boldly going everywhere" characterizes meditation with insight as active and progressive rather than passive and static. This is an essential point in Mahayana Buddhism. In her address to the pilgrim the goddess makes a point of her own multiphase cultivation of meditation; her diverse methods of stopping unhealthy passions, feelings, and thoughts in people; and her follow-up with development of positive motivations, thoughts, and intentions.

At last the night goddess sends the pilgrim to the next guide, another night goddess by the name of Pramudita-nayana-jagad-virocana, "Illumining the World with Joyous Eyes." This goddess puts on a magnificent display of pleasing, liberating, and enlightening activities, radiating emanations showing practices of the Ten Perfections, or Ten Ways of Transcendence, the parameters of mature Mahayana Buddhism: charity, morality, tolerance, diligence, meditation, insight, methodological skill, commitment, power, and knowledge.

The revelation of Illumining the World with Joyous Eyes is rich in detail and goes on for a long time. At length the pilgrim, now in ecstasy, begins to sing the praises of the night goddess, extolling her perfect integration of transcendental insight and compassion:

While you have no attachment to mind or matter,
You guide the world by emanating forms of perfection.
Detached from the internal and the external, having left the sea of
    mortality,
You manifest infinite reflections in the states of mundane existence.
You have no vacillation, no vain imaginings or false ideas;
To the ignorant attached to falsehood you show the essence of things.

After eulogizing the night goddess, the pilgrim asks her how she came to attain her liberation. In reply, she recounts a long series of buddhas from whom she learned in the course of her development, at last to be awakened by a night goddess emanated from the supernal being Samantabhadra, or Universal Good. This supernal being represents the prototype and totality of the work of all bodhisattvas, the great saints of Buddhism who remain in the world to work for the welfare and salvation of all beings.

At last the goddess sends the pilgrim on to the next night goddess in the esoteric circle, whose name is Samanta-sattva-tran-ojah-shri, "Radiance of Power Delivering All Beings." This goddess manifests herself to the pilgrim in a body of great beauty, radiating a light from between her brows, illumining the whole world and suffusing the pilgrim with light. This may represent mental contact between teacher and learner in spiritual communication. The story says that the pilgrim attained a state of concentration called "sphere of ultimate dispassion" when touched by this light, showing that the contact was spiritual rather than sensory or psychological.

In this state of concentration, the pilgrim has an immense vision of worlds within worlds, in which he perceives the interconnection of all conditions of existence. He also sees Radiance of Power Delivering All Beings in the presence of every being receptive to guidance in all those worlds, and he witnesses her adaptations of her communications to the conditions of the beings she is addressing. This is representative of the cooperative union of insight and skill in expedient means, a hallmark of Mahayana Buddhism.

Enraptured, the pilgrim is again moved to poetic eulogy of the night goddess, after which he asks about her liberation. She replies with a very long and detailed story of her experiences of the past and what she realized in the course of her own pilgrimage. At the end of her journey she realized a liberation called "offspring of contemplation of the principles of the realm of reality." From the last five hundred buddhas she attended, moreover, she received illumination "by the light of all-knowledge" called "womb of knowledge of past, present, and future, vast as the universe."

Through this illumination, she says, she perceives infinite buddhas in every moment of thought, and from seeing those buddhas fresh flashes of the light of all-knowledge enter her mind, "because apprehending these flashes of the light of all-knowledge is endlessly and infinitely revealing and instructive." In this way the image of the "womb" is here connected with receptivity, which is of the essence of intuitive insight. Buddhist scripture says that all things are teaching at all times, but we are generally too distracted by our thoughts and personal preoccupations to be receptive to the lessons of the world around us. The "womb of knowledge" is open to impressions of truth and therefore can "nurture the embryo of enlightenment."

Finally the goddess directs the pilgrim to call on the night goddess sitting next to her at Vairocana's site of enlightenment. This night goddess is named Prashanta-ruta-sagara-vati, "Containing an Ocean of Tranquil Calls," and she informs the pilgrim that she has attained "equanimity through purification of the ocean of mind."

In characterizing her equanimity, this night goddess illustrates the mentality of Mahayana Buddhism: "My mind is not fixated on anything and not dependent on anything. My mind is intent on serving all beings, and my mind is tireless in seeing all buddhas." In this context, freedom from fixation and dependency has no connotations of aloofness, negativity, or stasis, but is dynamically expressed in dedication to human service and progressive awakening. The goddess declares, "Stilling the intense pains of the mundane world, producing all happiness in everyone, producing the ultimate bliss of the enlightened for endless eons—this is my vow!"

This story also goes on at great length and into considerable detail as the goddess explains how she helps and guides people in many different ways according to their particular needs, and how she learns by observing the enlightened ones everywhere and watching the body of Vairocana Buddha, who represents the very embodiment of reality. Her liberation is called "supernal manifestations in a moment of thought producing vast floods of joy," which she says she attained as an "enlightenment tree goddess" in the past.

The pilgrim finally moves on to see the next night goddess, Sarva-nagara-raksha-sambhava-tejah-shri, "Radiance of Energy Empowering the Protection of All Cities." Her body is "unstained by all worlds" and "transcending all worlds," yet "adapted to developing and guiding all people, with a body proclaiming truth in all realms." Her liberation is called "entry into the profound miracle of enrapturing sound," which is a "medium of the light of the teaching."

This goddess is thus associated with intelligence and eloquence, and she carries out her educational work by means of countless *dharani*, mystical concentration spells in which vast constellations of meaning are stored by the association of letters or phonemes with specific teachings. The word *dharani* also means "mental command" and can be used in Zen to denote an awakened state, because the concentration spells were used to develop mental command of the teachings and to foster corresponding states of heightened consciousness.

Buddhist women in East Asia have almost invariably practiced *dharani* recitation or its equivalent for meditation. This is obvious in the case of the countless female adepts of Pure Land Buddhism, where chanting a buddha name is basic practice, but it is also found in Zen annals as well. The Zen master most known in history for the large number of his female disciples, Bankei Yotaku (1622–94), prescribed thousands of daily recitations of several *dharani* for the hundreds of Zen nuns in his congregation.

The Zen monks also recited *dharani*, but not nearly as much as the nuns. Curiously, this fact does not appear in public documentation of Bankei's famous school and even today exists only in a rare manuscript of his order. The mystic schools of Buddhism consider *dharani* to be powerful practical aids to personal liberation and enlightenment, and consequently dangerous for the disoriented or unprepared. The founder of Tantric Buddhism in Japan wrote that they could empower anyone, even an ordinary person, to attain enlightenment in this life, but many of them were kept secret.

It may not be possible to say whether chanting is especially useful or effective for women in all cases, or whether other factors might have been involved in the evident predilection of Asian Buddhist women for chanting spells, scriptures, or holy names. Classical models may be found in scriptural stories like this one of the night goddess, who recounts the names of the buddhas from whom she learned her liberation. This motif confirms her association with holy name recitation practice, and in the process illustrates the empowerment of memory, a by-product of *dharani* practice.

The pilgrim then visits the night goddess Sarva-vriksha-praphullana-sukha-samvasa, "Cohabiting with the Pleasure of the Blossoming of All Trees." The liberation of this goddess is called "manifestation of contentment with the treasure produced from great joy." She herself says of this

Parvati Seated on Shiva. Nepal, c. 1725–1750. Distemper on cloth. © The Jucker Collection.
Photography by Mischa Jucker.

Chitrini Nayika, from a Rasikapriya Series. India, c.1780. Opaque watercolor and gold on paper. Courtesy of the Arthur M. Sackler Museum, Harvard University Art Museums, gift of John Kenneth Galbraith, 1971.126. © President and Fellows of Harvard College.

Female Immortals (1909) by Wu Shujuan (1853–1930).
China, Qing Dynasty, 1909. Hanging scroll, ink and
color on paper. The Metropolitan Museum of Art, gift
of Robert Hatfield Ellsworth, 1986. (1986.267.143)

Buddhist and Taoist Nuns of the Past. China, Ming dynasty, dated 1454. Hanging scroll, ink, color, and gold on silk. Musee des Arts Asiatiques-Guimet, Paris. © Photo RMN—Ch. Larrieu.

Thangka with Green Tara. Tibet, c. 13th century CE. Color on cloth. The Cleveland Museum of Art. Purchase from the J. H. Wade Fund by exchange, 1970.156.

Prajnaparamita. Alchi, Sumtsek, c. 1200. Wall painting. Photography by Jaroslav Poncar.

Laila and Majnun at School by Bihzad (1450 or 1455–1536), Herat, Afghanistan, 1494. By permission of the British Library, R0.6810 f106v.

St. Anna Teaching the Virgin by Murillo (1617–1682), Spain. Engraving by Timothy Cole. © AISA-Archivo Iconográfico.

liberation that it is "known to those gone to peace, with tranquil minds, concentrated, ultimately calm and cool, practicing all the elements of meditation. . . . This is the liberation of those who know the path, whose minds have penetrated the essence of beings, whose minds are not imprisoned in the sea of existence, who are moons reflected in the minds of beings."

After a long story about her associations and experiences of the past, the night goddess sends the pilgrim to another night goddess at the enlightenment site, Sarva-jagad-raksha-pranidhana-virya-prabha, "Light of the Energy of the Commitment to Protect All Worlds." The pilgrim finds this night goddess on a seat of jewels reflecting the abodes of all beings, wearing a mesh of jewels reflecting the principles of the cosmos. Her body reflects all moons, suns, stars, and planets, and she appears to people in forms like them, according to their mentalities. By gazing at the body of the night goddess, the pilgrim attains "ten purities of thought" by which he gains "communality with the goddess" and "communality with all spiritual friends."

The story goes on to describe dozens of aspects of this experience of communality—communality of recollection, communality of enlightenment, communality of mental purity, communality of kindness and compassion, communality of independence, and so on. Finally it says that by the purities of thought attained by gazing at the goddess, the pilgrim gains communality with her "in as many ways as there are atoms in a buddha-land." This suggests the mystical method of enhancing consciousness or boosting awareness by empathic contact with a more developed mind.

Spiritual communion appears in scripture as a medium of teaching and learning at least as important as verbalization. This idea seems to be especially prominent in Buddhist goddess stories, probably because of the representation of formless insight as a goddess, and the associated recognition of a particular feminine power or predilection for this subtle mode of cognition and communication.

The pilgrim then switches to the verbal mode and asks the goddess explicitly about her liberation. She tells him it is a liberation "made of basic goodness fostering the development of all beings according to their mentalities." By this liberation, the goddess explains, she realizes the equality of the essential nature of all things, takes refuge in independence, passes away from all worlds, and comprehends the differentiations in forms of things while realizing their essential nature without difference. These realizations represent the basis of transcending the world while in its very midst, the Mahayana Buddhist way, and the night goddess goes on at great length describing the various embodiments in which she appears in order to guide people and foster goodness according to their individualities.

The goddess follows her description of her liberation and manifestation with an account of her past. This too is a prominent theme in Buddhist goddess stories. In one sense the recollection of the past represents an aspect of the practice of self-analysis as part of self-understanding. In another sense this motif represents the process of spiritual evolution through successive stages of personal growth. These two meanings coincide in the practice of reviewing one's life at different times in order to extract enlightenment from experience.

This goddess is the last of the night goddesses encircling the enlightenment site of Vairocana, the Illuminator, who stands for primal awareness. After giving her teaching, this night goddess finally sends the pilgrim on to another guide, a goddess of the grove where Buddha was born.

The goddess of the Lumbini Grove is called Su-tejo-mandala-rati-shri, "Radiance of Pleasure in the Sphere of Subtle Energy," whose liberation is "vision of the birth of enlightening beings in all objects throughout infinite eons." This represents the generic practice of awakening by way of objective observation of phenomena, common to many schools and methods of Buddhist meditation. The night goddess of the Lumbini Grove, site of Buddha's birth, explains to the pilgrim how the mind is prepared for liberation by special kinds of buddhistic "birth" or spiritual regeneration through commitment, will, meditation, purification of intent, mental power, communication skills, and entry into the perspective of unity of all enlightened minds in all times and the continuity of all worlds.

The goddess concludes her lesson with an account of what she witnessed on the birth of Vairocana, the supernal personality of Buddha, emerging directly from Lady Maya's abdomen, "manifesting an effusion of inconceivable infinite light, like the sunlight emerging from the horizon, like lighting from the clouds, like the diffusion of dawn from the mountains, like a great torch emerging from the darkness."

She recollects her personal history as the night goddesses did before her, then finally sends the pilgrim to his next teacher, a girl of human society by the name of Gopa, "Cowherd." Thus a most remarkable cycle of goddess teachings comes to a close, forming an epicenter within this great Buddhist scripture, projected as a protective circle of immense spiritual force surrounding the center of awakening and regeneration.

In the Sanskrit text, the formation of the circle of goddesses occupies more than one-fourth of this final book, the longest and richest in the whole scripture. The circle holds a vast wealth of teaching material and is of incalculable importance in fostering enlightenment. The scripture asserts that countless numbers of such "goddesses" accompany these prototypical goddesses, suggesting that innumerable unnamed girls and women on the Mahayana path followed these teachings in the course of their spiritual development and also subtly influenced the people around them through the tenor of their being.

Nighttime means darkness, and in darkness is invisibility and unknowing. All these images are related symbolically in referring to mystical experience. In the case of females in Hindu-dominated India, the nighttime may represent the social and religious submergence or suppression of women under orthodox Hinduism of historical times. The appearance of these "night goddesses" in Buddhist lore, from this point of view, could be a representation of the spiritual flourishing of women in Buddhism. Those who could not accept this, or would actively oppose it, were given, by the literary form of the scripture, the option of believing that it was all a bunch of mythology. In this manner the artistry of the illustration may have been, among other things, a way of protecting these precious people from Hindu hostilities.

10

Wakeful Women

THE HISTORICAL BUDDHA, GAUTAMA, did not observe Hindu taboos against the education of females, and the order of Buddhist nuns originating in his lifetime is considered the oldest such organization of women in the world. Throughout those parts of the East traditionally dominated by antifeminist Hindu and Confucian systems, Buddhism was a resort for many women seeking spiritual fulfillment. Although personal reputation has never been a part of this quest, and personalities in illustrative literature are often figurative and symbolic, nonetheless hundreds of notices of extraordinary historical girls and women are recorded in Buddhist annals.

Notices of outstanding women in Buddhism go all the way back to some of those who personally met Gautama Buddha. A canonical collection of ancient verses called Therigatha or "Hymns of the Eldresses" contains compositions attributed to about seventy early Buddhist illuminates. One of these compositions is also associated collectively with thirty nuns, whose tuition it is said to have formed, while another is similarly associated with five hundred nuns. Thus the entire collection is supposed to represent some six hundred women in all.

The eldresses who composed the hymns in this early anthology came from a wide spectrum of social and personal circumstances. Some were already homeless ascetics, some were divorcees, some had been prostitutes, some were menial workers. The group of five hundred were all women who had lost children.

Among the enlightened eldresses was Prajapati (or Pajapati), who is said to have been Gautama's aunt and nurse. She was the first woman to seek to join his order after he began teaching. The name Prajapati means "progenetrix," and she and Maya (supposedly Gautama Buddha's mother) are traditionally considered sisters and co-wives of Buddha's father, who was a king. Prajapati may have really been Gautama's birth mother, or the queen and principal wife at the time of Gautama's birth. The figure Maya may have been invented not only for metaphysical purposes but also as a dignified historical cover for a concubine of Buddha's royal father.

One of the great eldresses, Nandottara, says she had experienced both ascetic and sybaritic lifestyles before meeting Buddha and gaining spiritual freedom. She sings of how she used to worship the deities of the sun, the moon, and the fire, and how she used to practice immersion in the sacred river. She goes on about how she used to observe a plethora of religious rules and vows, shaving half her head, sleeping on the ground, and abstaining from food at night. Then she gave up the ascetic life, began to wash and perfume herself, and pursued a life of sensual enjoyment. Finally she became a Buddhist nun and abandoned desire, was freed from all bonds, and attained peace of mind.

One of the eldresses who speaks of having met Gautama Buddha in person had been a Jain ascetic. In her song this eldress, Bhadda, relates how she used to cut off her hair and smear herself with mud, wandering about with only one piece of cloth around her. She alludes to a pseudo-religious perversion of values, saying she "thought the blameless blameworthy, and thought the blameworthy blameless," a delicate way of describing morbidity in excessive asceticism or self-torture. Then she encountered Gautama Buddha teaching a group of mendicants and underwent a change of heart; approaching the Buddha, she entered the order at once. After that she traveled around from country to country for fifty years "without any encumbrance," living on alms. Ultimately she attained liberation from all bondage.

Hundreds of the early Buddhist nuns abandoned the world after suffering extreme depression on the death of a child. One of these was Ubbili, who had been a wife of a king. She was very depressed on the loss of her daughter when she met Gautama Buddha in person. The Buddha told her that an incalculable number of children with the same name as her daughter had been cremated on that very spot. Realizing the universal fact of impermanence and uncertainty, the lady recovered her sanity, joined the Buddha, and ultimately attained spiritual liberation.

An eldress named Vasiti had also once suffered from severe depression after the death of a child. Deranged by her grief, she took to wandering around naked with matted hair, haunting crossroads, garbage dumps, charnel grounds, and roadsides. She lived for three years in this distraught condition before meeting Gautama Buddha and attaining peace of mind through his guidance.

Today we might think the society of the time excessively indifferent to the plight of this woman and others like her, but there were naked Jains and other ascetics around in those days, including antecedents of the infamous Kapalikas or "skull wearers," in regard to whom the charity of the culture of that time was to consider them not necessarily mad but rather seekers, or perhaps indicators, of another order of reality. They survived biologically partly because the concept of charity also included a habit of giving such people something to eat.

It may have been that Buddha himself thought his own society and culture excessively indifferent to the plight of the demented, in view of the order he personally brought to the random experimentation in mind-alteration going on in his time.

Some eldresses allude to frustration in their married lives, others to frustration in their religious lives. One eldress had been an impoverished childless widow who wandered on her own as a beggar for seven years before being initiated as a Buddhist nun. Another eldress relates how she had been on the brink of suicide when she suddenly attained spiritual liberation at the moment she tied a noose around her own neck in order to hang herself.

The eldresses often had sharply contrasting pasts. Uppalavanna, who came to be known as foremost among nuns in spiritual powers, relates that she had been a partner in a bigamous marriage wherein her husband's two wives were actually mother and daughter. While her verses do not reveal which one she herself was, Uppalavanna does speak of her revulsion as her motivation for leaving. The eldress Sona, in contrast, had been married for a long time and had borne ten children before she left home and became a nun in old age, as if worn out with the weariness of the world.

Another distinguished eldress, whose name, Anopama, fittingly means "Incomparable," never married at all. A beautiful daughter of a rich merchant, she had been sought in marriage by princes and scions of wealthy families; her father had been offered as much as eight times her weight in gold and jewels for her hand. In her verse she does not openly express her evident aversion to being treated as an item of commerce, but simply mentions that she met Gautama Buddha and that he taught her. According to her own account, at that very first meeting Anopama attained the third of four stages on the path to nirvana. This is called the stage of those who never return, and she subsequently cut her ties with her family and society and became a nun. Her own verse records that it was composed on the seventh night after liberation from all fixations.

The rapidity of Anopama's spiritual attainment may indicate the depth of her disenchantment with the mundane world. People may think wealth and beauty desirable, but this woman saw an insufferable vanity, a spiritual unreality, in the attentions these attributes brought to her. Her suitors were obviously not looking for a whole person, but were eager for a beautiful body and a large dowry.

The commercialization of most forms of marriage through dowry and dependency systems has made the bride's part in such transactions resemble in some way a particularly arduous and personally unprofitable form of involuntary prostitution. This harsh actuality, abandoned by Anopama for religious mendicancy, may also explain, without paradox, the early careers of the eldresses who had been voluntary prostitutes before renouncing the mundane world to become Buddhist nuns.

The eldress Vimala, whose name means "free from impurity," alludes to her past as a prostitute in her song of liberation. She gives the impression that she herself was the entrepreneur, being conscious of her own exceptional beauty and considering herself more fortunate and more clever than others. Thinking herself better than other women, she says, she considered men to be fools. She portrays herself as having been like a huntress, using the arts of the courtesan to snare suitors, inwardly sneering at them while outwardly seducing them.

Vimala does not tell exactly why she left that life to become a nun, but in the end she portrays herself as sitting under a tree meditating, finally to be "released from the yoke of heavenly and human worlds," unattached to anything, freed from all defilement, clear and cool, attaining ultimate peace.

Another enlightened ex-prostitute, the eldress Ambapali, is explicit about her disenchantment and detachment from that life, illustrating a process of meditation. Her song, one of the longest in the entire collection, goes on at great length about the beauties of her physical attributes—her hair, her eyebrows, her eyes, her nose, her ears, her teeth, her voice, her neck, her arms, her hands, her breasts, her torso, her thighs, her calves—and then in every case she describes the deterioration of each part of her body and the disappearance of her beauties as she grows old, reflecting each time on "the truth of the words of the one who realizes truth."

The cases of these ancient Indian ex-prostitutes who became Buddhist nuns and eldresses appear to be quite different from those of noted ex-prostitute Buddhist nuns in late medieval Japan. These Japanese nuns had not been prostitutes on their own account, but had been young women of the upper class sold into prostitution by fathers fallen on hard times. Their stories revolve around the profound depression these women experienced as prostitutes, and how they reached out to Zen meditation for psychological salvation.

One of these famous Japanese prostitutes succeeded in attaining awakening while still enslaved in a brothel. She had had the fortune to obtain instruction from the popular Zen master Hakuin, who had also experienced mental illness. Subsequently she was manumitted by a man who married her. She became a Buddhist nun late in life, and her story was immortalized in a best-selling book on extraordinary people of the times.

A rather different story is told of a friend of this woman, another nun who had been a prostitute in the same brothel. She was also from a respectable samurai family, but her father had lost his position and they had become impoverished. When her father subsequently fell ill, she sold herself into prostitution to obtain money for his medicine and other needs.

After selling herself to a brothel, the young woman was taken by an unmarried client as an exclusive mistress, whom he kept in a separate place. This man's mother, fearful that his relationship with the courtesan would present an obstacle to a proper marriage, attempted to intervene. The young man did not disagree with his mother, but neither did he break off the relationship. At length the mother went to talk to the courtesan herself.

Expecting a flashy tart, the mother was surprised to find instead an unusually demure young woman, fine-featured but plainly dressed. The older woman said her piece, expressing her objections to the younger woman's relationship with her son. The courtesan replied silently with a letter and a bundle of her own hair, emblematic of tonsure on renouncing the world.

The mother was infuriated by this gesture, cynically interpreting it as a ruse. She thought the young woman was only faking her desire to become a nun in order to put off confrontation. The sad fact was that by their time the literary Japanese word for "nun," bikuni, had come to connote a prostitute. One reason for this may be revealed in this story, following the assumption behind the mother's supposition, that men might try to conceal their affairs with courtesans by disguising them as nuns and keeping them in remote mountain cottages dressed up as temples.

In this case, concerned others calmed the older woman down and persuaded her to read the young woman's letter. In it she found the particulars of the courtesan's case, revealing her condition as a consequence of her sacrifice for her father. Her father and mother were both dead by now, but the debt structure of brothel contracts generally made it impossible for a prostitute to redeem herself by her earnings, unless a man of means took a special liking to her and purchased her freedom. The older woman's son had indeed redeemed her from bondage, allegedly for her to fulfill her wish to become a nun; but he had been as yet unable to get over his own personal attachment to her. That was where matters stood.

The older woman, overcome by this revelation, personally saw to the construction of a mountain retreat where the young lady might live in peace and practice her devotions as a nun. All seemed well, at least on the surface. After a couple of years, however, the nun fell into a profound depression from which she never emerged. Refusing the offer of another place closer by the family, declining all solace and abstaining from medicine, she allowed herself to pine away and die, finally passing in peace.

Although orders of nuns were established throughout the Buddhist

East in tandem with orders of monks, it is generally more difficult to obtain information about nuns. This may suggest that orders of nuns remained truer to their ideal of renunciation, shunning notoriety and fame. As Buddhism became institutionalized in various countries, sometimes even adopted as a kind of state religion, the structures and operations of Buddhist monastic organizations came to reflect the imaginations, expectations, and ambitions of their patrons. The internal spiritual egalitarianism of Buddhist ideals was therefore compromised, in the overt institutional formalization of monastic Buddhism, by the pressures of the environment. This is one reason for the difference between scriptural pictures of Buddhism and historical forms of religious Buddhism.

In the Buddhist literature of India and China, where Hindu and Confucian polities generally prevailed, laywomen are more prominent than nuns. In the Buddhist literature of Japan, in contrast, where shamanism was completely dominant until the sixth century and never totally replaced, repressed, or absorbed by Confucianism or Buddhism, the conception of a group of ascetic women as a state treasure was already familiar.

The same was undoubtedly true in Korea, whence came the first Buddhist nuns to Japan, but it is more clearly evident in the records of Japan, where state Confucianism never had quite as much power over the culture as it asserted in Korea. The order of Buddhist nuns in Japan was instrumental not only in the founding of Buddhism in Japan but also in the very founding of Japan itself as a unified nation. The tutelary deity of the leading clan of the most developed ministate at that time was the sun goddess Amaterasu Omikami, "Honored and Respected Divinity Who Lights the Sky," and the ancient leaders of the ministate—as of many of the ministates of prehistoric Japan—were shamanesses.

The first Buddhist nuns in Japan were sent from the Korean nation of Paekche during the reign of the Japanese emperor Bidatsu (ruled 572–85). These nuns were part of a state gift of a cultural delegation that included teachers of Buddhist precepts, meditation teachers, enchanters, sculptors, artists, and carpenters.

The first nun to be ordained within Japan was an eleven-year-old girl, daughter of an immigrant from China who had settled in Japan. She was ordained at the insistence of Soga Umako, a top clan leader intimately involved in the founding of the Japanese state, who found a defrocked monk from Korea to be the nun's preceptor. Two more nuns were soon ordained, both daughters of Chinese immigrants, before a plague was blamed on the "foreign religion" and all three young women were defrocked, imprisoned, and scourged. Buddhist statuary was burned and thrown in the river to get rid of the curse.

Another plague followed, however, and this time the clans backing Buddhism blamed it on their opponents' act of desecration. Buddhism was thus reestablished, and the three nuns were turned over to the custody of their original patron, who built them a sanctuary and supported them. By the year 624, when an ecclesiastical hierarchy was first established late in the long reign of Empress Suiko, there were nearly six hundred Buddhist nuns under the authority of the newly centralized Japanese state.

The regulations imposed on nuns in early Japan illustrate something of the habits into which monastics had fallen in the thousand years since the founding of the order, and the measures that governments took to control Buddhism and subordinate Buddhist organizations to perceived interests of the society and state.

Nuns were forbidden to practice divination, fortune-telling, political commentary, and the study of military and strategic sciences. Nuns were not allowed to set up centers of teaching or preaching outside the official cloisters, to delegate lay people to teach or preach, to own private property, to engage in trade or money lending, or to excite the common people by displays of wonders or acts of self-mutilation.

The stipulation of such rules for both nuns and monks in the original foundation of Buddhist orders in Japan suggests that these forbidden practices were already known to be occurring in Korean and Chinese Buddhism. Later Japanese lore also confirms that these activities continued in Japan, whether covertly or otherwise, as time went by. They still occur, in fact, to the extent that many people consider these officially forbidden activities normal routines for Buddhist cults.

Nuns were also specifically forbidden, like monks, to "falsely claim to have attained enlightenment." It is not clear how the government proposed to enforce this rule, but it may explain why the higher spiritual capacities commonly cited in the songs of the ancient Indian eldresses are little mentioned in stories of Japanese nuns in spite of the shamanic roots of Japanese culture. It does not necessarily mean they did not have them; it may mean they did not reveal them because of the threat of persecution.

Buddhists known or believed to have extraordinary powers were highly sought by rulers in many areas of the East, but by the same token they were feared and suspected on account of the presumed possibility that they might use their powers to influence people directly or gain personal followings. Some unusual monks in China were actually imprisoned on account of this fear, and the nuns rarely if ever revealed what they experienced.

The order of Buddhist nuns in medieval Japan did have some social impact. For one thing, it developed a mechanism for women to obtain divorce. Japanese society was at that time under the martial rule of samurai warriors; marital sex was for reproduction and not expected to involve love, and a woman ordinarily had no choice in marriage or divorce. Under these circumstances, the only way a woman could obtain a divorce on her own initiative was to enter a *kakekomidera* or runaway refuge cloister and live the life of a Buddhist nun for two or three years. While it could be said that the entry of married women into the order of nuns always implied divorce, the medieval Japanese system was probably unique in providing for a designated period of purification after which the woman could start a new life.

This interlude approach to renunciation was a more reasonable practice of monasticism than the career ecclesiastic model into which most of the nations of the East forced their Buddhist orders. The problem with the lifetime monastic model was that it reduced the orders to organs of the secular society, cultivating all the attendant ills of personality politics and worldly ambition. This is clear from the writings of leading Eastern Buddhists themselves, who were nevertheless generally powerless to change government policies on secular rule of religions.

Thus, while there are those who grumble even in modern times about the feminist function of the order of nuns in divorce proceedings, their motivations may be mixed. These critics may not be simply fearful men, as they might appear to be, or religious purists, as they might think themselves to be. They may speak as careerists whose own inherited institutional model of monasticism, itself essentially if unconsciously secular, has become static, irrationally conservative, and therefore threatened by the dynamic of an active intervention in society such as that of the runaway refuge cloister.

An intimate portrait of an archetypal Buddhist nun in her spiritual role appears in the *Flower Ornament Scripture*, where a liberated nun named Sinha-vijurmbhita, whose name means "Lioness Awakening," is found teaching circles of gods and goddesses, demigods and demigoddesses, waning gods and goddesses, beings of the air, earth, and sea, women, men, girls and boys, preternatural beings, and enlightening beings of all stages. The nun is seen teaching each assembly separately, in accord with the needs and capacities of each audience, variously expounding purification of mind, penetration of phenomena, salvation of the world, rational knowledge of reality, mental awakening, joyfulness, compassion, and many methods of concentration.

The nun is seen in each assembly "calm, composed, mind and senses quiet." She is "restrained as an elephant, her mind pellucid and clear as a deep pool," while as a teacher she is a "granter of all desires like a wish-fulfilling jewel." Even as she sits in the midst of magnificent arrays of every heavenly and earthly glory, moreover, she is "unaffected by worldly things, like the lotus, to which water does not cling." Her very presence affects those who behold her, for she is "unshakable as a mountain, pure in conduct, soothing the minds of beings like intoxicating perfume, extinguishing the burning of afflictions, like sandalwood from the snowy mountains, alleviating the pains of all sentient beings like medicine good for everything, beneficial to all who see her, producing the physical and mental bliss of quiescence."

The enlightening liberation realized by this nun is called "removal of all vain imaginings." This is a classical definition of emptiness, identical to the statement of Nagarjuna that "emptiness is departure from all views." To distinguish this from nihilism Nagarjuna adds that "those who hold to emptiness as a view are incurable." Likewise, the nun Sinha-vijurmbhita explains the essential "middle way" of balance, integrating formal knowledge of existence with formless insight into emptiness in the course of everyday experience: "I see all beings with the eye of knowledge, yet I do not conceive any notion of any being, and do not imagine so. I hear all beings' verbal signals, yet I do not imagine so, because I do not get involved in the spheres of their discourses. I see all buddhas, yet I do not imagine so, because I know their body is reality. I remember the cycles of teachings of all buddhas, but I do not imagine so, because I am aware of the true nature of all things. I pervade the cosmos in every moment of awareness, but I do not imagine so, because I know the nature of phenomena as existing in illusion."

The nun Sinha-vijurmbhita is one of a series of guides in the epic pilgrimage capping the *Flower Ornament Scripture*. She in turn sends the pilgrim on to another spiritual teacher, also a woman but appearing to be the antithesis of a nun. This is Vasumitra, whose name means "Friend of the World." She is a courtesan, a devotee of the god Vishnu, and a wealthy woman.

In the mythology of Hindu Tantrism, as mentioned earlier, the esoteric rite of sacred sexual communion was introduced by the god Vishnu appearing as Buddha in China. The Buddhist image of the enlightened courtesan as a devotee of Vishnu is consistent with the Hindu myth. The courtesan lives in the country of Durga, named for the Inaccessible Goddess, the metaphysical matrix of the goddess Kali.

The historical priority of this Buddhist scripture may reinforce the Hindu claim that Tantrism originally came to Hinduism from Buddhism. Then again, this Buddhist scripture represents formal boundaries between religions and cultures as essentially notional rather than real, claiming that the advanced bodhisattvas, the so-called enlightening beings or major saints of Buddhism, may operate within any culture or religion.

The secrecy or esotericism of Tantrism may also be suggested in the scriptural story. The pilgrim finds that the local people were divided in their opinion of Vasumitra. Those who knew of the courtesan only by hearsay, unconscious of her inner qualities, considered her a bewitcher and a temptress. Those who actually knew her, in contrast, were keenly aware of her virtues.

The ambivalence of opinion pictured here could also be interpreted to lampoon monkish misogyny. The monkish misogynist may think he is holy, but he could be missing a vital spiritual contact on account of an unexamined preconception. Were that preconception examined, it would be found to construe women as a source of pollution precisely because the misogynist himself thinks sex is "dirty." It then becomes evident that the misogynist thinks sex is "dirty" because he himself has a dirty mind. Unable to clean his own mind of obsessions, he projects the notion of pollution onto others in his thoughts, to imagine himself apart from them.

This is obliquely illustrated in a famous Zen koan. A pious Buddhist woman once supported a hermit for twenty years, the story goes, employing a sixteen-year-old girl to bring him food and help out with the chores. One day to test him she told the girl to embrace the hermit and ask him, "What now?" When the girl did this, the hermit replied, "In a withered tree perched on a frigid cliff, there is not a breath of warmth in the middle of winter."

The girl reported this to the woman. Indignant, the woman said, "For twenty years I have just been supporting a worldly man!" Then she evicted the hermit and burned down the hermitage.

A famous Zen master commented, "A living dead man—positive energy does come back, but he didn't even know it!"

This scriptural motif, and the illustrative stories that bear its stamp, also represent two attitudes toward life in the world as a whole, contrasting the Hinayana and Mahayana viewpoints. The apparently "puritanical" Hinayana views the world in terms of temptation and trouble, and so seeks detachment. The seemingly "liberal" Mahayana views the world in terms of relativity and emptiness, and so feels free to learn from the world and act in its midst. The sacramental understanding of sensory experience and sexuality in the Left-Hand Tantric view is in this sense a normal facet of mature Mahayana Buddhism.

The manifestation and mission of the mystic courtesan Vasumitra illustrate the Buddhist use of sensory experience for a transcendental, liberating purpose. She has attained an enlightening liberation called "ultimately dispassionate," and she appears in the form of a beautiful female of every kind of being. Then, she explains, "all who come to me with minds full of passion, I teach in such a way that they become free of passion."

In Tantric Buddhism this is sometimes called "using a thorn to extract a thorn," that is, transcending the world by experiencing it consciously rather than by trying to avoid or escape it. Vasumitra illustrates various degrees of passion in people by the way her presence allays their discomfort. Some attain dispassion as soon as they see her, some by talking with her, some by holding hands with her, some by gazing at her, some by embracing her, some by kissing her.

Buddhist teaching is traditionally likened to medicine, prescribed according to individual ailments; the way of transcendence through experience, accordingly, is not a standard course but adapted to the particular person. From a Mahayana Buddhist point of view this explains why there are both Right- and Left-Hand Tantrism, not only in Buddhism but also in its Hindu derivatives.

The very fact that the courtesan Vasumitra is herself overtly a "Hindu" while esoterically a Buddhist teacher represents this same general principle of adapting forms and methods according to the needs of those to be liberated. Realization of emptiness, or nonabsoluteness, enables the Buddhist illuminate to live in the world without bondage and to adopt different occupations, different appearances, different cultures, and different religions without identity crises. It is therefore symbolically appropriate to represent this non-Buddhist Buddhist in a female form, because femaleness represents universal emptiness and intuitive insight.

This insight into emptiness ultimately liberates the mind from fixations and obsessions, "establishing people in this enlightening liberation of ultimate dispassion," in the words of the courtesan. Yet this is not fixation on detachment itself but rather clearing the mind of subjective distortions in order to see the world more objectively. Thus the courtesan further defines the enlightening liberation of ultimate dispassion as "setting people on the brink of the stage of unimpeded all-knowledge."

The symbolic association of emptiness and insight with the female makes it appropriate to represent insight into emptiness as a woman who allays passions. Because intercourse with her does not reproduce mundanity, though pictured as a lover she is not a mother. Nevertheless, the fecundity of woman is still echoed in the revelation that vision, contact, or intimacy with her is a prelude to unimpeded knowledge.

In technical terms, this reflects the teaching that the realization of emptiness—to the degree individually necessary for dispassion, or objectivity—is not a dissociated, static, or nihilistic state, but rather insightful penetration of impediments to direct understanding of absolute, relative, and imaginary realities. This is why, in a symbolic sense, the courtesan follows the nun in the succession of teachers and guides in this epic spiritual journey.

The same journey takes the pilgrim to numerous other female teachers, all of whom are lay figures and most of whom are girls. There is

Asha, whose name means "hope" and whose liberation is "sorrowless well-being." There is the girl Maitreyani, whose name means "friendly" and whose liberation is "access to perfect wisdom by way of the totality," also called "access to perfect wisdom by total mindfulness." Sorrowless well-being describes peaceful nirvana, while total mindfulness describes dynamic all-knowledge; thus these two teachers represent the complete cycle of release, the journey beyond the world to salvation and the journey back into the world for the salvation of others.

Further on, the laywoman Prabhuta, "Perfect," has attained a liberation called "inexhaustible treasury of manifestation of good." Achala, "Immovable," another enlightened girl, has attained a liberation "containing invincible knowledge." Goodness in the temporal world is not considered a self-defined absolute, but is effectively relative to needs and circumstances. Therefore goodness comes into being through the action of objective knowledge. By the same token, knowledge has no meaning in itself but assumes meaning relative to the effects it produces. Therefore knowledge comes into effective being through its manifestation in goodness.

Another guide, the girl Gopa, "Cowherd," knows a liberation called "observation of the ocean of concentrations of all enlightening beings." Bhadrottama, "Highest of the Good," teaches a doctrine called "baseless sphere" and has attained a concentration of "mystic empowerment" wherein "there is no foundation of any phenomena whatsoever." One of the avenues of spiritual progress in Mahayana Buddhism is ongoing expansion of perspective, often represented as travel through countless buddha-lands, or fields of awareness. This is made possible by the fluidity realized through fundamental nonattachment to any particular realm. That nonattachment is what renunciation or home leaving essentially means in the context of Mahayana Buddhism.

The meditations and concentrations employed by the practitioners of the Mahayana are so numerous as to be uncountable. "Cowherding" is a traditional metaphor for the discipline of concentration, derived from the image of controlling one's own mind; here the girl Gopa represents the unlimited scope of Mahayana meditation. The "baseless sphere" of "mystic empowerment" wherein there is "no foundation of any phenomenon" realized by the woman Bhadrottama, "Highest of the Good," symbolizes direct insight into the absolute truth, the "highest good" in a mystical sense. Thus she represents the penetrating insight of "emptiness"—experiential realization that no phenomenon exists on its own—freeing the mind from obsessive fixation on any temporal experience, idea, or state of consciousness.

These guides, like the goddess guides surrounding the site of enlightenment, play a prominent part in the unfolding of this epic Buddhist story. Their teachings, moreover, resemble those of the goddesses in featuring detailed recollections of personal history. The verses of the historical eldresses also make frequent mention of this enhanced power of recollection. This power is not peculiar to females, but its relative prominence in stories of Buddhist women could have been intended to connect the practice of recapitulation with the meditative process association with pregnancy.

The motif of recollecting successive lifetimes of effort represents growing consciousness of the process of psychological development and spiritual evolution. Just as embryonic development recapitulates biological evolution, the process of spiritual regeneration may be symbolized by pregnancy or gestation, which is naturally associated with the female. This association is explicit in Taoist meditation imagery, and may also underlie this particular theme in Buddhist imagery.

The dominant cultural milieu of Hinduism may have kept images of Indian Buddhist women within the circumscribed domains of mendicancy (in the case of the images of women of the Hinayana) and mythology (in the case of the images of women of the Mahayana). In the context of Chinese civilization, in contrast, preexisting Taoist feminism seems to have disposed the culture toward recognition of a broader spectrum of spiritual life for women in Buddhism, Confucian orthodoxy notwithstanding. As a result, a comparatively extensive body of historical notices of real women (and girls) known as living exemplars of Mahayana Buddhism is to be found in Chinese.

Not unexpectedly, some of the stories of great Buddhist women of China illustrate Taoistic themes. Spiritual healing, extension of life, and visionary experience are all featured in such stories, very much as in tales of Taoist immortal women. Because these women did not show off or court fame, notices of them were either hearsay or limited to what people thought about them. Records of early Buddhist women in China thus often resemble traditional lore about Taoist wizard women.

Nonetheless, Chinese Buddhism eventually developed its own rich and varied culture within an already diverse Chinese civilization, sometimes parting ways with Taoism. For one thing, Buddhists did not necessarily value longevity in itself, as Taoist immortalism did; healing and life extension thus do not play so prominent a role in Buddhist stories as in Taoist stories. Mention of visionary experience, on the other hand, is as prominent in notices of Buddhist women in China as it is of Taoist women.

The salience of visionary experiences in historical records of women of the Mahayana may be attributed to the fact that the majority of them were followers of Pure Land Buddhism, some forms of which foster visions and visionary dreams. It may also be attributed to a feminine facility for this type of mentation. This may be especially pronounced in cultures such as the Hindu and Confucian systems, where females have been systematically excluded from formal education and membership in the orthodox intellectual establishment.

Insofar as the function of the orthodox intellectual establishment is compulsory rationalization, this use of mind becomes a compulsive habit. That habit takes up the attention of those engaged in it, leaving no energy left for other possibilities such as intuition or creative imagination. Certain gender stereotypes, particularly those on the pattern of rational males versus emotional females, appear to have stemmed from alienation of these two modes of mentation. Corresponding social conventions, such as the general exclusion of women from formal education and public office, were rationalized on the basis of this alienation, even though these conventions were themselves the instruments of that very alienation.

Factors of this nature undoubtedly contributed to the formation of what were in part countercultural concepts and conventions, including institutionalized monasticism. The Buddhists were striving for a new outlook on life, sometimes a new chance in life; but the secular governments and the Confucian bureaucrats who served them considered it imperative to maintain control over the visible institutions of Buddhism, including the published literature. This pressure made it difficult for Mahayana Buddhism to fully unfold in the total psychic, social, political, and cultural life of the people. Nevertheless, the wider range of expression allowed to women within the Taoist and Buddhist spheres of Chinese and other East

Asian cultures clearly influenced the other religious and cultural traditions within their complex civilizations.

It is well known that women played an important role in the establishment of Buddhism in Tibet, as they also did in Japan slightly earlier. Buddhist culture was promoted in Tibet during the seventh century by princesses from China and Nepal. These princesses were presented to the king of Tibet as royal brides by courts hoping to civilize their neighbors the warlike Tibetans.

A great boost to Buddhism in Tibet followed in the middle of the eighth century with the arrival of Padmasambhava, a Tantric adept who was assisted by a number of female adepts and disciples. A considerable record of teachings attributed to Padmasambhava is supposed to have been written in a secret code by his foremost disciple, a certain Tibetan lady. This master, in various guises, is said to have worked with a number of women whom he recognized as spiritual beings known as Dakinis.

Padmasambhava is pictured as having relationships with both immaterial and physical Dakinis. The immaterial Dakinis seem to have appeared both in visions and in the persons of certain women he met. At one point in his development, according to legend, the Dakini Guhyajnana or "Secret Knowledge" appeared to him in the form of a nun. This may suggest that he contacted the spiritual reality of the Dakini in the person of a living individual. Their communication, in the normal manner of esoteric Tantra, can be interpreted as visionary, symbolic, or both. In response to his request for empowerment, she turns him into a mystic seed syllable (bija) then swallows him. In her abdomen, he is given three kinds of empowerment—outward, inward, and secret—and finally expelled through her vagina.

The imagery here, in appearing to mix digestion and gestation, may at first glance seem childish or primitive, but the actual relationship between the two elements of the symbolism is not based on a childlike confusion of biological functions. The image of "swallowing" or digestion can be interpreted as the "deconstructive" aspect of emptiness that dispels illusions of identity and stability, while the image of gestation or development within the woman can be interpreted to represent the "regenerative" aspect of emptiness that potentiates freedom of thought and action.

In pragmatic terms, this imagery is suggestive of the normal Tantric practice of emptying the mind and then projecting a "seed" letter on the field of the "sky" of the clear mind. The associations of meaning in the seed letter are then activated, generating an enlightening awareness envisioned as "emanating" from the letter mentally implanted in the "womb" of space.

Another one of the Dakinis associated with Padmasambhava met him in terrestrial rather than visionary time. Her name, Mandarava, is a flower of auspicious omen that often "rains" in Buddhist scriptures on the occasions of great revelations. She was the daughter of a king, but Padmasambhava saw her as a Dakini and induced her to come with him to a certain cave as his consort in longevity practice. This suggests a Taoistic conception of sacramental sexual communion, again reinforcing the Indian legend that Tantrism originally came from China. After three months together, Padmasambhava and Mandarava obtained a vision of Amitayus, the Buddha of Infinite Life, with the boon of a billion ecstasies and power over the duration of life.

Padmasambhava also had a Tantric relationship with a Nepalese princess, but demonic interference foiled their efforts for years. Eventually they succeeded in their quest nonetheless, whereby both partners attained the *mahamudra*, the bliss of unimpeded consciousness in the *dharmakaya* or "body of reality" of the immaculate mind. This suggests the meditative use of sexual ecstasy to purge the mind of random thoughts and heighten nonconceptual consciousness.

Padmasambhava is famous for having sojourned at several great charnel grounds, where he is supposed to have imparted instructions to resident Dakinis. It is not necessarily made clear whether these Dakinis were figments of his own imagination in need of refinement, or Kapalika women who frequented charnel grounds for their own practices, or concatenations of both. These scenarios do not contradict each other, and there seems to be no reason to rule out any of these possibilities arbitrarily.

Tibetan cultures featured both patriarchal and matriarchal practices, both polygamy and polyandry. Polyandrous women in Tibet (whose husbands were normally brothers) generally had more authority than their counterparts in the Confucian sectors of China. The relatively high status of females in this widespread form of marriage may have been a factor in the evolution of Tibetan representations of friendly and fierce Dakini personalities.

Dakinis are sometimes pictured mainly as symbolic or imaginary beings—bearers, guardians, and revealers of secret knowledge—who assist a practitioner in the process of spiritual refinement. They may appear, in this function, as esoteric inhabitants of a yogic mindscape. But Dakinis could also be real people. The semimythological personalities of the flesh-and-blood Dakinis would probably derive from their spirituality insofar as they were identified by their inner attainments rather than by their social identity.

Dakini is a Sanskrit word, figuratively interpreted into Tibetan as "sky dweller." In Tibetan Buddhism the Dakinis represent emptiness, or the empty essence of luminous awareness; hence the symbolism of the sky. Being representatives of emptiness, Dakinis are often represented as teaching in paradoxical, challenging, or even threatening ways. In this manner they illustrate absolute truth baffling the conditioned intellect; their appearance may be perceived as frightening, as conventionalized conceptualizations of reality flee the scene.

Dakini is a feminine word; the masculine form, Daka, is also used, but Dakas do not play the prominent role in Tibetan lore that Dakinis do. In stories of male adepts, of course, the prominence of Dakinis may be attributed to their role as spiritual consorts. The special significance of Dakinis in Tibetan Buddhist lore is also connected to the traditional symbolic association of emptiness with the female. The secular strengths of women in Tibetan family life and social structure may also have influenced the standardization of concentration on the Dakinis as spiritual facilitators of self-transcendence.

In actuality, Dakini is a feminine equivalent of the word Dakat, the name taken by the Kali worshipers who pursued robbery and assassination. As explained earlier, in Hindu mythology Dak is an emissary of Kali, a sort of Grim Reaper who helps her cull the population of earth. The professional bandits and assassins who called themselves Dakat, "From Dak," were referring to deprivation by death, in effect representing their gangs as "angels of death."

The Dakinis of Tibetan Buddhism, by symbolic transference, could also be said to be robbers and killers, in the sense that insight into absolute emptiness deprives the mind of its holdings—it is no longer possible to hold on to the subjective sense of the world and the self as absolute realities. This is their "terrifying aspect" in that it may be frightening at first and seems destructive. Yet it is in effect constructive, in that it enables the mind to view and assess the world and the self in new ways, thus making it possible to overcome the obstacles to understanding and efficiency created by rigidity and fixation of thought and emotion. Therefore the terrifying and the benevolent faces of the Dakini are ultimately inseparable.

Because Tantric Tibetan Buddhism shares so many externals with Tantric Hinduism, it has often been assumed that these elements of Tibetan Buddhism, or Buddhist Tantrism in general, reflect Hindu infections. It has even been claimed that certain Tantric masters instrumental in the development of Tibetan Buddhism were in fact Hindus. There is another explanation for this phenomenon, however, in the context of Ekayana or "One Vehicle" Buddhism, the original basis and fullest expression of the Mahayana or "Great Vehicle" that produced the Vajrayana or "Thunderbolt Vehicle."

According to the Flower Ornament Scripture, which predates the emergence of Tantrism, the higher adepts of Buddhism can and do enter into circles of other religions, even becoming leaders of such groups, in order to stimulate more universal understanding and ultimate liberation. That is why some of the original Tantric Buddhists also appear in other contexts as master alchemists, Kapalikas ("skull wearers" who practiced ascesis through radical acts of uncivilized and unsocial behavior), and Naths ("protectors," gurus of a neo-Hindu appearance, possibly precursors to the Tibetan Lama cultus), as well as secular tradesmen and workers of various kinds.

From the point of view of Ekayana Buddhism, these and other medieval "Hindu" movements may have been founded or infiltrated for local expediency by Buddhist adepts. As Ekayana Buddhism was articulated centuries before the emergence of any of these movements or cults, this particular hypothesis of their origin does not require historical retrofitting to fulfill its own premises.

In comparing the forms and functions of Dakinis in Tibetan Buddhism with Kali, Dak, and the emissaries of Dak in Hindu Goddess worship, similarities and differences suggest a connection at some level —certainly metaphysical and possibly historical—without obliterating

171

philosophical and practical distinctions between Buddhist and Hindu worldviews. Tibetan lore makes reference to non-Buddhist Dakinis as well as Buddhist Dakinis, so it is clear that some distinction was consciously maintained.

The symbolic or immaterial nature of many of the Dakinis in Tibetan Buddhism, the laconic representations of Tantric relations with terrestrial Dakinis, the secrecy of Tantric circles throughout the Buddhist world—all of these factors may intensify the mystery of these women and the origins of their way of life. In the annals of Buddhism in the historically minded cultural sphere of China and other Confucian countries, in contrast, are found notices of numerous identifiable flesh-and-blood women (and girls) whose portraits represent certain Dakini-like personalities and activities.

The Chinese Ch'an lore of the T'ang dynasty (619–906), when women were comparatively free, features both nuns and lay women who foster the progress of Ch'an by stumping overly intellectual monks and deflating the egos of pedants and zealots. Some of these stories are immortalized in classical collections of koans, literary tableaus designed to provoke, reflect, or test various facets and levels of Ch'an consciousness. Most of the laywomen are peasants, often supporting themselves as small-time entrepreneurs, particularly preparing and selling refreshments on pilgrimage routes. This type of occupation enabled them to meet people from all classes of humanity, and the spiritual awakenings of some of the most famous Ch'an masters in history came from conversations with these women.

The T'ang dynasty is commonly considered the golden age of Ch'an as well as an apex of Chinese cultural history. The Ch'an lore of those times became the foundation for Ch'an revivals of the following Sung dynasty (960–1278), also circulating in Korea and later in Japan. Sung society and culture, however, were quite different from T'ang times, being more xenophobic and conservative. Sung reactions against T'ang polity and culture included repudiation of the freedoms women had enjoyed in those times, labeling such trends "Turkic" and "barbaric."

In this more restrictive and threatening environment of Sung dynasty culture, the Ch'an women mostly appear in the lore as nuns or ladies of good families. Some of them were given formal sanction as spiritual successors of great Ch'an masters. These individuals may not have been spiritual superiors of the doughnut makers and tea vendors of the T'ang dynasty, but the pressures of Sung culture against free women evidently dictated a need for token formalities as a protective device. For certain purposes, these formalities naturally included images of enlightened women acceptable to the mainstream society of their time.

When Ch'an was imported from Sung dynasty China into Japan in the thirteenth century, already highly ritualized and bureaucratized, it was patronized as sectarian Zen by the dominant warrior class and adapted to their purposes. The martial rigor of the age was reflected in the cryptic stylization of confrontational techniques developed for testing teachers and students in Zen circles. This formalized obscurity further created a fog of esoteric elitism. Under these conditions, the manifestations of Zen among women, who were suppressed to an unprecedented degree under centuries of military rule, could present a shattering challenge to both secular and religious conventions, reminiscent of a Tantric goddess or Dakini in her terrifying aspect.

Dramatic illustrations of this type of personality in Zen women can be found in the vignettes of the nun Eshun. She was from the aristocratic Fujiwara clan and noted for exceptional beauty. She did not become a nun until she was thirty years old, a ripe age in those times, and must have been married or had a love life. Her older brother was a Zen master, and she went to him for initiation when she decided to "leave home" and become a nun.

When she asked her brother to ordain her, in the Zen manner of the times he tested her resolve with severity. "Leaving home is for powerful men," he said in the customary initial refusal, "not something children and women can do."

Hearing this, she withdrew without a word. She then heated up an iron chopstick in a brazier and branded her face with it. Now she went to her brother again and asked him to ordain her. Seeing the depth of her resolve, the Zen master shaved her head, initiated her, and admitted her into his company, where she eventually mastered Zen herself.

Although she was from an ancient aristocratic family rather than a samurai family, Eshun's traditional act of self-mutilation in demonstration of unbending will reflects samurai values. Her ferocity as a Dakini-like Zen adept does not necessarily mean she was all ferocity, any more than goddesses of Hindu or Buddhist Tantrism are always terrifying or always benevolent. The thinking of the times, whatever it is, may tend to foster or to notice a particular limited range of human expression. In the context in which Eshun lived, thought was largely dominated by the warrior caste. Other stories of her boldness similarly display characteristics admired by warriors, while as a Zen adept in the spiritual sense she uses the confrontational behavioral language of her time to point at incontestable truths beyond temporal conventions. In this way Eshun proved to be more of a warrior than the professional warriors themselves, in cunning, in bravery, and in Zen mastery.

On one occasion Eshun was sent to a great government-sponsored monastery in the military capital, a major Zen center with more than a thousand monks residing in its halls. The normal protocol for such occasions called for an open Zen dialogue with the visitor, a procedure that gave rise to a lot of latter-day Zen stories. This custom had arisen from the mutual testing of seekers and guides, eventually developing a confrontational style that became all the more stereotyped in the martial cultural milieu of medieval Japan.

A visit from an advanced Zen adept could thus create an embarrassing scene for a careerist monastic abbot. The redoubtable Eshun was well known for her sharpness, so the crowd at the great monastery wanted to catch her out. Their aim was to discountenance her and put her off before she humiliated them and their abbot with her superior perception and power.

In pursuit of this plan, one of the monks, on seeing her coming up the steps, suddenly pulled up his robe, exposed his penis, and caused it to become erect. Then he did a headstand and cried, "My thing is three feet long!"

Unfazed by this display, the nun lifted up her skirt to bare herself. Spreading open her intimate parts, she rejoined, "My thing is depthless!"

Taken aback, the monk got flustered and ran away; the quick wit and steel nerve of the nun had won the fray.

Another case of "sexual harassment" of Eshun—this time not a calculated ploy to repel the nun but an aggressive attempt at seduction—was rebuffed in a similarly striking manner, at once intimidating and educational.

It seems that Eshun was so lovely that even with her face branded men were still attracted to her. One particular monk was especially earnest in his pleas to be allowed to embrace her. To his great joy she assented at last, but only on the condition that their intimate union have a special venue, as she was a nun and he a monk. She wondered about his resolve—would he break his promise when the time came?

No, the monk protested—as long as she let him have his way, he would be ready and willing anyplace, anytime, even in a cauldron of boiling water or a pit of burning fire. Hell itself could not dampen his ardor.

Eshun said nothing more about the matter for several days. Then the time came when their Zen teacher, her brother, was to give a formal talk on Zen before a large audience. When the great assembly had gathered, unexpectedly Eshun appeared before the crowd stark naked. In a loud voice she called to that monk, "Hey, you! Come do what you want, as we agreed the other day!"

The monk was so stunned that he left the monastery altogether. In the process of being "expelled" in this way, of course, he probably learned more than he would have by conventional punishment according to monastic laws. In Zen terms, that is why the story is preserved, not because it is racy.

Viewed in the context of secular Japanese culture, though, these stories of Eshun demonstrate an interesting amalgam of the sensuality and playfulness of the older culture of the Japanese aristocracy with the austerity and rigor of the newer culture of the Japanese samurai. The older aristocratic culture was steeped in the aesthetic mysticism of Tantric Shingon Buddhism, while that of the newly ascendant samurai was bent on a more stoical, ascetic interpretation of Zen.

These differences in cultural inclination mirrored the different ways of life experienced by aristocrats and warriors. What we see in Zen vignettes such as these may not be considered exemplary in an absolute sense, from the Zen point of view, because they are clothed in the culturally conditioned expectations and perceptions of the time. In purely Zen terms, what the specific combination of the two cultures in Eshun's anecdotes illustrates is called "adapting to the time to cut off the current."

In ordinary terms of everyday life strategy, this Zen "device" means dealing with the world responsively according to contemporary conditions while remaining inwardly "above the time" and individually inaccessible to the psychologically distorting influences of those very conditions. This balancing act is supposed to enable the individual to be effective in getting along in the world as it is while breaking free of stifling preconceptions and mental habits to see with fresh eyes and fluid ideas.

In the context of the martial culture in which Eshun lived, the asceticism of Zen seems to have shaded off into what might be called anestheticism, or celebration of the capacity to disregard pain. This may be why states of oblivion appear with greater frequency in the Zen annals of the late Middle Ages than they do in classical Zen lore and Buddhist scriptures, where such phenomena are considered mere states of mind and are not identified with enlightenment except by the ignorant.

Actions that may appear to be extreme examples of asceticism or anestheticism—and may indeed have been interpreted that way by warriors trying to follow Zen—tend to appear in the death stories of adepts. In a Buddhist context, these stories represent several aspects of Zen: the practice of letting go of all thoughts and things as they occur and pass away; the belief that a lifetime's self-cultivation is expressed at the moment of death; and the ideal of self-mastery and conscious triumph over death, even while dying. These are vividly demonstrated in the dramatic story of Eshun's passing from this life in an act of self-immolation as forthright and fearless as her passage through this life.

In her later years Eshun lived in a hermitage near her brother and "received travelers," meaning that she counseled and taught Zen pilgrims outside the formal monastic system maintained by the government. Many of the greatest Zen masters known to history, both male and female, remained in such situations all through their lives, well aware of the technical difficulties involved in handling large crowds and dealing with the vagaries and pressures of state sponsorship.

In this milieu Eshun was free from the rites and ceremonies that dominated formal monastic life and could therefore demonstrate Zen more directly and effectively to the individual seeker. There is no telling how much she and others like her contributed in this way to the actual development of Zen understanding, except perhaps by observing that in Zen annals the great teachers who taught both publicly and privately are said to have been more effective in private. As a Zen proverb says, "Finding people is not a matter of having large numbers of them around."

While most of her Zen teaching was private, Eshun's final lesson was conducted in public, with all the audacity of her legendary warrior-woman image. When she was getting ready to go, she built a shelf of firewood on a huge boulder in front of the outside gateway to a monastery. Sitting on it, she set it afire herself. Then she went into *samadhi*, a state of absorption in meditation.

At this point we might suppose she entered a state of oblivion, cultivated no doubt over many decades of meditation practice as a Zen nun. But suddenly her brother shows up on the scene, calling out to her, "Hey, nun! Is it hot? Hey, nun! Is it hot?"

This is a Zen conundrum, and the occasion of its use here at the scene of a sort of "suicide" may prove that confrontation by means of conundrums was not regarded as a mere intellectual exercise in Zen circles.

In Zen terms, the conundrum is as follows: If the nun says it is hot in the midst of the fire, that means she is still clinging to feelings for this world; if she says it is not hot, that means she is clinging to denial. If she screams, she is a "shaven-headed worldling"; if she is silent, she is a "ghost in the pit of oblivion."

Zen consciousness at her core, Eshun fell into none of these extremes. Is it hot? "No raw wayfarer can tell if it's cold or hot," she replied, and then silently passed away in the flames.

Not oblivious, yet not overcome—this is the Zen attitude toward the world, illustrated in the life and the death of the nun Eshun. It is not that she couldn't tell if it was hot or not, because she was still alive. She could not have been oblivious, because she could still hear and speak. And yet her "mind" could not have been dwelling on the feeling of the fire, for that would have overwhelmed any natural organism, causing it to lose control of its own functions. This would all suggest that Zen is not just a way of training the body and brain to remain impassive, as it was sometimes taken by professional samurai adapting parts of Zen techniques to their own uses.

Whether or not we can judge the story of Eshun's death to be psychologically or neurologically possible from the standpoint of modern science, it faithfully represents the Mahayana principle of transcending the world in its very midst, "like a lotus in fire," and this is probably its main purpose (rather than encouraging people to marvel at wonders or to get ready to immolate themselves).

Yet visual documentary evidence of modern times shows one of the voluntarily burning Buddhists in wartime Vietnam reaching out to (successfully) right his own sagging body in a ball of flame before expiring sitting upright in the fire. This photograph suggests that even stories like that of Eshun cremating herself could have been literally true.

The war-torn times in which Eshun lived demanded such rigors, and the martial culture of the samurai dwelt on images of this sort. So it is that, apart from three or four anecdotes of steel will and shattering force, nothing is known of the lifetime teaching of the enlightened Zen nun Eshun.

A similar irony can also be seen in the story of the Holy Woman of Mount P'eng, one of the most revered female saints of Chinese Buddhist history. She did not live in the remote past but died as recently as 1613, late in the decadent Ming dynasty. She was not a nun and her case is on record in secular sources, furthermore, because the police were officially involved; and so it cannot pass as a mere fairy tale or sectarian hagiography.

Notice of this otherwise nameless "holy woman" seems folkloric in focusing on wonders. This might be attributed to the Taoist background of Chinese culture, or to the common human habit of developing fixations associated with the emotional impact of baffling, dramatic, or otherwise startling events or phenomena. Certain elements of the story are perfectly credible, and a degree of exaggeration might be considered natural under conditions of involuntary and cumulative emotional excitement in the oral transmission of stories.

If we look at the story as a representation, apart from past or present conceptions of what can be experienced, we can at least see a portrait of woman's "imprisonment" and outward helplessness in the society of the times. This "holy woman" had always aspired to mysticism and wanted to become a nun, but her parents would not allow it, marrying her to a man in the next village. Confucian ideology dictated marriage, childbearing, and obedience to her husband and parents-in-law, but Taoist and Buddhist sources are sympathetic to women of mystical yearnings even if those longings might lead them to leave home life.

The Holy Woman of Mount P'eng did obey her parents and get married. She did not ask her husband to be allowed to live apart—as some Taoist and Buddhist women did—nor did she leave home on her own. In a way her story might be used by mystics to illustrate the exercise of "absolute nonresistance" or "nondoing"—a method of getting through the external world with a minimum of internal stress in order to conserve mental and physical energy. There seems to be more to the matter than that, however.

After the marriage, the story continues, every night after the lights were out the man felt that a wall suddenly sprang up between the two in their marriage bed, so that he couldn't approach her. This went on for months.

Today we might imagine that the man had found himself inexplicably impotent. We might further imagine that this could have been on account of the young woman's aloofness, but we need no imagination to know that impotence is an absolutely and literally mortal fear of Confucian males. It is not difficult to resume imagining, therefore, that the degree of anxiety this man's reaction to his impotence produced in him may well have caused him to become paranoid and perhaps even hallucinate, especially late at night. It is probably not necessary, therefore, to suppose that such an apparently fantastic story as a wall springing up between him and his wife is no more than a magical or folkloric embellishment.

When confronted by her husband about the mysterious wall that came between them on their marriage bed, the woman simply laughed and replied, "How could there be any such thing? It's just that there is blockage in your heart."

If impotence was indeed the problem, from a modern point of view it may seem unexceptional to suspect a psychological origin, as the woman does here. When this story took place four hundred years ago, there was undoubtedly a need to consider the emotional factor of marital and sexual relations more deeply in Confucian society. The prominence of aphrodisiacs in latter-day Chinese folk medicine would suggest that impotence was a problem and a fear of considerable concern to Chinese males. As attitudes toward sexuality became more biased and mechanical in later times, with men in pursuit of imaginary techniques whereby they believed they could "take" energy from women by sexual means to heal their own illnesses and prolong their own lives, the ethereal element of emotional intimacy was overlooked in the scramble for power.

Against this background, the revelation that the "wall" between the woman and the man is mental—and that it happens to be in the mind of the man—becomes a profound social commentary as well as a lesson in human psychology. The woman's explicit diagnosis of the wall's mental nature strips it of its fairy-tale quality to enable the modern mind to acknowledge its meaning for mankind.

After the man in the story had confronted the woman and been told that the barrier between them was his own psychological wall, he was apparently unable to resolve the problem. Things went on the same way for another two months. Finally the man's family stigmatized her as a pixie or a sprite and filed a complaint against her with the prefectural magistrate.

While preternatural beings were nothing new to the cultural landscape of China, there seems to have been a special fear of sprites on the part of the government of the Ming dynasty, which has bequeathed more to modern times than its vases. There were rational reasons for this fear, moreover, in that the founder of the dynasty had himself risen to political power from leadership of an underground religious cult and had ever after made it a policy to suppress and control all religions in China. Over the following centuries, however, as a probably predictable reaction, charismatic mystics did emerge to create or lead popular liberation movements time and again, to the great discomfiture of the imperial government.

As a result of these historical circumstances, an individual with apparently supernatural abilities, such as the woman in this story, could be viewed with great suspicion by the authorities, in proportion to the awe in which she or he was held by local people. It may even be that the imperial honors and patronage given to some of these extraordinary individuals were really intended as a form of imprisonment, to isolate them from contact with commoners.

In the case of this woman, an investigator was dispatched to look into the matter. The woman made no protestations to the charges of her husband's family and was subsequently sentenced to imprisonment in a mountain cavern.

The cavern was no more than ten feet square and pitch dark inside. After the woman was put inside, the mouth of the cave was bricked up, leaving only a hole an inch in diameter, enough for slight ventilation but not enough to allow food and drink to be passed in to the prisoner.

Considering the sheer ignorance and cruelty of this treatment of an

innocent, one may wonder how deeply the humane and intelligent doctrines of Taoism and Buddhism had really affected Chinese culture over
so many centuries of currency. The survival of preexisting habits alien to
a historically accepted religion or ideology may be observed in the domains of all world religions over the centuries. This observation has resulted in some general cynicism about religion and has even led some
people to reject religion altogether. Others it has led to distinguish more
strictly between spirituality in religion and political exploitation of religious ideas and organizations.

Superstition seems to have played its role in the brutal imprisonment
of the Holy Woman of Mount P'eng, but then superstition among the
people was encouraged in those times as a method of retarding their
intellectual and social progress. The central government of the Ming dynasty even circulated books that were deliberately scrambled in order to
keep effective knowledge from the people without overtly appearing to
do so.

The element of superstition seems to underlie the excessive paranoia
that condemned the woman to such extreme imprisonment. Superstition
appears to emerge again in the form of curiosity, when people go to the
cave to check on her a few days later. The cave had not been bricked shut
with the intention of releasing the woman after a few days of confine-
ment; the people probably wanted to see whether she had turned "back"
into a fox, perhaps, or vanished altogether.

Instead of a magical vixen, an empty human shell, or a solitary shoe,
the people found the woman calmly sitting upright in the cavern, showing no signs of distress. Her mother and elder brother took pity on her
and left her some dates and chestnuts, which would fit through the hole
in the wall. She told them that her belly felt full and she had no desire to
eat. This matches typical descriptions of the results of Taoist breathing
exercises, which always precede and accompany Taoist fasting procedures. Based on the woman's early interest in mysticism—for which she
was now being made to pay with her physical freedom—she probably
had already gotten instruction in Taoist and Buddhist techniques of mental and physical training.

Now her brother asked when she would get out. She replied with a
cryptic statement predicting that the cavern would be opened when a

181

man with a particular name showed up. This was gossiped about, and soon everyone far and near had heard about the woman in the cavern.

The woman's sudden fame might also be attributed to superstition, since her prediction had not yet been proven. The image of a solitary in a cave making cryptic prophecies was already established in the culture and alluring to many people at every level of society. Even if the woman were no longer imprisoned in forced fulfillment of the cultural stereotype of the sprite, she could still have been kept imprisoned to fulfill the cultural stereotype of the sage. Thus three years passed.

Now it happened that a regional inspector making a tour of the region heard about the woman imprisoned in the mountain cavern and went to see her. His name coincided with her prediction of three years earlier.

When the inspector came to the cave where she was imprisoned, the woman told him that his son was in great danger at that very moment and was on the road in flight from his enemies. Later a messenger arrived with news that confirmed the woman's statement. The inspector's wife, a devout believer in Buddhism, insisted that the wall closing the cavern be taken down.

The woman's prediction about the removal of the wall had now been fulfilled, but she refused to come out, saying her sentence was not yet up. Perhaps she had more inner work to do, and she may have found it safer and more peaceful for this purpose inside the cave than she would have in the outside world. Asked when her sentence would be up, again she gave a cryptic prediction; she couldn't be induced to come out, so the cavern was bricked up again. After a long time the inspector assumed that the woman had died, and he returned to his native place in sorrow.

Four years later, another inspector came to the district, with a name matching the woman's second prediction. He too heard of the case and went to investigate. Finding the woman alive, he asked her for a word of instruction. This would show that by now she had the reputation of a holy woman.

She told the inspector she had nothing special to tell him, but simply asked him to relay news of her to the former inspector who had first tried to release her. Surprised and delighted to hear that the woman was still alive and well, the old inspector sent people at once to welcome her out of the cave. By this time she had been in the mountain cavern for a total of eighteen years.

Now the Holy Woman of Mount P'eng was a celebrity, treated as a sort of oracle whose predictions and advice regularly proved true. It is recorded that she ate vegetables and fruit like ordinary people but did not urinate or defecate. This detail, in the general Chinese cultural context, may reflect something of Taoist-influenced curiosities about physical changes produced by ascesis. In this particular story, its crudity may also reinforce the image of public "holy" figures as in effect prisoners of personality cultism.

Anonymity and inconspicuousness are recommended in both Taoist and Buddhist manuals, not merely for modesty but also for practical privacy, in order to work unmolested by curious idlers and people with superstitious obsessions.

In any case, the holy woman did not last long on this earth after her release from the cavern prison. After a little more than a year, one day she appeared to be slightly ill and announced to her large following that she was leaving. When the preparations had been made, she bathed, changed her clothing, then sat in her casket and passed away. No one knows how old she was, but if she had been shut in while a bride, she was probably then still in her teens. If she was in the cave for eighteen years, then passed away within two years of emerging, she may have been no more than forty years old when she died.

There is a Chinese saying to the effect that a beautiful flower can survive only in a hidden place, unseen and untouched by the eyes and hands of worldly admirers. From this point of view, spiritually gifted people who secluded themselves or made themselves personally unavailable to the world at large were not seeking to avoid worldly temptation, as recluses are thought to be doing; by seclusion they avoided becoming attractions or temptations to greedy worldlings seeking blessings, favors, attention, solace, satisfaction of curiosity, and so on. For this reason Zen Buddhists often pretended to be ignorant, citing the proverb, "Good merchants conceal their goods and seem to have nothing."

It stands to reason that notices are written only of people who are noticed, for better or worse. Even a local daily newspaper could not reproduce the full day-to-day texture of life in the smallest hamlet. Thus, we would do well to be wary of distorting our view of a society or people by generalizing too much from data that is by nature drawn from the distinctive and dramatic. The value of the data, after all, depends on what we make of it. If we only try to draw a social lesson from a spiritual story, in the struggle of spirituality for social expression we may simply see social sickness and misunderstand the psychology of spiritual survival.

Both the social and spiritual aspects of women's struggles took on many different forms in the context of Buddhism as it developed in Eastern civilizations. The tragic tale of the Holy Woman of Mount P'eng is sharply contrasted by that of another Chinese woman of the Ming dynasty, Hsia Yun-ying, who rose to high social standing by dint of her own talent before becoming a nun.

This woman learned to read both Confucian and Buddhist classics in childhood, mastering several major works by the age of seven. When she was thirteen she was chosen to be a consort of the crown prince of a minor state within the Ming empire. She eventually became head of the royal household after the crown prince had become king and his original princess had passed on. Not only did she manage the affairs of the royal household, she was often consulted by the king on matters of state as well. She retired when she was still only twenty-two years old, claiming illness and expressing a desire to become a nun. She received the bodhisattva precepts of universalist Buddhism and practiced the esoteric Vajrayana, then fashionable in Chinese high society through infusion from Tibet. Two of her writings, a collection of hymns on the Lotus Scripture and a volume of poetry, were circulated in society, and notice of her also occurs in literary annals.

This woman's story shows how talent could be and was in fact recognized and fostered in Chinese society, even in the generally repressive Ming dynasty. And yet it is impossible to avoid supposing that she had been given her education as a girl in hopes of grooming her for a palace position, much as boys were educated to groom them for civil service positions. The moral flaw in that educational system was precisely what led so many men to abandon Confucian academics for Taoist or Buddhist learning. Women were excluded from the Confucian examination system altogether, so it was natural for their intellectual and spiritual curiosities and aspirations to lean toward Taoism or Buddhism.

This story also raises the issue of the cost of recognition, albeit in a different way from the story of the Holy Woman of Mount P'eng. Here is someone who achieves great success and prestige early on in life, along with authority and influence, then retires at the age of twenty-two. It was common for highly sought-after Buddhist adepts to refuse honors and abbacies on account of "illness," which for them could simply be a whimsical term for "mortal existence." Under the circumstances of this woman's life, however, it is not difficult to believe that the stress of her position made her physically unwell. It could also be that her choice of Vajrayana Buddhism may have been based not on fashion but on a particular need for healing.

It may also be possible that the king would not let her go and had her ordained in esoteric Tantric Buddhism specifically so he could keep her there as a consort, confidante, and adviser while allowing her to substitute religious rites for the business and political affairs that had preoccupied her as head of the royal household and counselor to the king.

There are many, many more women of wisdom known for their journey on the Buddhist path, some of whom we will have occasion to meet in our observations of Tantric and Pure Land Buddhism. We find wide diversity of expression among these women, even when they come from the same cultural context; but every one of them makes us wonder what liberation may mean. The ideal of the Buddhist bodhisattva is to go to the "other shore" of ultimate truth beyond the reach of worldly sorrow, freeing the spirit from the follies and foibles of the world, but then to return to "this shore" of mundane reality to ameliorate the conditions of the world bit by bit while showing its inmates how to escape imprisonment.

In this sense the bodhisattvas sacrifice both this world and the next, so we can hardly judge them by conventional standards, either secular or religious. Perhaps this is why it is said of the true adepts that "outsiders secretly spying cannot find them out; even gods wishing to honor them find no path on which to strew flowers."

11

The Lotus and the Thunderbolt

I T IS GENERALLY BELIEVED that the widest scope for the expression of female spirituality in Buddhism has been found in Tantrism. Buddhist Tantrism, at least as controversial as Hindu Tantrism, is largely esoteric and subject to the same or similar problems of verification and interpretation as any secret movement or organization. Part of the freedom in Tantrism, of course, is in its secrecy. That can be a double-edged sword, however, for the investigator as well as the participant.

For those not culturally trained or bound to accept the authority of the Tantric texts, many of the questions surrounding Buddhist Tantrism concern its origins and derivations. A central issue revolves around the relationship of Tantrism to scriptural Buddhism, and indeed whether Tantrism is to be properly considered Buddhist at all. There is, naturally, a wide range of opinion on these points.

One of the difficulties in dealing with terrestrial Buddhist history is in trying to sense original strata of teachings and activities through the medium of systems and schemes of classification devised long afterward. These systems and schemata were constructed by people who inherited vast accumulations of diverse materials that had originated at different times and under different circumstances. As useful as these intellectual edifices may have been for certain purposes, over centuries of elaboration their monumental structures could become too enormous, too intricate, too rigid, and too overwrought for widespread utility even in their own cultural milieus.

In the mystical perspective of Indo-Tibetan legend, Tantrism was brought into the historical plane in the fourth century CE by Asanga, one of the greatest Buddhists of the time, and was transmitted secretly for some three hundred years before surfacing in the Tantric texts and the famous adepts. For the next four hundred years, from the sixth through the tenth centuries, Tantrism would influence the culture of the entire Indian subcontinent, reaching west as far as Afghanistan and Persia, south as far as Sumatra and Java, and north and east to Turkestan, Tibet, Mongolia, China, Korea, and Japan.

The Indo-Tibetan version of the origin of Tantra is based on the principle of vijnapti-matrata, which means "the quality of being only representation," a technical term used to describe the conceptual nature of our picture of reality. This term is fundamental to the stream of Buddhism called Yogacara or Yoga Practice, whose inception is attributed to this same Asanga and his brother Vasubandhu.

This association is important because the theory and practices of Tantric Buddhism, including its history and hagiography, are based on the realization that our experiences of the world and the beings in it are conditioned by our subjectivity. Tantric sacralization of the secular is thus based on the principle of "emptiness," according to which all things are pure in their essential reality; it is the relative purity or impurity of our own minds that make our temporal perceptions of the world and our interactions with it pure or impure. Tantrism applies this principle to the problem of personal integration by transforming the perception of the world that conditions our relationship to existence.

Questions of origin, whether mythical or historical, are thus of more than mere academic interest because they get at matters of context that can help to clarify meaning. Concern for scriptural origins of Tantra, therefore, are not necessarily concerned with sectarian polemics or intellectual history, but provide a larger background against which to view the mysteries, or otherwise apparently idiosyncratic elements, associated with the teachings and practices of Tantrism.

Indications of scriptural roots of Tantrism are generally sought in the appearance of elements such as incantations, pantheons, and mandalas in the Mahayana Buddhist sutras. These increased over the years, even in different versions of the same texts, reflecting a general trend in popular Buddhism. Spells had been separately collected by the "Dharma-Protection" sect as early as the second century BCE, and these evidently found their way into mainstream Mahayana texts from early times.

Many scriptures are cited in studies of proto-Tantrism in Mahayana Buddhism, but the full range of Tantric prototypes is to be found in the comprehensive *Avatamsaka-sutra*, the *Flower Ornament Scripture*, which we have already seen to contain the most extensive array of female teachers and their teachings. What can be discerned of the history of this sutra also sheds light on the terrestrial history of Tantra and the Hindu legend of its Chinese origin. But this discussion must be deferred for the moment in favor of an overview of the proto-Tantric designs in the *Flower Ornament Scripture*.

Certainly this scripture is not unique in containing the metaphysical bases of Tantra, the principles of emptiness and representation-only. It is unique, however, in containing within its range the patterns of all supposedly peculiar Tantric practices. There is empowerment and blessing (*adhisthana*), initiation and consecration (*abhishekha*), devotional service (*puja*), and attendance on teachers (*guru-sevana*). There is extensive formation of mandalas, projection and absorption of visions, teaching and learning in ecstasies and dream states, and other forms of mind-to-mind communication.

This scripture also represents the general processing of sensory experience for knowledge and liberation, as well as special processing of sensual and sexual experience for enlightenment. Associated with these is the use of architecture and iconography, decorative and fine arts, music and song, drama and dance. There is also the invocation of *dharani*, mystic spells like mantras, including the root letters, the so-called *bija* or "seeds" used in visualization and chanting for the creative reconstitution of consciousness.

The scripture also features occupational symbolism synthesizing worldly occupation with spiritual practice; mental and physical journeying, inside and outside this world; special places on or inside the surface of the earth itself; cosmopolitan perspective; and permeability of social, cultural, and religious boundaries. All of the many mandalas in the scripture contain females of every class of being, while the final book of the scripture, the "brain" or "crown" of the monument, is, as we have seen, richly adorned with the enchanting figures of all sorts of women and girls teaching the Dharma in a multitude of different ways.

And last but not least, there is the concept of the essence of intimacy, secrecy, or esoterism, in the invisibility of the whole scope of the teaching to the senses of limited thinkers.

All of these things are templates of Tantric Buddhism.

According to Buddhist mythology, the Flower Ornament Scripture was the first statement of Gautama Buddha after his enlightenment, when he poured out his whole realization to a dumbstruck universe. It was only after that initial outburst, legend continues, that Buddha proceeded to teach in a linear manner, in order to gradually refine the minds of the people to the point where they could perceive all the manifestations of the teaching by reaching its source in the relationship between inner consciousness and objective reality.

The factor of secrecy, therefore, is fundamentally based on perceptive capacity. It is not necessarily deliberate, but may have to be so under certain conditions. In practical terms, secrecy is as much a means of protecting unprepared people from ideas and practices not suited to them as it is a means of protecting practitioners from molestation by ignorant outsiders.

The historical background of the Flower Ornament Scripture, so far as it can be determined, seems to prove that Tantrism is even older than sectarian mythology claims. While Buddhist texts are notoriously difficult to date, and the oral traditions behind them virtually impossible to trace to original sources, Chinese translations can nonetheless provide "latest possible" dates for many of them. The national or ethnic origins of most of those who translated Buddhist texts into Chinese are also known, as are outlines of their travels, studies, and works, thus providing some clues about historical distribution of teachings.

Parts of the Flower Ornament Scripture were translated into Chinese as early as the second century CE, generations before Asanga was born in India and centuries before Tantrism is believed to have emerged as a distinct movement. These portions already contain proto-Tantric mandala formation and Buddha visualization.

The first translation from the Flower Ornament Scripture was made by a monk named Lokaksin, who traveled to the old Chinese capital of Loyang in 176 CE and worked there from 178 to 189. Lokaksin was from the

Kushan Empire, where one of the greatest of Buddhist cultures flourished between the first and third centuries.

The Kushan Empire, which occupied Afghanistan, Pakistan, Kashmir, and most of northern India, was founded by a Central Asian people, the Tukharians, known to the Chinese as the Yueh-chih. Speaking an Indo-European language, the Yueh-chih were probably descended from one or more of the ancient Scythian tribes. Driven out of Central Asia by Huns in the second century BCE—the Huns themselves migrating under pressure from the new expanding Han dynasty of China (founded 206 BCE)—the Yueh-chih conquered Greco-Persian Bactria (centered in Afghanistan) before pushing into India around the middle of the first century CE. Linking Persian, Indian, Chinese, and Central Asian civilizations, the Kushan Empire became a center of trade on the Silk Route and a hub of the world.

The most famous of the Kushan rulers was Kanishka, who ruled from what is now Peshawar in Pakistan. This was the region of Gandhara, whose Buddhist culture flourished under Kanishka, synthesizing Greek and Indian aesthetics to produce an unmatched standard of beauty in Buddhist art.

Kanishka also convened the Fourth Buddhist Council in Kashmir and had the Pali Canon of Hinayana Buddhism engraved on copper plates. There may also have been a "secret" Mahayana convention at the same time, reflected in the compilation of the monumental Ekayana or unitarian Buddhist texts *Saddharmapundarika-sutra* and *Avatamsaka-sutra*, the *Lotus of Truth Scripture* (popularly called the *Lotus Scripture*) and the *Flower Ornament Scripture*.

The *Lotus Scripture* presents a scenario in which the elders of the Hinayana walk out on the Buddha as he begins to expound the comprehensive teaching. The *Flower Ornament Scripture* presents a scenario in which the great congregation of unitarian sages was not even visible to the congregation of Hinayana elders. While these images unquestionably relate to the correspondence between capacity and perception, events of this nature may very well have taken place at the time of the Fourth Buddhist Council in Kashmir, as unitarian lay Buddhists attempted with limited success to communicate their broader vision of Buddhism to sectarian monastics.

Further Chinese translations from the *Flower Ornament Scripture* were made two generations later by another Kushan, a layman who came to China in the year 220. Mastering six languages, he produced no less than fifty-one translations from Buddhist works. These included two books from the *Flower Ornament Scripture*: one focusing on the deconstruction of formal religious practices, and one organizing the whole range of Buddhist teachings into a series of ten grades.

The appearance of such erudition and motivation in a layman would seem to indicate that lay Buddhism in Kushan culture was not limited to pious almsgiving. This strengthens the belief that the Kushan Empire may have been the source of the great composite scriptures of unitarian Mahayana Buddhism, the *Lotus* and *Flower Ornament* scriptures.

The proto-Tantric elements in these syncretic scriptures suggest that this creative Kushan culture was a primary historical homeland of Tantric Buddhism. Strengthening that association with Tantrism is the fact that this lay translator of the third century was not only an accomplished scholar but also a master of many arts.

Among the numerous translations attributed to this Kushan layman, furthermore, are several scriptures with female interlocutors; an early version of the *Scripture Spoken by Vimalakirti*, an analogue of the *Flower Ornament Scripture* already mentioned in connection with the goddess who changed Buddha's disciple into a female; six volumes of translations from the major sutra on *prajnaparamita*, the abstract supreme goddess of Buddhism; and several texts of *dharani* or mystic spells, one of the mainstays of esoteric practice. All of these interests suggest a strong undercurrent of proto-Tantrism in Kushan Buddhism.

The fall of the Kushan Empire to Persia around 240 did not exactly put an end to the influence of Kushan/Gandhara Buddhist culture, but rather caused it to spread even further as refugees fled to other parts of the Buddhist world. A Kushan monk named Kalasivi, for example, arrived in Tonkin (northern Vietnam) in the year 255, shortly after the end of Kushan rule, and translated an important text related to practical application of the *Lotus Scripture*, which like the *Flower Ornament Scripture* is unitarian in outlook and contains many Tantric templates.

The work of another post-Kushan translator of the third century, Dharmaraksha, also suggests that this culture was the source of both the *Lotus Scripture* and the *Flower Ornament Scripture*, and the original homeland of Tantric Buddhism. Dharmaraksha's ancestors were Kushanese, and he was raised in Dunhuang, a Buddhist center on the Silk Route now famous for its cave temples and the gigantic cache of writings discovered there.

Ordained at the age of eight, Dharmaraksha traveled widely and ultimately learned as many as thirty-six languages and dialects.

Dharmaraksha made a translation of the whole *Lotus Scripture* as well as three books of the *Flower Ornament Scripture*. Among its proto-Tantric elements, the *Lotus Scripture* contains a chapter of *dharani*, but instead of transliterating the Sanskrit sounds as a "mystic spell," Dharmaraksha renders the formulas in meaningful Chinese. This is a most interesting detail, showing that the mystification or esotericization of spells, or concentration formulas, was a secondary development.

Dharmaraksha's translations from the *Flower Ornament Scripture* include a reworking of the "Book of Ten Abodes," an early version of the "Book of Ten Stages," and a rendition of the "Book of Ten Concentrations." The "Book of Ten Stages" is one of the most important books of the *Flower Ornament Scripture*, organizing the totality of Buddhist teachings, beginning in a linear or sequential manner but culminating in the "all-at-once" integration of complete consciousness from which the "fundamental continuity" of Tantra emerges. The "Book of Ten Concentrations" begins with this immensity and pursues its potentiality in a manner suggestive of the fullest development of the capacities of extra-dimensional perception, visualization, and conscious projection associated with Tantric practice.

In addition to these works, Dharmaraksha translated a scripture centered on a thunderbolt bearer called Secret Traces. The image of a thunderbolt bearer whose presence and activity are invisible is clearly suggestive of the ideal and practice of esoteric Buddhism, which may be "hidden" by nothing more than skillful integration with the ambient society and culture.

Dharmaraksha also translated several scriptures with female interlocutors, whose association with Tantrism and the restoration of the feminist element in Buddhism need not be emphasized, except to say that it rounds out the picture of Kushan Buddhism as a primary source of both unitarian Ekayana Buddhism and esoteric Tantric Buddhism.

Translators from Kashmir, formerly within the Kushan domains, continued to produce Chinese versions of unitarian and proto-Tantric works for centuries after the fall of the Kushan Empire, as did translators from Khotan, Kucha, Kashgar, and other Buddhist oases on the Silk Route north of Kushan on the way into Central Asia, China, and the Far East. The first comprehensive rendition of the *Flower Ornament Scripture* was made around

418 from a text obtained in Khotan, which was the next stop to the north of Kashmir, at the northeast edge of Tibet. When the most complete Chinese version of the *Flower Ornament Scripture* was made nearly three hundred years later at the behest of Imperatrix Wu, one of the greatest women in Chinese history, both the text and the translator were imported from Khotan.

Thus Khotan was clearly an important center of Kushanese or Gandhara Buddhism for centuries after the fall of the Kushan Empire itself. It was also a Buddhist connection and distribution point for Indian, Chinese, Tokharian, Turkic, and Tibetan cultures, whose interaction produced impetus for the evolution of syncretic movements later to be classified as Tantric.

Elements of South Indian Dravidian cultures, which seem to have an important role in the evolution of Tantrism, were also incorporated into Kushan civilization, further enriching the fabric of Buddhist expression and extending its capacities of cultural outreach. A powerful Dravidian dynasty had conquered Magadha, the ancient center of Buddhism, about a century before that part of India was taken over by the Kushan Empire under Kanishka.

The infusion of Dravidian elements added considerably to the cosmopolitanism of Kushan civilization and enhanced the luxuriousness of Tantrism. Some aspects of Tantric feminism may have been influenced by Dravidian cultures, among whom matriarchal and matrilineal systems seem to have existed in ancient times. Dravidian cultures may have also influenced the Tantric sacramental uses of meat and liquor, music, drama, and dance. The institution of temple courtesans (called *devadasi*, "divine servant") has also been attributed to South Indian culture.

Another source of southern input into Tantrism was through the Buddhist master Nagarjuna. Cited earlier as the most eminent metaphysician of emptiness, in the Far East Nagarjuna is considered an ancestor of Tantric Buddhism. Tibetan tradition reckons him the first to pass on teachings in secrecy to a disciple. He is also considered an ancestral teacher of Zen, Pure Land, T'ien-t'ai, and Flower Ornament schools of Buddhism. This multifaceted versatility is in itself redolent of integral Tantric diversity.

Before he became a Buddhist, furthermore, Nagarjuna was supposedly a Hindu sorcerer or wizard of sorts, who used to spirit himself into the royal seraglio to disport with the ladies. The *Kama-sutra* affirms that neglected concubines in old India did indeed make it a practice to conceal youths in their apartments for sexual sport, so this legend of Nagarjuna may have some basis in fact, even if it is only meant to illustrate a cultural background.

Some accounts say that Nagarjuna was originally a Brahmin from South India. Other accounts say he was from West India and received the Buddhist teaching from Master Kapimala before traveling to South India to convert the Dravidians. Kapimala was the successor of Ashvaghosha, the great Buddhist poet at the court of Kanishka, the Kushan emperor. Thus whether he was originally from the South or the West, in the story of Nagarjuna the living connection between Kushan-Gandhara Buddhism and Dravidian civilization is clearly affirmed. Medieval Zen tradition in Japan, where the early masters all studied esoteric Buddhism, makes open reference to "secret teaching from South India" on the basis of belief in transmission of Tantrism through the great master Nagarjuna.

Nagarjuna is also associated with the practice of arousing the kundalini "serpent power," which in one form or another is common to the psychic circulatory system of Tantric Hinduism, Tantric Buddhism, and alchemical Taoism. This connection also places the origins of Tantrism even further back in history than later sectarian visionary history alleges.

Nagarjuna is supposed to have "recovered" two major bodies of Buddhist scripture associated with Tantrism, the corpus on *prajnaparamita* or transcendent insight, and the *Flower Ornament*. The former is the major repository of the teaching of emptiness, essential grounding for Tantrism, while the latter, as we have seen, outlines the complete structure of Tantra.

The Tantric and Dravidian association is, moreover, explicitly confirmed in the *Flower Ornament Scripture*. In the epic journey of the scripture's final crowning book, in which all the teachings are integrated, one of the earliest teachers visited by the pilgrim is a "grammarian" in a Dravidian city named Vajrapura, "City of the Thunderbolt" (or "Diamond City"). It is well known that Tantric versions of Buddhism, sometimes called Vajrayana, the Thunderbolt or Diamond Vehicle, can often be identified by the "vajrafication" of all sorts of names; thus it is clear that the location of the "Vajra City" in a Dravidian country openly acknowledges the debt of Tantrism to Dravidian civilization.

The image of the Dravidian guru as a grammarian is an interesting touch of historical realism, because one of the great works of ancient Tamil, one of the principal Dravidian languages, is a grammar. This grammar, the Tolkappiyam, also contains a great deal of anthropological and sociological information and thus would have been a good source of material for the new cultural synthesis of Tantrism. In the Flower Ornament Scripture the Dravidian grammarian says that he knows the languages of all peoples, as well as the variety, unity, and mixture in the languages of all individuals. He knows the terms and concepts of all cultures, the ideas of all sages, and the ideas of all ignoble people. This interweaving of linguistic, intellectual, religious, and psychological understanding mirrors the image of a grammar-ethnology textbook very well and places this worldly knowledge in the context of an even more comprehensive labor of global expansion of consciousness.

According to tradition, Nagarjuna "recovered" the Flower Ornament Scripture and the Scripture on Perfect Insight from among the Nagas. The name Naga, translated as "dragon" in Chinese, is popularly taken to mean "water spirit" or "rain spirit," but also refers to a Tibeto-Burmese people by that name. Their homeland, now the state of Nagaland in the farthest east of India, once part of Assam, is a remote mountain forest region bordering Burma (modern Myanmar).

There is no way to rule out a literal interpretation of the name Naga in certain Buddhist scriptures and traditions, even if a symbolic interpretation is coherent. The notion that advanced teachings could be "stored" among a supposedly "primitive" and preliterate people does not recommend itself to minds trained to regard literacy as a mark of civilization. In ancient India, however, writing was for political and commercial purposes; sacred literature was customarily transmitted orally and held in memory. The use of writing for religious works in India seems to have been started by Buddhists, using both vernacular and classical forms, even as oral traditions continued in tandem with, and periodically fed into, the evolving traditions of written literature.

Given this cultural milieu, it does not seem logical to exclude the possibility that the Nagas from whom Nagarjuna is said to have recovered generally unknown teachings were in fact real people, human Nagas. The supposition that they were may be strengthened by the observation that Kamarupa, one of the most holy sites of Tantrism and Goddess worship, was in the western part of Assam, where Nagaland is located. Interaction with Nagas and other hill tribes, as part of the Tantric "weaving" of diverse societies and civilizations into a "continuity," may have been part of the purpose of the pilgrimage for Buddhists.

The evolution of Tantric sign languages may indeed have been encouraged by the phenomenon of ritual pilgrimage to such sites. Comparatively simple signal codes may have been fostered by temporary but recurrent interaction among small but internally diverse cross-sections of peoples from radically different cultures, with languages of completely different root families, perhaps without written forms for transmission and study, making it relatively difficult for full-fledged creole languages to develop.

Legendary or real, the Nagas are represented as regular attendees of Buddha's universalistic discourses. One of the most important symbols of spiritual egalitarianism in unitarian Buddhism is found in the figure of an eight-year-old Naga girl who attained enlightenment when she met Buddha. This well-known story, which illustrates a Buddhist ideal of consciousness transcending barriers and biases of race, culture, gender, and age, comes from the popular Lotus Scripture, which emphasizes the universality of the buddha-nature in all people.

The Buddhist historian Taranatha places the Nagas in Kashmir in the time of the third grand master of Buddhism in India, Shanavasa or Shanavasika. The likelihood that the Lotus Scripture was compiled in Kashmir has already been mentioned. We cannot consider it impossible that the modern Nagas, now remote from Kashmir, are descendants of people who migrated from Kashmir. In the process they may naturally have intermarried with other mountain tribes from among whose descendants emerged some of the Tibetan and Burmese peoples.

It is also possible that the name Naga itself, with its association with the "dragons" of the mist and fog, clouds and rain, may have been a generic plains or city term for mountain tribes of the Himalayan chain, many of them possibly interrelated, of whom the modern Nagas could be one group who retained an ancient ethnic and cultural identity by virtue of the inaccessibility of the region they eventually settled after having left Kashmir.

The Nagas may have been driven out of Kashmir in the first place—if that is where they were in Buddha's time—by the military incursions and disruptions, or the boom in the caravan trade through the mountains, that came along with the establishment and expansion of the Kushan Empire in the first centuries before and after the Common Era.

While the historical reality of Nagas in Mahayana Buddhist scriptures may not be necessary to the appreciation of the symbolic meaning, it is of some use to pursue the consequences of literal interpretation. Even if the results are inconclusive, it can still be demonstrated that literal interpretation should not be pursued at all unless it can yield plausible hypotheses. When literal interpretation leads to absurdities, that should be a signal to us that we are looking at figurative representations never intended to be understood literally. This helps us to make sense of the literature on both spiritual and cultural or historical levels, which in turn helps us to relate spiritual concerns to the course of history, the evolution of human consciousness, and the achievement of civilization.

The story of the Naga girl who attained buddhahood has an element that brings the problems of symbolic versus literal interpretations into a sharp focus, particularly as the interpretative possibilities appear within specific cultural contexts.

According to the scripture, this enlightened girl was challenged by Shariputra, one of Buddha's mendicant disciples, who claimed she could not attain buddhahood in a female body. According to the Chinese translations of this scripture—whose largest historical readership has been in the geographical regions served by the Chinese Buddhist canon—in response to the monk's challenge the Naga girl suddenly turned into a male bodhisattva.

This vignette has at times been cited by professional monks to "prove" that a buddha cannot have a female embodiment, and by modern scholars to "prove" that Buddhism was traditionally male-oriented. It could also be used, however, to "prove" the reverse of these contentions—yet without, paradoxically, needing to disprove them in the process. In terms of the Buddhist philosophy of vijnapti-matrata, "representation only," based on the premise that we construe reality according to our mental patterns, the subjective plausibility of an interpretative premise all depends on the perspective of the perceiver. Who names a buddha? Who were the Buddhists? What is Buddhism? Just as there have been different answers to these questions about the nature and reality of buddhahood and Buddhism, people have also held different opinions regarding the understanding of womanhood in relationship to buddhahood and Buddhism.

To the credit of Chinese Buddhist commentators on the Lotus Scripture—with the exception of the usual drones who compulsively organize material without regard to spiritual meaning—they have not been unduly boggled by the transformation of the Naga girl. Those who deal with the story in any depth regard it as emblematic of the universality of buddhanature and the potential for instant enlightenment. One of the great lay scholars, using Taoist terminology familiar in the Chinese cultural sphere, asserts that the "male body" is merely a symbol of a condition of "pure yang" or pure positive energy purged of mundanity.

That is not to say that enlightened understanding was enjoyed by all in the interpretation of materials such as this. Once a woman in China famous for her spirituality was challenged by a monk who demanded to know why she didn't "change into a man," in accord with the scriptural model, if she were really an enlightened buddha. The woman calmly replied that she was not a ghost or a sprite, so she had no business doing weird things. This is not simply an expression of social or religious feminism, of course, but a reminder that the aim of Buddhism is enlightenment, not sorcery or wonder working.

One of the classical principles of interpretation in Mahayana Buddhism is "resort to the meaning, not the letter." The Chinese translations of the story of the Naga girl are somewhat crude and inaccurate, but this adversity renders more admirable the ability of many Buddhists using these versions to see through the distorted literal surface to apprehend the spiritual meaning.

In the Sanskrit version of the scripture, according to a manuscript from the Silk Route Buddhist oasis of Kashgar, the Naga girl does not change into a man. What she does, in response to the monk's challenge, is to cause herself to appear to him as a bodhisattva with the feminine energy muted and the energy of the universal soul manifest.

In the Chinese, the story is worded to make it seem that the Naga girl actually transformed her body. In the Sanskrit, it is explicit that she causes herself to appear in a new way to the perception of everyone, including that elder. One implication of specific mention of the elder monk in addition to the more inclusive "everyone" may be that the change in her appearance has a particular meaning relative to the monk as perceiver, effected to cure him of his subjective prejudice and professional monkish bias against females. For this reason, one of the great lay Buddhist writers of the T'ang dynasty asserted that the context of the *Flower Ornament Scripture* is superior to the *Lotus Scripture* because there is no longer any need for change in appearance in the *Flower Ornament* perspective.

Even in the Sanskrit version of the *Lotus Scripture* the story is worded so that a literalist could read the passage to say that the girl appeared to the monk and everyone else as a bodhisattva with the female organ hidden and the male organ manifest. Apart from suggestions of spiritual androgyny, which would not explain the change, unless we take the absurdities consequent upon this level of literalism as a Mahayana joke on monks and their sexual taboos, or a joke on different communities and their cultural taboos, we are obliged to seek further for more substantial meaning.

The resolution of this interpretative problem does not reject either literal or figurative understanding, but requires greater depth in the domain of literal interpretation. The primary meaning of the word used for "organ" here is "power" or "force," and the word used for "male" also means "universal soul." If we go back to root meanings to interpret the literal presentation, therefore, we find completely coherent meaning in the expression without violence to either literal or figurative dimensions of the story.

As it happens, the vast majority of Buddhists throughout history have never had the opportunity to read the *Lotus Scripture* in the original Sanskrit, whether because their local schools rejected all Mahayana texts, or because their canonical languages were different, or because their local schools were actually based on the writings of later interpreters rather than original scriptures. Similar phenomena have also occurred in the institutionalized handling of the scriptural traditions of other world religions, which have appeared in diverse forms within different cultural and linguistic areas, often relying almost entirely on later local interpreters for their sectarian emphases.

While the peculiarities of local manifestations have their purpose in the context of the cultural projection of the teachings, over time these temporal prostheses may usurp the function of the original body of the teaching, allowing unused parts to wither away, ultimately to the detriment of later generations who may need them.

In the original *Lotus Scripture*, after the Naga girl had caused herself to appear as a bodhisattva with the energy of the universal human manifest, she then caused herself to appear to have gone south to a realm named Vimala, or "Free from Pollution," where she realized complete perfect enlightenment. Again the association of the South, where matriarchy allegedly survived among Dravidian cultures, with the "nonpolluted" status of the female, suggests that this great scripture represents an original historical matrix of Tantric Buddhism.

There may also have been yet other cultural sources for the Tantric feminism whose roots can be observed in the monuments of unitarian Buddhism. The Tukharians who founded the Kushan dynasty, wherein unitarian Buddhism flowered, may have inherited some remnants of matriarchal custom from their Scythian ancestors, as did the Cruthin, a most ancient Celtic people claiming Scythian descent.

Even among Christianized patriarchal Celtic tribes—who traditionally claimed Scythian descent—women retained considerable degrees of status and influence, as noted by outside observers past and present. From this point of view, we cannot completely rule out the possibility of some remnant of ancient Scythian culture involved in the development of Buddhist feminism in the so-called Gandhara or Kashmir schools of unitarian Buddhism emanating from the Kushan dynasty.

The Scythian heritage, which extended east into China, south into India, and west into Europe, is not always identified as such because the Scyths did not write and their offshoots took on different names as various tribes parted ways and intermarried with other peoples over the ages. The Sakas seem to be the last Central Asian group now commonly called Scythian, but it is difficult to establish that the Tukharians, parents of the glorious Gandhara culture of the Kushan Empire, were not a Scythian people.

The Tukharians were contacted by the Chinese court two hundred years before the formal introduction of Buddhism to China in the first century CE. The Tukharians played a major role in the translation of Buddhist lore into Chinese, and they apparently maintained a cultural force in Central Asia for over a thousand years. If they themselves did not retain some sort of Scythic feminism, the Tukharians were undoubtedly in contact with peoples who did have matriarchal or feminist elements in their cultures.

One such people were the inhabitants of Supi, a queendom surrounded by India, Bengal, Burma, China, Tufan and Khotan. It was centered around Lhasa, the capital of modern Tibet, and was ruled by two queens. Men were of lower status than women in Supi, and their only political function was warfare. Supi sent an embassy to the court of the Sui dynasty, which reunified a China long divided between Chinese and other Asian rules, in the year 586.

The Sui dynasty fell in 618, and Supi's loss of her connection with China, or the scramble for alliances with the new T'ang dynasty taking over from the Sui, may have played a part in the dissolution of Supi. A civil war between factions of the two queens of Supi enabled the king of neighboring Tufan or Tubo (Tibet), Songzen Gambo (617–50), to incorporate Supi into Tubo.

The peoples of Tubo and Supi were both descended from the ancient Ch'iang, whose immensely far-ranging tribes are traced all the way back to the Fire Goddess or Fire Emperor (depending on a matriarchal or patriarchal reading), an ancestor in common with the Chinese of high antiquity. Their very wide and sparse distribution is attributed to the fact that they remained largely hunting peoples for much of their history, gradually taking to herding, trade, and agriculture through contact with other civilizations in the various reaches of their migrations.

The fact that Tubo was patriarchal while Supi was matriarchal may suggest that their common forebears, the Ch'iang, had tribal organizations that were balanced within themselves but could have developed either matriarchy or patriarchy according to external conditions. Those conditions might be natural, having to do with the climate and environment. It is said, for example, that the Tibetan form of polyandry, in which one woman marries two or more brothers, was formulated to keep land holdings intact while minimizing population growth under the harsh conditions of the Himalayan mountain chain. This system would naturally have maintained a matriarchal structure even with a patriarchal polity superimposed upon it.

The conditions that influenced the development of Ch'iang society in different areas could also be social or cultural. The Ch'iang of Central Asia had fought savage wars against Han dynasty China from 107 to 118, after the grandees and officials of the Chinese Empire had taken to abusing and oppressing the primitive Ch'iang tribes. The Ch'iang were conquered by Hun cavalry in Chinese service, but over the next five centuries they formed three great nations rivaling China in power. The development of

201

the patriarchal institution of hereditary *gambo*, or king, among the Ch'iang of Central Asia who established Tubo, may have been a consequence of contact and conflict with China.

Another pre-Tibetan Ch'iang state also challenged China. That was the Tuyuhun or Tughukhun, which formed during China's Western Chin dynasty (265–317). This nation was named after its founder, who led a migration of seven hundred families of Hsien-pei from the border of Korea west to Gansu, where they established ascendancy over the scattered Ch'iang tribes and founded an independent state. The titles *khaghan* and *khan*, later used by Mongols, Turks, and Pathans, originated in the lineage of the leaders of Tuyuhun. Like Supi, Tuyuhun divided internally in the beginning of the T'ang dynasty of China, and was similarly incorporated into Tubo/Tibet by the powerful Songzen Gambo.

The Hsien-pei ancestors of the ruling class of Tuyuhun are commonly referred to as Turkic. Another branch of the Hsien-pei, the T'o-pa, ruled northern China from the late fourth century to the middle of the sixth century, forcing the Chinese to adopt Hsien-pei surnames and attempting to impose Hsien-pei culture on the Chinese even while becoming Sinicized themselves. The ruling house of the Chinese T'ang dynasty is reputed to have been partly of Turkic ancestry, and the relative freedom of women and comparatively liberal sexual mores of T'ang dynasty China were attributed by later Confucian historians to Turkic influences.

From this point of view, the Hsien-pei or Turkic element in pre-Tibetan Tuyuhun may have been another source of feminism, or egalitarianism, in the diverse cultural pool with which Buddhism was in contact in the course of its evolution of the great plurality of religious expression found in universalist Mahayana, unitarian Ekayana, and integral Tantric forms of Buddhism.

The different histories and cultures of the three states eventually forged into Tibet all seem to indicate the presence of elements that might account for the overwhelming attraction of Tantrism to Tibetans. These converging histories also seem to suggest that Buddhism, Taoism, and Hinduism were all filtering into different sectors of the pre-Tibetan peoples long before the unification of Tibet in the seventh century.

The Buddhist kingdoms of India, Afghanistan, Kashmir, Bengal, and Southeast Asia still patronized Hindu priests and pundits for state and social functions, just as their counterparts in China, Korea, and Japan patronized Confucian scholars for political purposes. Tantric Buddhism could not have ignored the Hindu elements of ambient cultures any more than it could ignore the shamanic elements, if it was to serve the purpose of integration. While neither Brahmanism nor Confucianism were overtly established in Tibet, equivalent roles could be played by Buddhist lamas within the scope of Tantric practice.

There may have been a source for integration of Taoistic elements into the early Tantrism of Central Asia through the fourth-century kingdom of Ch'eng in Ssu-ch'uan in the west of old China. The kingdom of Ch'eng was founded around 304 by a leader of the aboriginal Pa people. He invited a Chinese Taoist to be his top adviser, and together they established a nation known for low taxation, social justice, and pacifism.

Many Ch'iang people have settled in Ssu-ch'uan, which borders directly on Tibet, since time immemorial. Not all of them were absorbed into Tibetan civilization, but many of them were. Today there are two autonomous Tibetan prefectures and two autonomous Tibetan counties in Ssu-ch'uan (Siquan), as well as one autonomous Ch'iang (Qiang) county. There is thus a certain historical probability that Taoist concepts and practices filtered into Tibet for centuries before it was unified by the thirty-second *gambo* of Tubo in the 600s and given deliberately intensified infusions of massive amounts of cultural material from all quarters.

Of the three proto-Tibetan nations, the queendom of Supi was closest to the older centers of Gandhara culture, which is suspected of spawning both Ekayana and Tantric Buddhism. Supi was also closest to the Himalayan mountain tribes, perhaps including Nagas in the process of migrating from Kashmir to Assam. Of the three pre-Tibetan cultures, Tuyuhun may have been more Turkicized, Tubo more Sinicized, and Supi more Gandharicized. This may account, to some degree, for the relative affinities of different Tibetan regions and peoples for Bon shamanism, Tantric mysticism, and celibate monasticism.

Tantrism and early Tibetan Buddhism are particularly associated with Uddiyana, one of the former centers of the Gandhara Buddhist culture of the Kushan dynasty. From there the eighth-century giant Padmasambhava and others injected old-fashioned Tantrism into the culture of the new united Tibet. Some further hints about Tantric secularism and feminism may be gleaned from traditional tales about Uddiyana in the lore of the

Old School of Tibetan Buddhism, the Nyingma-pa, who trace their spiritual descent from Padmasambhava, once a prince of Uddiyana.

According to Old School tradition, the mystically minded realm of Uddiyana was at one time depopulated on account of the large numbers of people who dematerialized under the tutelage of the Buddhist gurus there. One theory is that this legend refers to the Arab invasion of Buddhist Afghanistan, which began in the seventh century and took a hundred years to complete. Beleaguered Buddhists took refuge in neighboring Tibet, where Buddhism was just then being officially promoted by the kings of the newly united Tibetan Empire.

The emigration of entire communities from old Buddhist Afghanistan into new Buddhist Tibet may well have given rise to the legend that the people of Uddiyana dematerialized into the "rainbow body" under the guidance of their spiritual preceptors, thus depopulating the land. The warriors who fell in battle against the invading Arabs, and the monks who were executed by the conquerors, ostensibly as idolaters but actually as property and power holders, may also have been counted among those who dematerialized for religious reasons.

Another explanation of the dematerialization/depopulation story is based on Afghan legend that the Buddhist hierarchs who managed the monumental sanctuaries of Buddhism in Afghanistan were exploiters who made as many people as they could into monastics, enslaving the general population of producers to the support of these overblown establishments. This exploitation of the general population, it is alleged, was accepted in exchange for the promise of a better life after death, according to a belief ingrained in the people by these very hierarchs for the purpose of making them submissive to this arrangement. According to this view, the depopulation of Uddiyana was due to the inhibition of reproduction by excessive monasticism, along with the drain on the labor and resources of the general population made to support it.

Similar arguments, of course, have been advanced against all sorts of political, religious, and professional hierarchies. Every history is complicated by the paradigms employed to interpret it.

A third view of the depopulation of Uddiyana takes a combination of the foregoing factors into account. Invasions undoubtedly reduced the population of Buddhist Afghanistan, but so did monasticism.

It is implausible to overlook either the factual reality or the external causes of removal of Afghan Buddhists to Tibet during the seventh and eighth centuries, and this historical displacement must be considered in relation to their legendary dematerialization.

The impact of this emigration on the formulation of early Tibetan Buddhism undoubtedly played a part in the appearance of lay lamas and Tantric gurus who were wealthy landowners, grandees, and castellans. Reaction to this by entrenched interests—Bon shamans and warlords— led to the suppression of Buddhism in Tibet for over a century. When Buddhism was reintroduced into Tibet, it was largely from East India and Bengal, another side of the Tantric world of Gandhara Buddhism, with its own blend of poetry, philosophy, and tropical sensuality. Bengal and East India, it will be recalled, were also sacred homelands of Hindu Goddess religion.

Other factors also contributed to the disappearance of Buddhist mo-nastic communities in Afghanistan. The heirs of Gandhara pan-Buddhism, the Buddhists of the Mahayana, Ekayana, and Vajrayana Tantric domains, were emerging into public view with great momentum by this time, with their own severe criticisms and repudiations of career monasticism and other exoteric religious institutions commonly sponsored by secular gov-ernments for political purposes. The fall of the Roman Empire and the consequent decline of trade along the western stretches of the old Silk Route also weakened the great merchants of India who had long been among the most generous patrons of Buddhist monasteries.

Some of the feminism and sexology of certain Tantric Buddhist texts seem to be directed specifically at ex-monastics-to-be, or people under the spell of monastic values or monastic elitism. The feminist themes include a reverence for women in all roles, sometimes emphasizing the significance of motherhood, sometimes extending love to all females of the human family, sometimes emphasizing the blessings of marriage to a woman, especially the raptures of emotional and sexual communion.

The sexual themes in this lore include normal advice on love play, but some of them seem to be addressed to a special audience dealing with conditioned aversions to women's bodies cultivated by monastic regimens. Some material addresses certain confusions about women's bodies arising from immature or arrested psychosexual development in males consigned to monasticism from childhood. This material can be quite shocking if its purpose is not understood, but it must be remembered that the actual transmission of Tantric texts was normally accompanied by verbal instruction elucidating inner meaning in accord with the spiritual state of the initiate. Shocking or puzzling surface content in esoteric material could conceal meanings to thwart meddlers; it could also be used to test the relative sophistication of aspirants.

In terms of institutional professional religion, Tantric protocols may have been designed to reintroduce monastics and ascetics to the fullness of life to mature their empathic powers. In terms of social and sexual mores, Tantric protocols may have been intended to restore balance and harmony between the sexes where militarism and politics had divided them. Sexual initiative was restored to women, and chivalry was restored to men. Feminine flirtation and male courtship were reconstituted apart from socioeconomic power structures, based on spiritual attractions and affinities.

Tantric spiritual relations by no means invariably included sexual relations. This point must be emphasized to avoid conveying a mistaken impression of Tantrism. For those who actually became lovers in Tantric communion, however, sexuality was refined physically as well as psychologically and spiritually. Sophisticated foreplay, including an extremely erotic form of advanced cunnilingus called "sucking the lotus," was emphasized to ensure the complete satisfaction of the woman and the mutual attainment of bliss. The bliss itself was not sought for its own sake, but used to attain mental quiescence and clarity for the awakening of subtler perceptions.

Like Hindu Left-Hand Tantra and Taoist chamber arts, Tantric Buddhist sexual etiquette emphasizes prolongation of the man's erection. In some contexts this may be referred to as preservation of male vitality, but in relation to the woman the purpose of prolongation is to enable the man to satisfy the woman's body completely. The emphasis on sexual satisfaction seen in the secular lore of India and China is connected with enhancement of marriage, and this certainly carries over into the domain of Tantric lore; and yet still finer dimensions of serenity, release, and spiritual expansion in mutual embrace are paramount in Tantric Buddhism.

The timing of sexual climax in men and women tends to differ in the uncultivated state for reasons of natural evolution. Because natural reproduction requires the man's body to inject semen into the woman's body, male orgasm is biologically essential. Orgasm in the female enhances the rates of impregnation, other factors being equal, but its biological necessity in this process is not as critical as that of the male semen. Since reproduction depends on the efficiency of the male ejaculation, the biological result of this necessity has been the readiness of male orgasm.

From this point of view, Tantric and Taoist lovemaking is a form of high culture, raising human beings above animal brutality as well as the cultural brutality of mechanical marriage matches made by insensitive systems of human control. The Tantric and Taoist attempts at balancing the orgasmic experiences of men and women and translating their climactic emotions into psychically and spiritually uplifting energies was nothing short of an effort to continue human evolution on the mental plane, elevating conscious mastery of self beyond the elemental demands of nature.

The emphasis on prolonging the man's erection is explicit in a religious song of one of the adepts, which declares, "I am a man perpetually erect inside a woman." The need for the woman's cooperation is nonetheless implicit in the song of another adept who says, "If the tortoise is milked, the pitcher cannot hold any more." Thus the methodical Tantric control of the man's climax is not a chore or distraction on the part of one partner, but a spontaneously mutual psychophysical expression of spiritual intimacy.

The Tantric refinement of sensual experience to facilitate the control of climactic peaking begins with meditations on conventional and ultimate realities, in which one learns to detach, analyze, and reintegrate. In sacramental sexual relations, the relative and absolute truths are pragmatically combined in visualization of partners as supernal beings. This process is intended to elevate the mind beyond superficialities, in preparation for the most intense of human intimacies, particularly the mutual perception of spiritual communion within the experience of physical union.

The "psychic nerve" system envisioned in certain Buddhist Tantric practices, as in some Taoist and Hindu Tantric and yogic practices, also plays a practical role in the sacred sexual maturation of the practitioner. This is especially true of the spine or main trunk of the Buddhist version of the system, which may be referred to as the three channels of perception, dalliance, and clarification. These three channels are visualized as psychophysical locations of visualization and meditation processes, such as the three-step practice of focus, analysis, and resolution.

In the context of sacramental sexual communion, the stage of perception is the onset of erotic sensation and the initial arousal of sexual response. The stage of dalliance is the diffusion of erotic feeling throughout the body and mind, like a stream of waves with cyclically changing frequencies. The stage of clarification is the experience of perception and dalliance from an extradimensional point of view, referred to in Buddhist psychology as that of the witness of the self-witness of the perceiver, such that consciousness is not carried away by what it perceives and enjoys.

Tantric sexual communion requires preparation in learning to apply the contemplative exercise of perception, dalliance, and clarification in the course of everyday life, focusing on the relationships of mind and objects, the ordinary thoughts and things of life. Because of their universal context, therefore, the spiritual relationships of Tantric Buddhists may or may not include personal relationships.

This is illustrated in the legends surrounding the *mahasiddhas* or Tantric adepts of the Bengali schools, who reestablished Buddhism in Tibet after its initial suppression. Most of the teachers of the adept Lui were women, and the adept Shabari had two female gurus. The adept Kambala was mentored by his mother, who was herself a Dakini. The adept Tilopa was converted to Buddhism by a Dakini woman who directed his spiritual journey to several teachers, including an enlightened Dakini living as a courtesan in Bengal. Tilopa, one of the founders of the Kagyu sect of Tibetan Buddhism, was also associated with an unnamed woman who was his lover and spiritual companion.

There are many more examples of adepts whose teachers and students included exceptional Dakinis and yoginis. The great Saraha was taught by a woman known only as the Arrow-Making Yogini. Atisha, who was instrumental in the revival of Buddhism in Tibet, spent three years in Uddiyana living among yoginis. The adept Kanha had an equal number of male and female disciples, but his foremost disciple was a woman. The famous Naropa, another founder of the Kagyu, had two hundred enlightened male disciples, but one thousand enlightened female disciples. Naropa's own greatest teacher was a woman named Niguma, who would meet him only in dreams and visions. Clearly she had no interest in a position in the hierarchies of academic and religious institutions.

In the final analysis, Buddhist Tantrism cannot be defined in terms of any limited cult, sect, rite, or order. Nor can it be understood solely from a sociological or anthropological perspective. The original root of the word *tantra*—*tan*—means "to extend," "to spread," "to be diffused," "to shine," "to continue," "to prepare a way," "to direct oneself," "to make manifest," "to accomplish." These meanings are all appropriate to the description of Tantrism as the practical extension of spirituality into all domains and activities of life.

This complete integration is illustrated in the *Flower Ornament Scripture* by the figure of the boy guru Indriyeshvara, "Master of the Faculties," who has attained "the light of knowledge of enlightening beings, characterized by higher knowledge of all arts and sciences." This boy reveals that he has been initiated into wisdom encompassing higher knowledge of all practical arts. This includes all the various arts and crafts and sciences in the world—the young teacher mentions writing, mathematics, symbolism, and logic; physical and mental health; city planning, architecture, and construction; mechanics and engineering; prognostication, agriculture, and commerce; conduct and manners, ethics and morals, and causes of happiness and misery; and even the requirements of the paths of buddhas, Buddhist disciples, and individual illuminates; the essentials of complete enlightenment; and behavior linking reason and action.

The *Flower Ornament Scripture* subsequently links this theme of extension or diffusion to formal Tantrism through the figure of another young bodhisattva named Shilpabhijna, "Higher Knowledge of Arts." He is the teacher of Vishvamitra, "Friend of All." In the imagery of the scripture, Higher Knowledge of Arts, the teacher of Friend of All, employs the practice of using "seed" syllables for concentration formulas. These are the basic elements of the Tantric concentration formulas known as mantra or *dharani*, which are chanted or repeated silently to evoke certain states of mind.

Shilpabhijna, Higher Knowledge of Arts, is represented as yet a youth. This symbolizes the further extension and evolution of arts and sciences in the future, as part of the continuity of Tantra. On concluding his recital of the doors of wisdom opened by the sounds, therefore, the youthful adept disclaims any finality or completeness to his knowledge, deferring to those who attain the perfection of all worldly and transcendental arts, extolling their expertise in all the arts, including writing and mathematics, applied sciences, mental and physical healing, pharmacology, chemistry, and mineralogy; design and construction of parks, groves, villages, towns, and cities; astronomy, physiognomy, geology, meteorology, agronomy, and prediction of trends; and the analysis, communication, understanding, and actualization of nonordinary phenomena.

Such is the expansive and pervasive light of Tantra, illuminating the continuum of mind and matter. This light is the living presence of enlightenment, directed toward the progressive regeneration and ultimate emancipation of the whole body of humanity.

12

Kissing Kannon

TANTRISM IS MOST ARTICULATE in its expression of the suffusion of all aspects of life with spirituality, but in practice the increasingly complicated use of prosthetic devices such as art and ritual was subject to economic constraints. The formalities of monastic organization and religious ceremonialism eventually reconstituted elitism and recaptured institutionalized Tantrism. Pure Land Buddhism, in contrast, evolved from more complex into more simple forms, diffusing into the lay population at large and spreading throughout East Asia to become the most popular path of Buddhist practice.

Tantric Buddhism and Pure Land Buddhism are similar in certain ways, especially in production of bliss for educational purposes by means of devotional meditation, visualization, and recitation of sacred formulas. Like Tantrism, Pure Land Buddhism also developed the use of occupational themes in meditation practice as a means of integrating spiritual exercise with everyday life.

Pure Land, in its many forms, includes the largest lay movement in Buddhism, with the greatest number of female followers and adepts. Like Tantrism in India and Bengal, both Hindu and Buddhist, Pure Land Buddhism was also very popular among the lower classes of East Asian societies, including followers of occupations outcast by the mainstream polity.

As in Tantric Buddhism, while there are specialized Pure Land texts employed by later sectarians, the roots of Pure Land Buddhist practice can be found in the great Ekayana or unitarian texts, the *Saddharmapundarika-sutra* or *Lotus of Truth Scripture* and the *Avatamsaka-sutra* or *Flower Ornament Scripture*. The *Lotus Scripture* teaches the practice of invoking the name of Avalokiteshvara, the personification of active compassion, for salvation in this world and beyond. The *Flower Ornament Scripture* also has a segment on Avalokiteshvara that extols this practice. In China and the Far East, this Avalokiteshvara was transformed into Kuan-yin, vulgarly paraphrased in the West as the Goddess of Mercy. From a Tantric point of view, Kuan-yin is a reflection of Tara, the Savioress, who is the consort and female counterpart of Avalokiteshvara. This savioress, who is held to appear in many forms according to the needs of the needy, is still greatly beloved as one of the most popular objects of devotion in East Asian Buddhism.

The *Flower Ornament Scripture* probably contains more visions of pure lands than any other Buddhist scripture. It also contains a section on the practice of "Buddha remembrance," which is the basis of Pure Land Buddhism. In the scripture's segment on the Vows of Universally Good Practice, moreover, one of the most important traditional Buddhist prayers, specific mention is made of Sukhavati, the Land of Bliss, which is the Pure Land of Amitabha, the Buddha of Infinite Light. The prayer concludes with a vow to lead all beings to this land, which is none other than the special object of devotion, meditation, and visualization for Pure Land Buddhism.

Several devotional works related to Pure Land Buddhism were composed by women of the eleventh and twelfth centuries from Uddiyana and Kashmir. Vajravati, an ex-Brahmini from Uddiyana, developed a practice based on devotion to a terrifying version of the Savioress Tara, called Wrathful Red Tara. Siddharajni, also from Uddiyana, developed a yoga focused on Amitayus, the Buddha of Infinite Life, another name of Amitabha, the Buddha of Infinite Light. Lakshmi the Great, a princess of Kashmir, initiated a ritual fast devoted to Avalokiteshvara, the consort of Tara the Savioress, ambassador of Amitabha Buddha, and personification of universal compassion.

Uddiyana and Kashmir had been within the great cultural basin of the Kushan empire, where the *Lotus Scripture* and *Flower Ornament Scripture* were compiled. The presence of a living, creative stream of Pure Land Buddhism nearly a thousand years after the Kushan Empire is an eloquent testimony to the residual force of the spiritual impulse of Gandhara Buddhism. As this force flowed into Tibet from Uddiyana and Kashmir, the works of these women were preserved within Tibetan Buddhist tradition.

In the East Asian Buddhist cultures of China, Korea, and Japan, where Pure Land Buddhism was promulgated among the masses by mendicants, some irony has been found in the fact that the central scriptural text adopted by these mendicant preachers to popularize the Pure Land teaching, a specialized devotional work called *Sukhavati-vyuha* or *Lay of the Land of Bliss*, specifies that there are no women, or even the very name of woman, in the Pure Land of Amitabha. Some observers take this as evidence of the transmission or filtration of this scriptural tradition through monastic media, which they see as imbuing the teaching with monkish antifeminism in the process. Others believe that it represents the absence of social or cultural gender bias in the realm of purified consciousness.

The generality of women of East Asia, who practiced Pure Land Buddhism in great numbers, evidently did not take a literal interpretation of the absence of women in the Pure Land, and so did not hesitate to embrace the teaching on this account. One of the scriptures of the Pure Land specialization says that seeing the Buddha is seeing mind, for mind is Buddha and mind makes Buddha. Zen masters of East Asia who taught Pure Land methods said that the Pure Land is purely mental, or that the Pure Land is none other than this very world as experienced by the mentally pure.

Under these cultural conditions, even unlettered people were able to appreciate the symbolic nature of scriptural imagery. Some of the greatest Buddhist adepts of all time, in fact, were themselves illiterate peasants, innocent of the qualms and quibbles of literalist scholars. A considerable number of the people who are supposed to have attained rebirth in the Pure Land of Amitabha were children, particularly girls, who passed away consciously in serene peace before their majority.

All Pure Land Buddhists of old Asia, literate or not, would normally have been familiar with the story in the unitarian *Lotus Scripture* about the transformation of the Naga girl, which the great commentators and founders of schools had described as symbolic. Likewise, the pilgrimage in the final book of the *Flower Ornament Scripture*, with its extensive visits to numerous female teachers, was also widely cited in all the great Buddhist schools of East Asia and deeply admired as a monumental epic of symbolic fiction.

Both of these unitarian works were primary sources of the Pure Land type of Buddhist thought and practice long before the later sectarian developments of East Asian schools. Their contents are directly linked to those of the specialized Pure Land scriptures, and they were widely used as sources of scripts for public educational dramas enacted by traveling dharma-dharas or Holders of the Teaching at shrines and other sites in the old world of Silk Route Buddhism. This cultural background helped to mitigate literalistic abuses of symbolic expression among both educated and uneducated people in the old Buddhist East.

While Pure Land Buddhism does not display the open eroticism of Tantra, in its encompassing outreach as a largely lay movement Pure Land embraces married life, and there are many stories of beautiful marriages of devotees who shared high attainments of faith. There are also many stories of abusive or indifferent spouses transformed by the devotion of a partner, or by the Teaching itself through the inspiration of the other.

In Japan, Pure Land Buddhist sects were championed by monks of the old monastic orders, but they eventually developed new institutions more consistent with the life of the ordinary people, including coeducational cloisters and married clergy. It may not be coincidental that this took place shortly after the establishment of the first national military government, which officially banned the practice of Left-Hand Tantra in Japan.

The name Kannon, the Japanese version of Kuan-yin, the so-called goddess of mercy, the supernal personification of the compassion and mercy of Infinite Light, came to mean, first in secret, then in slang, the private parts of a woman. To "adore Kannon" thus meant to make love to a woman; and to make love to a woman was an act of adoration of Kannon.

In this way the religious aspect of eroticism, sexuality, and marriage was maintained in popular Pure Land Buddhism after the military government had eliminated it from the Tantric Shingon school of Buddhism, which was influential among the old Japanese aristocracy.

The carnal aspect of Japanese Kannon worship appears to have been initiated, at least in illustrative history, by the great medieval Zen master Ikkyu. He is known for bowing to the private parts of women as the "place where all Buddhas are born," overtly implying reverence for motherhood while covertly alluding to Tantric practice. Ikkyu himself had female lovers even into old age, and he is believed to have fathered at least one son. He seems to have been a major influence on the great Pure Land leader Rennyo, who fathered as many as twenty-eight children by several wives, remaining sexually active into his eighties.

Ikkyu lived in a time when Japan was ruled by military men, but he himself came from the old aristocracy, known for its artistic sensuality. The poet-scholars of earlier times had accepted impermanence with tenderness and compassion; the warriors who supplanted them embodied it with harshness and cruelty. The social and political subordination of women reached unprecedented levels under centuries of military rule in Japan, echoed by antifeminine developments in cultural imagery and sexual mores. The idea that women are inherently sinful, originally a rationalization for their oppression, even became a standard part of what Japanese people generally came to take for Buddhist belief. Under these conditions, the Pure Land embrace of women and children, family and home, was a mercy and a blessing to the masses of people laboring under the harsh and repressive social disciplines of the ruling warrior caste.

13

Twin Souls

"O humanity, be conscious of your Lord,
who created you from one soul,
and created its mate from it."

—QUR'AN 4:1

FROM A THEOLOGICAL POINT OF VIEW, the apparent polytheism of Hinduism, religious Taoism, and Tantric Buddhism seems to present a sharp contrast to the strict monotheism of Islam, but the Sufi point of view distinguishes their different levels of discourse. The imagery of gods and goddesses as married couples appears particularly alien to monotheistic Islamic, Jewish, or Christian ways of thought, but the nature of their apparent contradiction is a matter of interpretation.

Buddhism, which uses both concrete images and metaphysical abstractions with equal facility, resolves this problem of perception by understanding ideas of gods and goddesses as representations rather than realities. This is also characteristic of the attitude demonstrated by Sufi mystics working in multicultural and multireligious contexts.

The Sufi point of view agrees with Buddhist metaphysics in distinguishing the illusion in mistaking a representation for a reality. The great eighteenth-century Sufi Shah Waliullah of Delhi, in his brilliant *Altaf al-quds*, explained that "popular mystics" had failed to understand the differ-

216

ence between subjective association and objective meaning.[1] This corresponds to the unitarian Buddhist idea of humanity's error in mistaking representation for reality. In the context of religion, this refers to confusing expressions, ideas, or images of divinity or reality with divinity or reality itself. This confusion of subjectivity with objectivity, while perhaps unavoidable at some stage in the process of thought, is eventually undesirable because it can ultimately lead to individual and mass delusions that in extreme forms are prone to produce fanaticism, tyranny, and irrational violence.

Shah Waliullah elaborates further on the confusion of the subjective with the objective in the context of contemplation. He explains that the imagination may form an explanatory picture for the intellect in the interest of certitude, but if that picture comes to dominate the mind, then its form may be taken by the enraptured contemplative for the actual presence of truth or reality. The Sufi admits that the imaginary form can be a useful tool, but acknowledges that the problem of distinguishing the imaginal abstraction from purely immaterial reality is not solved by every ecstatic.

In Buddhism, the problem of the mind of the contemplative becoming overmastered by the imagery employed, or the states of rapture experienced, is referred to as "being reborn under the sway of a meditation state." In terms of Tantric Buddhist meditation, this may be described as "dwelling in the vein of dalliance and failing to open the channel of clarification." Gautama Buddha himself broke with his Hindu gurus over this issue, but meditation states were again systematically reified by followers of Buddhism until Zen arose a thousand years after Buddha's time to reassert the distinction between subjective states and objective realities.

Seen in this light, there is no direct comparison between the apparent bitheism of Hinduism and the monotheism of Islam, because the former represents a projection of human imagery and the latter represents a transcendence of human imagery. More precisely, from the monotheistic point of view represented by the above passage in the Qur'an, the gender dualism in Hindu gods and goddesses represents a perception of the sacredness of the pair in the design of the natural order. In this sense, or in

1. Shah Waliullah, *The Sacred Knowledge of the Higher Functions of the Mind*, trans. G. N. Jalbani, ed. David Pendlebury (London: Octagon Press, 1982), p. 52.

terms of this way of understanding, the god/goddess pair is not different from the Qur'anic articulation of mates or pairs as a sign of God.

As in Taoism, with its complementary principles of yin and yang, this pattern of mating or pairing is seen as part of a design of nature pervading different realms or orders of being. The Qur'an says, "Glory to the One who created mates, all of them, from what the earth produces, from their own kinds, and from what they do not know" (36:36).

The relationship between the genders, from this point of view, is part of the divine design. The longing of a lover for the beloved, often used in Sufi poetry to symbolize love and longing for reunion with the divine, also intimates the longing of the fragmented soul for completeness. Realization of the oneness of the original soul can be experienced in reunion with its mate, of which it is part and which is part of it. As the Qur'an tells men and women, "You are from one another" (2:195).

Further depth in perception of these ideas can be gained by examining the root and ramifications of *nafs*, the original Arabic word used for "soul" in the citation opening this chapter: "Your Lord . . . created you from one soul." The meanings of the grammatically feminine noun *nafs* include "soul," "life," "animate being," "person," "essence," "nature," "identity," and "self." The passage thus implies that we are all created from one soul, one life, one essence, one nature; and so we are originally one being, one self. The identification of the individual self with the universal self may be experienced and expressed in the selfless dedication of chivalry and in the selfless admiration of love. For in the recognition of the soul mate is found the recognition of the original soul itself, of whose very essence the mate partakes by nature.

The verbs yielded by the same root further articulate the nature and operation of the *nafs* as the "self." The first base of the root gives a verb *nafusa*, which denotes that something is precious or valuable; and also a verb *nafisa*, which means to be sparing of something or to begrudge something to someone. These verbs together suggest potential worth that may be prized and cultivated or protected and defended.

The second base of the root yields a verb *naffasa*, which means to cheer someone up or to comfort someone. The second base of an Arabic root commonly conveys an intensive or a causative meaning; the idea of cheer or comfort deriving from this root for "person" or "individual" may suggest the sociable nature of the self or soul. This sociable nature might be understood, in this context, as a subconscious memory of the "one self" or "one soul" from which humanity was created.

The third base of the root yields a verb *naafasa*, which means to strive, to compete, or to desire. The third base of an Arabic root construes meanings of doing something to someone, or attempting to do something to someone; the notion of striving and competition deriving from this root of "self" seems to illustrate the outcome of divisive fragmentation of the consciousness of "one self" or "one soul" into individual egos. The habit of sensing and viewing ourselves and others as ultimately separate entities lies at the basis of competition and strife. This is also emphasized in the verb deriving from the sixth base of the root, which is similar to the third but emphasizes reciprocity in verbs, implying an "other" in their action. The sixth base of the root of "self" yields the verb *tanaafasa*, which means to contend.

From this constellation of associations it is clear how important the issue of purification of the *nafs* is on the Sufi path. Do our selves or individual souls yield value and comfort, or rivalry and strife? Do we consciously remember our whole original soul, or is our awareness forever refracted into a multitude of partial selves?

In technical Sufi terminology, the *nafs* has been called *ar ruuh al hayawaniyya*, the animal spirit or animal soul, defined as that which bears the power of life, sense perception, and voluntary activity, the intermediary between the rational or reasonable soul (*an nafs an naatiqa*) and the body. For the body to obey the rational soul, the mediating self or animal soul has to be receptive to the promptings of the rational soul. Thus the clarification and refinement of the animal soul is sometimes referred to in terms of taming or training, and sometimes in terms of regeneration or evolution.

As many as seven stages in the development of the *nafs* have been defined in Sufi works. The first stage is called the compulsive self, meaning the unruly animal soul dominated by instinct and habit. The second stage is called the critical self, meaning the stirrings of conscience and self-reproach. The third stage is called the inspired self, wherein intimations of greater potential become accessible after conscience dislodges compulsion from its throne of assumed authority. The fourth stage is called the tranquil self or serene self, which has achieved stability and poise and is thereby able to accept inspiration without the distortion of compulsion.

Some representations of the development of the self conclude with the tranquil self, citing the Qur'an verse of the chapter *Daybreak*, which addresses the serene self in the divine voice, saying, "O tranquil soul, return to your Lord, satisfied and satisfying; join My devotees, and enter My garden." The last three stages defined in the more detailed representation, called the satisfied self, the satisfying self, and the purified and completed self, can also be derived from this verse. The satisfied self has recognized its place in the scheme of things and acquiesced to the divine design; the satisfying self accepts and undertakes the imperatives of that design, fulfilling its true potential.

The end result of this satisfaction and fulfillment is the fully mature *nafs*, called the purified and completed self. The full operation of this purified and completed self is metaphorically compared to the entry of the devotee of the divine into the company of the community of souls in paradise.

The Qur'an declares openly that both men and women have a place in paradise and are assured of divine rewards on the same terms: "Anyone who does good and is faithful, whether male or female, will enter paradise and will not be wronged" (4:124). This entry of the "noble pair" into paradise is further described in terms of their radiance, their righteousness, and their reward: "One day you will see the faithful men and faithful women with their light streaming before them and by their right hands. 'Good news for you today—a garden beneath which rivers flow, wherein to abide forever.' That is the great triumph" (47:12).

Everyday elements of the practical path to this attainment are also described in terms of "noble pairs," highlighting the spiritual egalitarianism of goodness and the spiritual companionship of God-conscious men and women:

> For men who surrender to God and women who surrender to God,
> pious men and pious women,
> truthful men and truthful women,
> patient men and patient women,
> humble men and humble women,
> charitable men and charitable women,

men who fast and women who fast,
men who guard their privates and women who guard theirs,
men who remember God much and women who remember too,
God has arranged absolution for them, and a tremendous reward.
  (33:36)

14

Reverencing the Womb

And We have made humankind responsible for their parents—
their mothers carry them, sapped and weakened,
and their weaning takes two years.

—QUR'AN 31:15

A S SEEN IN OTHER TRADITIONS, an elemental aspect of spiritual
feminism is respect for motherhood. Elevated to religious and metaphysical terms in the East, this reverence maintained a reserve of respect
for women even under the patriarchal regimes of Brahmanism, Confucianism, and militarism. An analogous phenomenon is found in monotheistic tradition, where reverence for motherhood is extolled on a
medium of human harmonization with the divine.

Once someone asked Muhammad the Prophet, "Who is most deserv-
ing of good treatment?"

The Prophet said, "Your mother."

The questioner asked, "Then who?"

The Prophet said, "Your mother."

The questioner asked, "Then who?"

The Prophet said, "Your mother."

The questioner asked, "Then who?"

The Prophet said, "Your father."

The Prophet is also reported to have said, "Paradise lies at the feet of mothers."

In the Qur'an, the ancient sage Luqman says of respect for parents, "Lower the wing of humility to them both, mercifully, and say, 'My Lord, have mercy on them, as they took care of me when I was small!' " (17:25).

While the teaching of the Qur'an certainly honors the biological function of motherhood as a sign of God, the psychological, social, and spiritual aspects of motherhood are also emphasized, and perhaps even more, for their significance in the development of human consciousness.

The nurturing archetype of motherhood as a symbol of compassion is set forth by the Prophet as a universal manifestation, or reminder, of divine mercy: "God rendered mercy into a hundred parts, keeping ninety-nine and sending one down to earth. By virtue of that one portion, creatures are merciful to each other, to the extent that even the mare lifts her hooves away from her foal, fearing she may step on it."

This is illustrated in the Arabic language used in the Qur'an, which was the sacerdotal language of the keepers of the shrine at Mecca before it became the vehicle of the Islamic revelation. The root of *rahim* or *rahm*, the Arabic words for womb—r-h-m—is also the root of the verb *rahima*, which means to have mercy. It is thus the very same root of the most frequently used epithets of God—ar-Rahmaan, ar-Rahiim—The Supremely Compassionate, The Supremely Merciful.

The root and ramifications of the Arabic word 'umm for "mother" also yield insight into the archetype and associations of motherhood in this system of thought. The primary verb derived from the same root is 'amma, which can convey three basic meanings: to betake oneself; to lead the way; or to be or become a mother. The first meaning, to betake oneself, is associated with the role of the mother as the first resort of the child. The second meaning, to lead the way or to lead by example, is associated with the role of the mother as the first teacher of the child. Thus the meaning of being or becoming a mother is intimately associated with the responsibilities of being the first resort and first teacher of the child. The word Imam ('imaam), which means a leader, a guide, or a plumb line, is also derived from this root.

The meaning of 'umm does not refer only to biological motherhood but also signifies origin, basis, foundation, matrix, or source in a wider context. It is used to mean the original version of a book, as well as the gist or essence of something, or that which is principal or most important. The 'umm ar-ra's or "matrix of the head," for one example, refers to the brain. The Sufi code name of the popular 'Alf Layla wa Layla or Thousand and One Nights, for another example, is 'Umm ul Qissa, "Matrix of the Story," indicating the presence of stories of special significance within the matrix of this work. In these and other expressions the association of the original with the essential imbues the root of the word for "mother" with an unassailable dignity and depth of meaning.

The noun 'umma, from the same root, is also of great significance. This word means a way of life, and it also means a people, community, or nation. The root association of motherhood with the people and the community as a whole focuses attention on the social nature of humans and other animals. "There is no animal on earth, and no bird on the wing, but are communities ['umam] like you," says the Qur'an (6:38). The connection of this basic realization with the awakening of compassion and mercy is self-evident. When asked if people are rewarded for the way they treat animals, Muhammad the Prophet said, "You are rewarded for your treatment of every living thing."

The fecundity of earth, like the fecundity of woman, is viewed as a sign of God. Fecundity itself is not the primary focus of concern, but is a mirror of the divine agency, which is the primary focus of the mystical ascent beyond material form: "It is God who has produced you all from a single self" (Qur'an 6:98). The divine agency is seen as the ultimate source of all life and reproduction: "And among the signs of God is having created you all from dust; and there you are, humankind, propagating widely!" (Qur'an 30:20).

The divine agency is also seen as the source of the life and fecundity of earth itself, and so the fertility of the living earth is seen as a reflection of the living presence of the absolute Reality: "And a sign for them is the earth when it is dead; We enliven it and bring grain forth from it, of which they partake. And We have placed gardens of dates and grapes on it, and caused springs to flow therein, that they may eat of its fruits, though they did not make this themselves. Will they not be thankful?" (Qur'an 36:33–35).

The theme of gratitude and ingratitude as fundamental indicators of the quality of human life, be it material, psychological, or spiritual, is prominent in the teaching of the Qur'an, and in the mystical projection thereof in Sufism, which has been called the creed of Love. Gratitude for both material and spiritual opportunities of life is fundamental to the development of conscience and morality, as an everyday mode of consciousness of the divine presence and divine agency.

This applies, naturally, to the rigors of life as well as to the bounties thereof, just as elemental goddess images balance the benevolence of creation and nurturance with the chastisement of disruption and destruction. Like a mother, the goddess of the elements not only gives nourishment, warmth, and comfort but also instructs, admonishes, and punishes. In the language of the Qur'an, while the compassionate nurture of motherhood and the fruitfulness of earth, as reflections of the divine design, are understood as foundations for the cultivation of conscientious mindfulness, likewise the inevitable end of the world and dissolution of life on earth are considered for their impact on the moral intelligence of humanity.

In this context, the earth is viewed not simply as a medium of the divine power of creation but also as a repository of temporal phenomena and forces produced by human deeds. When the end of time arrives, or when causes produce their results, this repository will disgorge its contents to "accuse" its perpetrators and show them their responsibility for their actions. Just as the Hindu or the Buddhist believes in the inevitable consequences of karma, or action, the Qur'an illustrates the notion of the judgment of humanity as a representation of the natural outcome of the deeds of humankind: "When the earth convulses in her shock, and the earth disgorges her burdens, and the people wonder what is wrong with her, that day she will tell her news: That your Lord has inspired her. On that day, humanity will go forth divided, to be shown their works. And whoever has done any good at all will see it; and whoever has done any evil at all will see it" (99:1–8).

While their manners of expression may differ, each of the traditions considered demonstrates a certain commonality or universality of concern, arising from the nature of human life. There tend to be areas in which differences in mode of discourse can sometimes obscure similarities, particularly when engaging in theological debate. The poignant realities of motherhood, however, both concrete and symbolic, transcend these cultural differences to a degree that lends a special value and a particular importance to the mindfulness of motherhood.

15

Saintly Women

The best of you is the one with the best character.

—MUHAMMAD

Sufism is character; so whoever is more advanced than
you in character is more advanced than you in Sufism.

—ZAIN UL-ABIDIN

S UFIS THROUGH THE AGES have affirmed sainthood as a reality in
this very life. The great Sufi expositor Ali al-Hujwiri goes so far as to
say that the very foundation of Sufism, and gnosis itself, rests on sainthood. In some sense, therefore, sainthood is a goal of Sufism, although it
must be admitted that both sainthood and Sufism have been defined or
described in various different ways. However these spiritual realities may
be temporally defined, it is nevertheless universally recognized that
women can attain them, and the highest authorities affirm that women
have been included among the ranks of saints and Sufis.

Abu'l-Hasan Nuri said, "Sufis are those whose spirits are pure, and
they have attained to the primal purity in the presence of the Truth." He
also said, "The Sufi is one who neither possesses nor is possessed." Ibn
al-Jalla said, "Sufism is truth without form." Murta'ish said, "Sufism is
goodness of character." These classical statements, preserved in the origi-

nal Arabic in *Kashf al-Mahjub*, the first Persian treatise on Sufism, succinctly demonstrate the essential universality of the Sufi outlook, which does not discriminate against people on account of race, class, or gender.

An interesting Sufi affirmation about sainthood, mentioned by Hujwiri and others, is that there are a number of unknown saints on earth at any given time. they are unknown (as saints) not only to society at large but also to each other and even to themselves. Because their sainthood and their beneficial effect on the world are not part of their own personal view, they are thereby preserved from falling prey to conceit on account of the excellence of their spiritual station.

Tradition reckons the unknown saints at four thousand, but such numbers can be representational. Sufi stories often feature characters resembling the traditional picture of the unknown saint, including humble and inconspicuous women whose inner illumination shines forth only in response to a genuine need in the search for truth. In this respect, as teaching figures these anonymous Sufi women resemble the *lao-po* of Ch'an Buddhist tradition, who generally appear to be insignificant peasant women until an occasion arises when a sincere question or an authentic dilemma deserves an answer, or an occasion arises when an academic idiocy or ecclesiastical ego requires a shattering.

Sufi tradition also refers to the existence of some thirty thousand saints, called Friends, who have no formal territorial jurisdiction but are associated with, or subservient to, a secret world hierarchy of adepts. At the head of this esoteric hierarchy, which can only act by mutual consent of its members, is the Qutb, the Axis or Pole, the leader of all Sufis. It is held that the identity of this individual is generally unknown, except to other members of the hierarchy. This secrecy is maintained, it is said, for practical purposes; Sufis do not court fame, and indeed may seek to be disregarded or even disapproved by the generality of humanity, so that they can work undisturbed by the curious and the greedy.

This concept of a hidden Sufi hierarchy is somewhat similar to that of the Taoist idea of an esoteric government staffed by realized people whose true spiritual status and function is generally invisible except under certain special circumstances. Only when they perceive a real need, and a glimmer of genuine receptivity, are these adepts able to make themselves known to humanity in a beneficial way. Often the work must be done in a completely subliminal manner, as the oldest Taoist works suggest. This inconspicuous efficiency is also reminiscent of the Buddhist image of bodhisattvas assuming various guises for the edification of others, working for the good of the world without seeking social standing or recognition for their labors.

While the esoteric Sufi leadership is therefore shrouded in secrecy, some theologians have asserted that the first Axis of this hierarchy was in fact a woman. According to the great fifteenth-century Sufi master Jami, there have also been women among the saints in this occult hierarchy of the rank known as Abdal, Changed Ones or Substitutes, who are said to number forty souls.

The extraordinary woman said to have been the first Axis was none other than the saintly Fatima, one of the Four Exemplary Women of Islamic tradition. Fatima was daughter of Muhammad the Prophet by his first wife, Khadija. As the mother of the Prophet's grandsons, Fatima is also the mother of the Prophet's personal heritage, known as the People of the House, the Sayeds and Sharifs, descendants of the Prophet, among whom are families in which the Sufi sciences are said to be preserved.

Fatima's husband was Muhammad's cousin and disciple 'Ali, a great Sufi later known as the Door of Knowledge. 'Ali was the Fourth Caliph of the Sunnite Muslims, the First Imam of the Shi'ite Muslims, and traditionally counted among the first generation of classical Sufi masters known as the Seven Great Ones. Fatima and 'Ali were part of the Prophet's original inner circle, through which inner dimensions of the teaching were transmitted in private. The Prophet said of her, "Fatima is the mistress of the women of the people of paradise."

While Fatima is universally revered as a perfect woman in exoteric Sunnite Islam, the educational organization called House of Wisdom established in Fatimid Egypt about a thousand years ago may have been connected with a particular formulation of the belief that Fatima was the first Axis or Polestar of the secret Sufi hierarchy of saints. Sufism was supposedly taught at one of the upper levels of the curriculum of the House of Wisdom, and it has been suggested that the modern version of the Sufi organization known as the Mu'assissa or Foundation—associated with the hidden leadership—was itself founded or reconstituted in Fatimid Egypt.

Some believe that the House of Wisdom was either created or inspired by agents of the Foundation, or that the Foundation was a product of the House of Wisdom, or that the Foundation and the House of Wisdom are both merely traces of the activity of the hidden leadership. These apparent obscurities, sometimes called veils, screen the workings of the saints from the eyes of the world; this is sufficient reason to realize that, from this point of view, we cannot presume to define saints in terms of gender, class, race, ethnicity, or personal identity of any of the usual kinds that we have learned to project upon ourselves and others.

The fact remains, nonetheless, that in Islamic lore there are indelible traditional indications of women in the assembly of saints. In the religion of Islam, with which Sufism has widely been associated for the last thousand years, women are not excluded from the sacred and the spiritual, as they are, for example, in orthodox Hinduism and Confucianism; and Islam also grants women more legal rights than do traditional Hinduism and Confucianism. Where Muslim women were in fact accorded their Qur'anic rights, there was no need for special religious cults to emancipate women spiritually as seen in Hindu-dominated India and Confucian-dominated China, where movements such as Buddhism, Tantrism, and Taoism were resorted to as alternative ways of life by many of the socially and religiously disenfranchised.

The case of the Bektashi order of dervishes, which made a particular point of holding mixed meetings for the purpose of overcoming extremism in segregation of the sexes in Ottoman society, may be considered special in this context, considering the social nature of their stated aim. When the dervish orders were suppressed in republican Turkey after the end of the Ottoman Empire, the Bektashi authorities declared that they were closing their own doors because their mission had been accomplished. Never, perhaps, has the old joke "You can't fire me, I quit!" been used with greater effect.

The designation of marriage, family, and social relations as a framework for spiritual practice is explicit in the Qur'an and the Sunna or Custom of the Prophet, and this recognition is evident in notices of the lives and works of the great Sufis of the last thousand years, who are considered the "modern" Sufis. Sufi centers for special studies have formed and dissolved from time to time over the centuries, nonetheless, for the purposes of particular concentration. These centers, however, according to reports past and present, also reflect the balance of human types, including the archetype of the "noble pair," having for centuries included separate centers for women and men as well as mixed assemblies.

Fatima's esoteric position as the first Qutb, the Axis, Pole, or Polestar of the Sufi saints, is paralleled by her exoteric position as one of the Four Exemplary Women, also referred to as the Four Perfect Women, named in Islamic tradition as exemplars of feminine integrity. In this role as an exoteric feminine model, Fatima is joined by her own mother, Khadija, beloved first wife of the prophet Muhammad; by 'Asiya, the independent-minded wife of an ancient Egyptian grandee; and by Mary, the God-inspired mother of Jesus.

Khadija, who was not only the first wife of Muhammad but also his only wife during her lifetime, was a successful international business-woman fifteen years his senior. Twice widowed before marrying Muhammad, at one time the astute and self-possessed Khadija employed the young prophet-to-be in her business, which she had inherited from her father when she was thirty years old. Through their professional relationship, Khadija became well acquainted with the morals and character of her future husband.

Although she was already forty years of age when she and Muhammad were married, Khadija bore him six children. Their first child, a son, died at the age of two; their last child, also a son, died in infancy. The saintly Fatima, mother of the Imams, was the youngest of their four daughters.

Khadija and Muhammad had been married for fifteen years by the time he began to receive revelations during his meditations in a mountain cave outside Mecca. Muhammad was already a mature man of forty, known in the community for his reliability, but what he experienced in that cave created a profound turmoil in him. It was to Khadija, beloved wife and mother of his children, that Muhammad hastened in his turmoil. Retaining her own composure and keeping her presence of mind, Khadija calmed the nascent prophet, reminding him of his reputation for trust-worthiness and assuring him that he could not be mad, as he at first feared.

Beneath the color and drama of this famous incident lies a reminder of a human reality whose poignancy is inescapable regardless of how one may feel about the reality of prophecy; and that is the plight of a woman whose husband, the father of her children, has lost his mind. Since the man himself, even if divinely inspired, first thought he was going mad, how sublime must have been the sobriety and how profound the insight of the woman who saw the truth of the matter and did not waver or doubt.

If Khadija herself had plunged into anxiety and fear, as any ordinary human being might understandably do under the circumstances of an apparent breakdown of her spouse and parent of her children, the intense agitation and distress in Muhammad's mind and body might have spiraled to a degree that could have damaged him irreparably. The sustaining wisdom and fortitude of this exemplary woman were therefore to have far-reaching consequences.

Over the next ten years, until her death at the age of sixty-five, Khadija continued to maintain her unflinching loyalty and steadfastness as the wife of the Prophet and the first to embrace Islam. At an age when she might reasonably have expected to enjoy the fruits of her labors, including a comfortable life and domestic tranquillity, instead Khadija shared the pains of ostracization and persecution visited upon the family and followers of Muhammad by opponents of his message.

Khadija did not live to see Islam's ultimate triumph, but this only highlights the purity and power of her certitude, as though her spiritual perception had penetrated the veil of time. Khadija's outstanding strength of character as "Mother of the Believers" shines through the darkness of those days of trial as a beacon of a brighter future. As a truly exemplary woman, she is not obscured by the brilliance of her husband in his prophetic role. As we see her in tradition, the light of the revelation is reflected in the clear mirror of her spiritual perception, which had sensed the verity of the message from the first. By virtue of her qualities, therefore, Khadija became the first earthly matrix of the historical dissemination of the message through her partner the Prophet.

'Asiya and Mary, the other two of the four Exemplary Women exalted in Islamic tradition, are also associated with prophets, namely, Moses and Jesus. It may seem incongruous that pre-Islamic people should figure so prominently in Islamic lore, but this is consistent with the Qur'an's recognition of Moses, Jesus, and others as divinely inspired prophets. According to Islamic tradition, there have been 128,000 prophets on earth and 104 books of true revelation. Similarly, the Illuminist school of Sufism considered the Sufi message identical or parallel to the teachings of certain ancient sages, including Hermes; and people of many different religions have been known to follow Sufism in historical times. A similar phenomenon is seen in the contexts of Zen, Taoist spiritual alchemy, and Tantrism, to which disciplines people of different religious backgrounds have often resorted for special illumination.

The figure of 'Asiya honored in Islamic tradition comes directly from the Qur'an, where she is depicted as a wife of a pharaoh of ancient Egypt. 'Asiya is believed to be the woman who saved the infant Moses from the Nile River, where he had been set adrift in a basket in an attempt to escape the mass destruction of male offspring of the Jews in Egypt as ordered by the pharaoh. Symbolically, Sufi lore uses the figure of Pharaoh to represent worldliness, or the compulsive self. Moses, in contrast, stands for the critical self and the inspired self. The struggle of Moses to lead his people to freedom from the tyranny of Pharaoh thus represents the struggle of conscience and inspiration to free the soul from the chains of compulsive habit. A "Moses basket," in Sufi parlance, referring to the basket in which the infant Moses was placed for safekeeping by his mother, means a cultural artifact in which a liberating teaching is concealed for preservation until such time as it can be retrieved by those who can perceive its value and apply it in life.

'Asiya, who retrieved the infant Moses from the river and returned him to his mother for nursing, represents this process of restoration and renewal. This can be done only by someone who has recovered her own integrity, has freed her soul from the web of the world and its opinions, and is thereby able to see what others cannot. In the Qur'an the lady 'Asiya prays, "My Lord, build me a house in heaven, delivering me from Pharaoh and his deeds, and delivering me from a tyrannical people" (66:12).

In Brahminic Hindu ideology, a woman's god was her husband; she was systematically excluded from personal contact with the sacred lore, hence the need for new religious movements to restore her right to higher truth. Similarly, the pharaohs of Egypt, like the emperors of Greece and Rome, proclaimed themselves gods not only of their women but of all their subjects and slaves. Here, in the example of 'Asiya the perfect woman, she acknowledges that truth transcends the world; the demands

232

of individual conscience, an inner and finer sense of truth and justice, supersede the commands of the social order.

Transcription of 'Asiya's name from Egyptian into Arabic illustrates the twofold symbolic value of this figure. The primary transcription of the root [a]-s-y seems to be 'ain-saad-yaa, which yields meanings of resistance, opposition, defiance, rebellion, inaccessibility, escape. This cluster of ideas represents 'Asiya's relationship to Pharaoh, spiritual resistance to material dominion. When this root is decoded by the standard abjad method used for mystical exegesis, it yields 'ain-qaf, from which is derived the verb aqqa, meaning to split, be disobedient, be recalcitrant. Thus the original root and the decoded derivation have substantially the same meaning, fortifying the image of 'Asiya in defiance of injustice.

A secondary transcription, based on linguistic semblance for didactic purposes, uses alif-sin, the "softer" correlates of 'ain-saad, for the a-s in 'Asiya's name. This reading of the root with "soft" consonants yields various derived verbs meaning to nurse, to treat, to make peace; to console, to comfort; to share one's possessions, to be charitable, to assist; and to find solace. This "soft" reading of 'Asiya's name illustrates her relationship to the infant Moses, for it was she who retrieved the baby from the river and convinced her husband to spare him and take him in, telling him the child would be a help and a comfort to them.

These two ways of transcribing 'Asiya's name thus present a picture of the two sides of her character as a traditional figure. She rejects the absolute authority of her husband for his iniquities, seeking a higher state in proximity to God. At the same time, she rescues and protects the endangered infant prophet who is to lead his people to freedom and bring them divine guidance.

Like 'Asiya, the example of Maryam, or Mary, mother of Jesus, is also featured in the Qur'an. Her story, like that of Pharaoh's wife, is invoked as a sign of God. One chapter of the Qur'an is even named after Mary; in it the holy book of the Muslims speaks reverently of Mary and Jesus, and also of Zacharias and his son John the Baptist, referring their spiritual tradition back to the ancient prophets Moses, Ishmael, Enoch, Noah, and Adam.

Mary also appears early on in the Qur'an, where her mother is referred to as a woman of 'Imran. This means that Mary was descended from the family of Moses and Aaron, who were the sons of 'Imran. That was a priestly Jewish family, and the Qur'an says that Mary's mother dedicated her to exclusive devotion to the service of God while Mary was still in her womb. When Mary was born, the story continues, she was given to the care of the priest Zacharias, who was the husband of Mary's cousin Elisabeth. John the Baptist was the son of Zacharias and Elisabeth, born to them in their old age.

The Qur'an goes on to relate how Zacharias used to find Mary mysteriously supplied whenever he looked in on her, and how she would say that God had provided for her. This seems to signify her independence from worldly things, and accordingly this scene is followed by angelic visitation. Unfettered by the compulsive self, impeccable to the critical self, Mary experiences the inspired self. Angels speak to her now, with news of a word from God called the Messiah Jesus.

Later on in the book, in the chapter of Mary, she goes through her birth pangs guided by a voice from the unseen. Then she brings the infant Jesus to her people, and as they wonder at the event the baby speaks up and tells them who he is: "I am a servant of God, who has given me the Book and made me a prophet, and made me blessed wherever I am, and made prayer and charity incumbent upon me as long as life goes on, and made me kind to my mother, and not oppressive or mean. And peace is upon me the day I was born, and the day I die, and the day I am resurrected" (19:30–33). In this address not only does Jesus vindicate his mother to her people at the very outset of his projection of divine inspiration, but he also includes kindness to his mother among the first of God's teachings, along with prayer and charity, to be commended to the whole human community.

Jesus is considered a Sufi and is featured as such in classical Sufic literature. Some bigots have accused Sufis of being secret Christians, but there is nothing in the Sufic recognition of Jesus that is contrary to orthodox Islam. Muhammad the Prophet is reported to have said, "I am the closest of all people to Jesus son of Mary, in this world and the hereafter; for all the prophets are brothers, with different mothers but one religion." The word "mothers" here also means communities, thus echoing the Qur'anic statement that prophets arise from time to time among the peoples they are to inspire; and also yielding the Sufic statement that all religions are originally local adaptations of the same transcendental truth.

From this perspective, the perfect woman Mary, mother of Jesus, represents the epitome of sole devotion to God and the formless spiritual matrix of Judaism. For even though the Jewish priesthood and patriarchy are male, Jewish descent is through the female. Thus, as the mother of Jesus, who is called a word from God, an inspiration from God, and a spirit from God, Mary mystically represents the matrix of clarity and purity required for the reception, concentration, and emission of divine inspiration.

The name of Mary, transcribed into Arabic as Maryam, also contains the seed concepts of her symbolic presence. Decoded by the *abjad* method, M-r-y-m yields the letters *ra-saad*, from which is derived the verb *rassa*, which means to compress, to pile up, to join together, to align. These ideas are suggestive of concentration, including the sense of accumulation of focused energy and the sense of alignment of attention and objective. The same letters can also produces the verb *asarra*, which means to persist, to resolve, to determine, or to prick up one's ears. These ideas strengthen the association with concentration, as perseverance, will, intent, and attention are all necessary to the development of concentration.

Considering Mary as an archetypal mother, the encoded association of her name with concentration parallels the Taoist use of pregnancy as a metaphor for meditation. In this light, it is also interesting to note that *rasaas*, another word derived from the code root of Mary, refers to the element lead, which is used in the metaphorical language of Taoist alchemy to represent true knowledge as a stabilizing factor in the production of enlightened consciousness.

Thus the Sufi technique of *abjad* decipherment of the root matrix of the name of Mary yields a Taoistic mystical explanation of the reality behind the use of the term Mother of God for Mary, as representing the embodiment of total concentration on divine truth or absolute reality.

In terms of Taoism, moreover, it is interesting to recall that Mary was already devoted exclusively to God while in her mother's womb. This is reminiscent of the ancient Taoist practice of "fetal education." According to this theory, it will be remembered, the psychological conditions and activities of the expectant mother influence the development of the unborn child, so "education" of the infant is begun during pregnancy.

Mary's mother was descended from Jewish prophets herself and was clearly conscious of the mother's role as a transmitter of Jewishness (which in its Arabic form means "Turning to God"). The Qur'anic story of the mother of Mary dedicating her to God's service while yet in the womb thus contains within its simple structure a profound meaning of maternal, meditative, and mystical import.

Another word from the derived root, surra, conveys the same idea of an earthly matrix containing a charge of higher value. Surra means, literally, "a money purse." A money purse is something of worth by virtue of what it contains, but the ability to hold that worth depends on the soundness of the container. Mary's innocence, her purity and transcendence of the world, made her a fit receptacle for higher inspiration.

Concentration, according to the inner traditions specializing in these matters, must be a sound vessel for insight if it is to be an effective tool for human development. Concentration without clarification of mind can magnify vanity and other negative characteristics, so the image of purification preceding inspiration is important from a technical point of view, even if theological terminology is not employed. In this sense, while the Mary of the Qur'an may generally represent total concentration on God, she particularly stands for sobriety. That is to say, in Sufic terms, while Mary is wholly devoted to God, she is not intoxicated by ecstasy and is therefore conscious of both domains, the divine and the human.

This, in essence, is what makes her an example of what Sufis call al-insan al-kamil, the complete human being. Mystically, then, Mary's singleness stands for her completeness as an individual. The apparent paradox of her fecundity in singleness, from this point of view, represents the infinite extension of the "journey with God" (safar bi-llah) in the final stage of Sufic self-realization. This journey entails return to the world after transcending it to serve as guides for other people, leading them from chaos to order and thence to realities beyond the familiar confines of life in this world.

Another way of deciphering the name of Mary is based on a semantic Arabicization in which the first ma is reckoned as a prefix rather than a part of the root. The meaning of the name Maryam, analyzed in this way, is said to be a woman who enjoys the company of men but is not flirtatious, immodest, or unchaste with them. This suits the exoteric Qur'anic image of Mary mother of Jesus, who associated with her people but remained untouched by men. In mystical terms, the name illustrates transcendence of the world while in its very midst, a central Sufi practice, particularly that mode of its exercise known in Persian as khilwat dar anjuman or solitude in company.

When Mary's Arabic name thus interpreted is subjected to abjad decipherment, it yields the root letters ra and nun. These consonants produce verbs meaning to cry out, to resound, and to hearken to a cry. According to the chapter on Mary in the Qur'an, Mary cried out to God when an angel came to her with the message of Jesus, announced by the angel as a "blameless boy" or "sinless child" given by God. The angel hearkened to Mary's cry and assured her that Jesus is a gift, a sign, and a mercy from God. Then when Mary gave birth to Jesus, she cried out in her pain, this time to be answered by a call from the unseen, guiding her to comfort and safety.

According to the chapter on Mary, at the time she was visited by the angel she had withdrawn from her people "to a place in the East." In Sufi symbolism, the East is the place of illumination. When the angel appeared as a man to her, Mary said, "I take refuge in the Merciful [God] from you, if you are conscientious." In mystical terms, this expression of external chastity represents the internal chastity of the mind wholly devoted to the absolute and thus unwilling to be enticed by any relative phenomenon, however subtle or sublime. Thus the mystical Mary, wholly devoted to God from even before her birth, gains access to angelic inspiration by temporary withdrawal of consciousness from the familiar world to the realm of the primary light that illuminates everything. Then, upon the dawning of inspiration, she retains her sobriety by questioning and verifying the source of the inspiration instead of succumbing to fascination with the messenger.

Upon her acceptance of the divine inspiration and her consequent conception of the divine word, the chapter on Mary continues, she withdrew "to a remote place." In mystical language, the "remote place" would suggest spiritual detachment "beyond the world." This transcendental station would be the abode of Mary's pregnancy and thus the realm of the fetal education of the sinless child.

As the final journey of Sufism takes place back in the world for the sake of others, in the story Mary's presence suddenly shifts from the remote place to the pains of childbirth. The pains drove her to the trunk of a palm tree, where she cried out, "Oh, would that I had died before this, oblivious and forgotten!" The palm tree (nakhla) stands for the Sufi way by association, because another, rarer word for palm tree (tariqa) is homonymous with the word for path (tariqa).

Death and oblivion, in the context of the Sufi path, allude to fana'—often figuratively translated as "annihilation," like the Buddhist nirvana, overcoming the tyranny of the compulsive self as a necessary prelude to inspiration, serenity, satisfaction, fulfillment, purification, and completion. Thus in mystical terms Mary resorts to the Sufi path to transcend her self in order to bring a sinless spirit into the world.

When she cried out for oblivion, Mary was answered by a voice from beneath the palm—the root of the Sufi way—drawing her attention to a stream beneath her, provided by God for her refreshment, and instructing her to shake the palm for dates to sustain her. The word for "stream" is associated with two roots—s-r-y and s-r-w—which also yield verbs meaning to travel by night and to dispel anxieties. Travel by night is a metaphor for the mystic path to certitude, by which instability of the self is overcome, thus dispelling anxieties. And just as drinking from this stream thus suggests treading the path of purification and transcendence, shaking the palm for nourishment also signifies the practice and experience of the Sufi way.

Viewing the Qur'anic story of Mary as a kind of outline map of the mystic path may also shed light on the mystery of the virgin birth of Jesus. Symbolic understanding of Mary's purity poses no problem for mystics of any tradition, but literalists may balk at devotional interpretation of the virgin birth as a historical miracle. It may be possible, nonetheless, to satisfy the requirements of religious myth and history both, by reference to certain Sufi concepts and practices.

The story of Mary in the Qur'an appears to accept the virgin birth as a fact and as a miracle, even though it does not apotheosize Jesus on that account. Read closely, however, the original text of the chapter on Mary leaves room for a time gap between her declaration of virginity and Jesus' conception, which seems to take place in the presence of an angel who appears to be a man.

Could it be that the pure-hearted Mary was "chosen" by a mystic society to mother a pure child by a spiritual adept, to undertake a special mission? Sufi masters have sometimes said that a completed and purified saint is human only in the most obvious sense. Hadrat Ali, for example, spoke of those who while physically still in the world are mentally "suspended in the highest liberation." Shah Waliullah also wrote that some of the mystics of ancient times had attained a state like that of the lesser angels. Just as Mary's mother devoted her to God in the womb, Mary may have repeated the same process herself, to achieve an even further level of devotion in her own offspring.

But what about the opprobrium attached to an unwed mother? In Christian tradition, Mary's husband, Joseph, is portrayed as an old man, signifying public belief that Jesus was not his son. In the Qur'an, Mary separates herself from her people before Jesus' conception, and she is greeted with suspicion when she returns to them with her wondrous child. If Jesus were in reality the son of an angelic spiritual adept, why was this father hidden, leaving his mother exposed to ridicule and ostracization? What kind of religious practice is that?

The answer may lie in one of the most misunderstood of Sufic practices, the so-called path of blame, the deliberate acceptance of opprobrium. The Sufi authority Hujwiri refers to this path (rahi malamati in Persian) as a method for concealment of the true condition of saints, not only from the eyes of the vulgar, but also from the eyes of the saints themselves.

The external instrument of this method is the carping of cavilers, who exist in all times and societies; the internal instrument is the so-called critical self or accusing self. The intermediating instrument, according to Hujwiri, may either be a superficial eccentricity or a sincere propriety. (There is also a third possibility he mentions, the true impropriety, that of the reprobate-impostor who claims "path of blame!" to justify personal waywardness under the sway of the compulsive self.)

As to the difference in method, Hujwiri points out that there was a time when it was necessary to do something unusual or disapproved to court opprobrium in defense against conceit. Hujwiri states with a hint of irony, however, that in his own time, eleven centuries after Mary, simply following the prescribed duties of religion, or perhaps lengthening voluntary prayers slightly, was enough to earn one the reputation of being a hypocrite and an impostor. How might this apply to Mary, mother of Jesus?

According to statements attributed to Jesus in the Bible, in his time there was an excess of formalism in religion, even to the point of ostentation in piety for profit. Jesus' saintly cousin John, for example, popularly known as the Baptist, was killed and cut apart by colonial authorities who feared his influence among the common people. Could it be that Mary purposely appeared unchaste in the eyes of the worldly and the pretentious, precisely in order to be rejected by mainstream society? If so, it may have been partly as an individual ascetic exercise in the course of her self-purification, and partly to cover the trail of her mission and make the authorities believe she was a nobody, without connections.

If this theory seems farfetched, whether in comparison to belief in the virgin birth of Jesus or in comparison to the dictates of reason, that impression may be due in the main to the calculated unfamiliarity of procedures pursuant to the path of blame. In any event, the sexual nature of the human Mary is veiled, as suggested in the statement of the Qur'an that she "screened herself" from her people. Her disappearance from the eyes of men was a prelude to spiritual inspiration, as her outward chastity mirrors her inward purity.

Modern humanists might think of the veiling of Mary's sexuality as ideological Christian cleansing of the holy mother's image, but from an educational point of view this mode of invisibility may be essential to her representational role as a Maryam or a woman who socializes with men without any sexual innuendo or involvement. Her son Jesus, according to traditional ideas of his life, is similarly pictured as a man who associated with women without any sexual innuendo or involvement.

Conventionally religious-minded thinkers have inferred from these images a certain sanctity in celibacy itself, but the original intention may have been to celebrate the beauty of platonic or spiritual relationships between men and women. An obsession with celibacy per se, ironically, can actually spoil spiritual relationships between men and women, insofar as such an obsession is itself of a sexual nature.

Spiritual intimacy does not suggest or require personal or sexual intimacy, but for lovers spiritual intimacy is essential to their religious experience of sexual intimacy. Thus the message of social and spiritual meaning in fraternal and platonic relations between men and women, as witnessed in the stories of Mary and her son Jesus, may have something of value to offer a society that is rapidly exhausting its current concepts of sexual freedom without having resolved the problems of personal relationships.

Considering that Jesus is considered by Sufis themselves to be a Sufi of the highest rank, there can be no doubt of the importance of his mother, Mary. As we have seen, this holds true in both exoteric and esoteric dimensions of religious reality. We use the symbolism of her name and its *abjad* transmutation to interpret the image of Mary because her historical person is veiled from us, whether by virtue of necessity or by necessity of virtue. In this way, landmarks of the mystic path can be illustrated, and hidden mysteries of Mary and Jesus can be elucidated.

The coherence of the coded meanings gives pause for thought, since Muhammad could neither read nor write and could not have constructed these terms. Jesus is recognized in the Qur'an as a prophet, and Mary is a completed human being and a perfected woman. If we turn one last time to the root elements r-n derived from *abjad* decipherment of Mary's name, we find they also generate the word *ar-runnaa*, which means humankind, or all of creation. Viewing Jesus as a Sufi, this may be the secret of his Arabic name Son of Maryam, yielding by decipherment of "Mary" a name Jesus is said to have used for himself—Son of Man.

It has been suggested that the latter-day cult of Mary in the Catholic Church may have been built on an outgrowth or remnant of a Sufic projection of a spiritual love theme through the troubadour movement, designed to promote a model of higher human development that would counter the unbalancing effects of Pauline antifeminism in the Catholic lands. However that may be, on account of the veil around Mary there is room for speculation and imagination in regard to her life story and religious experience. It may nonetheless be argued, as we shall see, that the traditional image of Rabi'a, the most famous of the female Sufis of the classical era, exhibits Sufistic similarities to the Qur'anic picture of Mary.

Rabi'a al-'Adawiyya, who lived from 713 to 801 of the Common Era, is recognized as a great saint and Sufi. Rabi'a's Sufi teaching is particularly reminiscent of the mystical message of Mary in its emphasis on divine love and intimacy with God. She emphasized pure devotion without fear of punishment or hope for reward.

Rabi'a was born the fourth daughter of a poor family of the city of Basra, which became a cultural center in her time under the reign of the famous Harun al-Rashid. She left Basra during a famine, after her father had already passed away, and was taken captive by bandits while traveling with a caravan. Then she was sold into slavery.

The themes of estrangement from her people and reduction into

241

bondage are also reminiscent of Mary. These images evoke visions of Mary viewed as an individual self and as a Jewish woman of a prophetic lineage whose homeland is ruled by agents of an ungodly empire. In ancient times, Simeon son of Judah led his tribe out of their homeland to escape a famine, like Rabi'a, only to fall into bondage in Egypt, as Rabi'a was taken captive and sold into slavery. In biblical accounts, Mary also goes into exile in Egypt with Joseph and the baby Jesus, at the behest of an angel in a dream, to escape the murder of the sinless child at the hands of Herod's men.

While yet captive in servitude, Rabi'a took to habits of intensive devotion after hearing a voice from the unseen in response to her cry of distress. Again we might be reminded of Mary crying out in her solitary travail, answered by a voice from the unseen guiding her to the palm tree and the stream running beneath it, representing the mystical journey of the Sufi path. The voice that answered Rabi'a gave her tidings of divine favor, as the angels gave Mary, leading Rabi'a, like Mary, to adopt a life of individual devotion.

After hearing the voice, Rabi'a took to passing her nights in prayer, having spent the days at work. At some point her sanctity became so evident that her master became ashamed of keeping her as a slave. Overcome by her spirituality, he offered to give her the house and work for her as a servant, reversing their present positions. Otherwise, if this arrangement were not to her liking, he told her, she was free to go. Rabi'a chose freedom.

Numerous illustrative stories featuring Rabi'a represent her seeking unmediated vision of God. For example, she is seen rejecting the holy shrine of the Ka'ba in favor of vision of God per se, and repudiating the supposed sanctity of pilgrimage and prayer undertaken for publicity. She also discounts any absolute value in supernormal happenings and capacities, for which she herself was famous, and generally disapproves of excessive emotionality in religious exercises.

Rabi'a remained unmarried by her own choice. In response to a proposal of marriage, she said she could not consent to marriage because she was not the owner of her body or her life. This meant she was wholly devoted to God, and she suggested that if her suitor really wanted to marry her, he should ask God for her hand. Presumably she meant he should embark upon a life of total devotion himself if he wished to be her spiritual mate.

The intentional and devotional singleness of Rabi'a the Sufi is in the spiritual mode of Mary as the virgin, pure and holy. The existence of Rabi'a as a publicly known saint is in the mold of Maryam as the "woman who socializes with men without being coy or unchaste."

The fact that the biblical Mary had a husband, Joseph, does not abridge her virginity in any way. The relationship between Mary and Joseph is represented as an ethical one on the exoteric plane and a spiritual one on the esoteric plane. According to the Gospel of Matthew, when Joseph married Mary he found that she was already pregnant. His first reaction was to shield Mary from public ridicule, for Joseph was a just man. Then, as he pondered the problem, evidently being a thoughtful man as well, Joseph was visited by an angel, who informed him that the sinless child in Mary's womb had been conceived of the Holy Spirit.

Thus Joseph's justness represents not only the quality of his character but also the quality of his external relationship with Mary, while his receptivity to angelic communication represents the quality of his own spirituality as well as the quality of his spiritual relationship with Mary. Somewhat later in the story Joseph is warned in a dream by an angel who tells him to flee with Mary and the baby Jesus. This also represents the moral and spiritual qualities of the paternal element of Joseph's natural manhood, the qualities that made him a worthy companion for Mary and guardian for Jesus.

Rabi'a the Sufi saint also had her Joseph, a moral and spiritual companion of high attainment. Rabi'a's Joseph was a man called Hasan al-Basri, or the Good Man of Basra. Hasan was one of the so-called Four Guides or Four Crowns, who were four eminent teachers of the second generation of classical Sufis. It is claimed that he was initiated by 'Ali, the so-called Door of Knowledge, whose wife and spiritual consort was Fatima, reputed to be first secret Polestar of the Sufis. Although Hasan is reported to have died in 728, when Rabi'a was only fourteen or fifteen years old, Sufi lore portrays her as his spiritual associate.

Joseph and Mary were also pictured as an old man and a young maiden, representing the platonic or spiritual nature of their relationship. According to one account, Hasan would refrain from lecturing if Rabi'a were not in attendance, and he is supposed to have credited her with helping him to attain spiritual rapture. Like her, he emphasized pure devotion to truth itself, without selfish hope or fear. Some of the tales of their conversations have her scolding Hasan for this purpose, to rid him of egotism and hidden hypocrisy in his religious practices.

From a Buddhist point of view, in this relationship Rabi'a stands for *shunyata* or emptiness, whereas Hasan stands for *upaya-kaushalya* or skill in means. This is particularly reminiscent of the *prajnaparamita* or perfect insight teaching of Buddhism, and the derivative Zen approach to doctrinal transmission. In terms of the pragmatic application and experience of the Buddhist metaphysical equation of relativity and emptiness, the purpose of projecting this type of teaching is realization of ultimate emptiness to prevent transmutation of temporal expediency into frozen formalism.

Sufic representations of Hasan as a candidate for religious egotism also put practices into perspective. Sufi tradition associates Hasan with procedure and therefore includes anecdotal antidotes to potential side effects such as personal pride in piety. The representation of both serum and antiserum, so to speak, is also characteristic of Zen prescriptions for remedial practices. When the functional relationship between seemingly opposed elements is not understood, their coexistence in Sufic or Zen lore may be misinterpreted as paradox or mystification.

The lore of saintly women in this tradition includes a broad spectrum of personality types and social situations. Both saintly individuals and saintly relationships appear in this lore, their underlying spiritual dedication transcending their historical and cultural differences. The question of human possibilities, including the possibility of completeness, is so deep that no formal religion or philosophy has answered it fully and definitively for the whole human race throughout all time. The essential values in the traditional stories of great hearts and lofty spirits of all cultures and climes, nonetheless, may somehow ring true to the nobler senses of our universal human nature, wherever we may find ourselves on the face of the earth.

16

The Marriage That Pervades All Creation

> And among the signs of God is having created for you mates
> from yourselves that you may live in peace with them, and
> having put affection and mercy between you. Surely in that
> is a sign for a reflective people.
>
> —QUR'AN 30:22

ONCE THREE MEN VISITED the houses of the wives of Muhammad the Prophet and asked about his devotions. When these men had heard the accounts of the Prophet's devotions from his wives, they felt they were far from him in their own worship.

One of the men declared he would thenceforth spend nights in prayer.

The second declared that he would thenceforth fast indefinitely.

The third declared that he would avoid women and never marry.

When he heard about this, the Prophet went to those men and said, "I am more God-fearing than you are, and more conscientious. Yet I fast but also break fast, I pray but also sleep, and I marry women."

The eminent "Western Master" Jalaluddin al-Rumi wrote of the Sufi path that the way represented by Jesus is in solitary struggle, while the way of Muhammad is in company with the people. Go the way of Muhammad if you can, Rumi counsels; otherwise, take the way of Jesus.

Going the way of Muhammad implies being in the world without being spiritually imprisoned by the world. This is a hallmark of Sufism, as it was of Mahayana Buddhism earlier on in history.

This is not comparative religion in the academic manner, much less a plea to embrace Islam in preference to Christianity. As a Sufi statement, it is a symbolic representation of the modern preference of the path. This particular contrast between the way of Jesus and the way of Muhammad in symbolic Sufi terminology for practical processes corresponds to the contrast between the narrow separatist path of monastic Hinayana Buddhism and the broad integrative highway of lay Mahayana Buddhism.

The great Spanish Sufi Ibn al-Arabi (1165–1240), once known to the learned of the West as Doctor Maximus, provides a metaphysical and contemplative elucidation of this distinction in his classic *Fusus al-hikam*, or *Bezels of the Wisdoms*. This work derives a series of symbolic teachings from stories of the prophets from Adam to Muhammad, including Seth, Noah, Moses, Solomon, Jesus, and other prophets of the ancient Near East. Ibn al-Arabi's explanation of the metaphysical and contemplative significance of intimacy between man and woman is contained within the chapter on Muhammad. Here he takes as his point of departure a well-known saying of Muhammad naming women, perfume, and prayer as three things made lovable to him in this world.

The Prophet mentioned women first in this statement, according to the Sufi, because one must know oneself before knowing God. Thus the essence of intimacy between man and woman is self-knowledge.

The Sufic dictum "Whoever knows his self knows his lord" has two levels of meaning, psychological and spiritual. First is a matter of knowing the compulsive self for what it is and does, in order to become able to get beyond the range of its dictates and their distorting influence on perception and behavior. This begins with the activation of the critical self. On a complete path this would be followed by the awakening of the inspired self, after which one may come to realize the higher and finer selves, up to the completed and purified self, whose spiritual purity is capable of reflecting the sublime origin of the soul. This subtler perception is the second meaning of the dictum, the avenue of knowledge of God through the knowledge of the higher selves. As another saying often cited in this connection goes, "God is closer to you than your jugular vein."

In the Prophetic saying about women, perfume, and prayer, the Sufi explains, Muhammad symbolizes God in the same way that every part of the universe symbolizes its origin, which is God. The affection of Muhammad for women is thus likened to the affection of a whole for its parts. Just as God created the universe out of divine desire to be known, making the universe a medium of the knowledge of God, so is woman a medium for the self-knowledge of man, who loves her as a being loves itself.

The Sufi also uses imagery reminiscent of Taoist yin-yang complementarity to construct a contemplative presentation of self-knowledge and God-consciousness in the contest of the relation between man and woman. When man contemplates God in woman, the Sufi explains, he focuses on the passive, while when man contemplates God in himself, he focuses on the active. When one contemplates God alone, he continues, without the medium of a created form, this corresponds to a state of passivity toward God. Thus the Sufi concludes that man's contemplation of God in woman is most perfect, as in this way he contemplates God in both active and passive modes.

The Sufi qualifies his reference to direct contemplation of God without any medium by recognizing that it is technically impossible insofar as God is independent of the universe and is therefore inaccessible in essence. This is why contemplation must resort to substance for a medium; so contemplation of God in woman is most intense and most complete, just as sexual intercourse is the most intense and most complete union of man and woman.

The Sufi mentions several levels of contemplative visualization associated with the relationship between the complete man and woman.

One level of contemplation envisions the irradiation of primal potential with the energy that quickens the universe. In theological terms, God causes the forms of the world to appear by projection of divine will. In the material world this manifests itself as sexual intercourse. Sexual intercourse is thus envisioned as a participation or enactment of the vivifying process of creation. This resembles the Taoist visualization of sexual intercourse as a union of yin and yang as microcosmic reflections of cosmic forces.

At another level, this is likened to the active projection of spiritual will in the realm of the spirits of light, or higher faculties and spiritual experiences. Intimate access to extra-ordinary domains can destabilize an immature mind, whether by the seductions of ecstasy, the sensation of personal power, or paralysis by an unmanageable flood of impressions. The image of being madly in love is sometimes figuratively used for such conditions.

In the context of sexual intercourse itself, this represents the man's ability to experience its pleasure without losing self-control, just as the inner meditation of the Taoist or Tantric Buddhist man enables him to maintain presence of mind and preserve potency through peaks of personal pleasure, thus prolonging intimacy to the point of his partner's perfect satisfaction.

On the strictly contemplative plane, this imagery concerns the ability to avoid loss of potential through indulgence in subjective sensations. Such a loss of potential is a peril encountered in all areas of life, not only mysticism and marriage, but it seems to have a crucial relation to the third level of analogical contemplation of intercourse set forth by the Sufi, which is the realm of reason. In this domain, the reflection of intercourse is seen in the production of a logical conclusion by the coupling of premises.

Here the cosmic and microcosmic interface. Spiritual, psychological, and sexual intimacy all imply an internal coherence of relationship, according to their intrinsic laws. When all of these dimensions of experience are consistent with one another, that harmony leads to the sublime feeling of "being at peace" with "soul mates" sharing "affection and mercy" mentioned in the Qur'an as a sign of God. Thus the Sufi master says that to love women in the manner of Muhammad is to love by divine love. Without the element of divine love, he says, love by natural attraction alone is like a form without a spirit.

Along with women, the Prophet also named perfumes as one of the three things made lovable to him in this world. Doctor Maximus elucidates this predilection of the Prophet in terms of the broad meaning of tayyib, the Arabic word for "sweet-smelling," contrasted with khabith or "foul-smelling." In general terms tayyib means good and khabith means bad, so the Sufi uses their application to fragrance to represent the "perfuming" or "fouling" influences of good and bad in the world. This usage is reminiscent of the expression "fragrance of morality" commonly found in Mahayana Buddhist scriptures.

In elucidating the nature of good and evil, the Sufi stresses that divine mercy manifests itself in both good and bad. As a consequence of this fundamental fact, there is no possibility of eliminating bad from the world. The real moral issue, therefore, is in practical distinction between good and bad in everything. The power of practical distinction, further-more, depends on the realization that temporal manifestations of good and bad are not absolute like God but are relative to their subjects, for there is something good and bad in everything, according to conditions.

To illustrate, the Sufi cites angelic distaste for the grossness of human materiality and the scarab beetle's repugnance for the rose. If a man is like a scarab, the Sufi says, he cannot bear the truth, just as the scarab cannot bear perfume. Thus the Sufi master understands the Prophet's pre-dilection for perfume to represent the divine inspiration to love only the good in everything.

Prayer, the third thing made lovable to the Prophet, is also experi-enced religiously as a medium of divine love and inspiration. In prayer, the Prophet said, he found the "coolness of his eye," which means conso-lation and joy. Here remembrance of God is equated with being remem-bered by God, just as the experience of loving God is itself experience of God's loving. This spiritual communion is illustrated in certain special traditions according to which God says, "Remember me, and I remember you," and "I keep the company of whoever remembers me."

The notion of maintaining mystical contact with subtler dimensions of reality while still manifestly in the ordinary world may be illustrated by these Prophetic perceptions of divine favor, grace, and mercy in the midst of the life of the world. Buddhists of the unitarian and integrative schools also sought avenues of experiencing and communicating what they called nonobstruction between the realms of the mundane, the spiri-tual, and the absolute.

If one heard an expression of love for women, perfume, and prayer in a Buddhist context, one would ordinarily think of Tantric Buddhism. Far more important than the superficial resemblance between these tradi-tions, however, is the essence of their clarity of vision penetrating the sensory to the spiritual. Sufis speak of "being in the world without being of it," which Buddhists symbolize by a lotus growing up from the mud unstained and blooming even more brightly in fire.

The question of how to live in the world of material sense while maintaining integrity of spiritual sense is one that has concerned seekers of all the traditions we have viewed. Those who have achieved balance have done so in their own ways, but the factor of balance nevertheless remains their common ground.

Shah Waliullah, the modern Sufi, wrote that the mysticism of the masses was unbalanced, based on an oversimplified struggle with the self in the form of exaggerated asceticism. Some of them attained states comparable to lesser angels, he acknowledges, but failure to give due consideration to all aspect of the total human being, including the legitimate requirements of the self, made the ascetic mystics of the past weak and effete. This Sufi credits Junaid (d. 910) with correcting the imbalance of popular mysticism by adopting the "middle course."

This sort of restoration of balance, in its own context, is analogous to what Buddha did for the popular mysticism of his time with his doctrine of the Middle Way. Restoration of balance was also the aim of subsequent developments in the progressive lay schools of Buddhism as they outgrew the self-involvement of their monastic predecessors. Taoists who reintegrated diverging trends of concentration on energetic and spiritual exercises were also after the restoration of balance and the achievement of human completeness. The Hindus who abandoned discriminatory ideology also struck a middle way between the tensions of the competing doctrines of tyaga and bhoga, renunciation and enjoyment.

Among the early Sufis who lived in the time when Sufism was "a reality without a name," as Hujwiri described it, the mystic Polestar, Fatima's husband, 'Ali, articulated this ideal of balance and completeness with particular clarity and beauty, integrating spiritual awareness into the very basis of our experience of everyday life. His words shed light on the spiritual struggles of all the mystics we have met thus far, and on the whole question of how to relate to the world without either grasping or rejecting it, as the Buddhists would say.

When 'Ali heard someone finding fault with the world, he said, "You who revile the world, blinded by its deceit, duped by its falsehood—do you rebuke the world after having been deluded by it? Are you accusing it, or is it accusing you?" If a desire to transcend the world is only a manifestation of disappointment, that means one is still in the circle of selfish concern and emotional reaction. 'Ali continues, "In fact, the world is an abode of truth for one who is truthful with it, and an abode of well-being for one who understands it. It is an abode of riches for one who learns from it, and an abode of counsel for one who takes a warning from it."

In terms of a religious view of life, or life lived in a religious way, 'Ali also says of the world, "It is the house of worship for those who love God, the place of prayer of God's angels, the place of descent of God's inspiration, and the place of business of God's saints. Therein is mercy earned, therein is paradise gained."

In this way, the world can be transcended without being repudiated, for the ultimate limitation of this world is intrinsic to it, not a product of human conception or emotion. Thus 'Ali teaches how to employ both sorrow and joy in the quest for understanding: "So who reviles the world when it has already announced its departure and declared it would leave? It has announced its own death and that of its people; by its trials it has given them an example of tribulation, and by its pleasures it has filled them with longing with pleasure. It started out with well-being and created misfortune, awakening desires and fears, causing alarm and alert. So some people revile it on a morning of remorse, while others will praise it on the day of resurrection, for the world reminded them, and they bore it in mind; and it spoke to them, and they verified what it said; and it cautioned them, and they took the warning."[1]

Love, Human and Divine

Ashiq nabud keh jan nabazad.
He is no lover who does not stake his life.
—ARIFI OF HERAT, *Hal nameh* (*The Book of Ecstasy*)

Sufism has been called the creed of love, and images of enraptured lovers have often been used in Sufic literature to represent mental states of the seeker of intimacy with reality. But then Sufis have sometimes been thought to make a religion of reveling in emotion; so while the classics relate human and divine love by analogy and metaphor, they also make a point of distinguishing the difference between the human and the divine.

1. Thomas Cleary, trans., *Living and Dying with Grace: Counsels of Hadrat 'Ali* (Boston: Shambhala, 1995), pp. 21–23.

In the process the Sufi classics clarify the distinction between subjective psychological feeling and objective spiritual experience.

Among the most popular themes in the romantic literature of the East emanating from the Sufi world are the story of Layla and Majnun and the story of Joseph and Zulaikha. Both of these romances illustrate the power of love as a purifying element, in the process contrasting the instability of the human condition with the permanence of divine truth. In between these two poles are discovered successive refinements of love, including the emanations of love that produce romance, chivalry, and domestic tranquillity, on up to the highest flights of mystical rapture. Mystical vision of God is not, however, an extension of these feelings of love, not even of the feelings of mystical rapture. Sublime human feelings and noble human sentiments are viewed as gifts of God, not subconsciously taken as tokens of godhood. They intimate the presence and power of God without letting the afflatus of exaltation aggrandize the self.

The story of Layla and Majnun illustrates this point in the ambiguity of the condition of Majnun, the lover. *Layla* means "night," the domain of the unknown, signifying the transcendence of the essence of divine reality beyond anything conceivable. *Majnun* means "mad," which can signify enraptured contemplation, indifference to the vanities of the world, or loss of sobriety and consequent incapacitation.

Indifference to the world may thus signify concentration on essence rather than form, or then again it may signify loss of ability to reintegrate constructively with ordinary life. One view represents a temporary procedure of the mystic path, while the other view shows what happens when procedure is taken for policy and pursued without balance, excluding all else.

A particular illustration of this may be seen in an episode where Majnun swoons into senselessness when he gets a glimpse of the hem of Layla's robe. In one sense, this may represent a kind of mystical sensitivity, vision of essence within form, through which all creation is seen as evidence of the Creator. In another sense, this may represent a kind of weakness, an inability to withstand true mystical vision or incorporate it constructively into conscious life.

The seed of the Sufi romance of Joseph and Zulaikha comes from the Qur'an. Zulaikha is the wife of an Egyptian man, apparently a grandee, and Joseph is a Hebrew whom he bought in youth as a slave. When the enslaved Joseph attains manhood, he is extremely handsome, and Zulaikha becomes infatuated with him. When she tries to seduce Joseph, he spurns her on moral grounds; she then denounces him. Joseph is tried and imprisoned.

Eventually the case is reopened when the imprisoned Joseph interprets some dreams of the pharaoh. The ladies of the grandee's household attest to his innocence, and finally Zulaikha herself confesses. Her confession is a candid recognition of the human condition: "Indeed," she says, "the self does compel to evil." This is the Qur'anic locus classicus for the Sufi term "compulsive self."

Earlier in the story, when Zulaikha had overheard other women of the household talking against her for her infatuation with Joseph, she arranged for them to see him and register their own reactions. Announcing a banquet, Zulaikha had Joseph appear before the women while they were in the kitchen preparing food. When they saw him, the women were so smitten by his beauty that in their distraction they cut their own hands. In this way the commonality of the compulsive self is demonstrated, not to condemn humanity for its foibles, but to surmount the lower self with higher understanding.

Sufi poets have followed up on the theme of Zulaikha's repentance, representing the activation of the critical self, to play out the drama of her spiritual purification. Her gaze of passion turns from outward to inward beauty, from appearance to reality, from desire to fulfillment. Her pining is the wasting away of her worldliness, until she realizes love as self-transcendence. When she is purified in spirit, Zulaikha is restored to youth and beauty and united with Joseph, whose soul mate she now has become.

The crucial distinction between ordinary and spiritual love, illustrated poetically in the story of Joseph and Zulaikha, is explained by the Sufi master Shahabuddin Suhrawardi (1145–1234) using the terms "common love" and "special love." The primary difference between these two forms of love is that in ordinary love the gaze of the heart is on beauty of qualities, while in special love the gaze of the soul is on beauty of essence. Figuratively, Suhrawardi likens common love to a light that adorns existence, and special love to a fire that purifies existence.

Some Sufi usage clarifies the distinction between human and divine love by avoiding the use of the word "love" for the latter, according to Hujwiri. Instead the masters have called divine love by the name purity. To describe the abnegation of self-will in favor of the will of the beloved, love of God is also called by the name *poverty*. The terms *purity* and *poverty* were employed, Hujwiri explains, to shield the doctrine of divine love from association with conventional usage. This approach to the terminology is based, in other words, on the practice of distinguishing ordinary love from divine love.

Hujwiri describes two kinds of lovers of God whose difference also reflects the distinction between common and special love. There are those, he says, who are led to love God as Benefactor by regarding God's favor and bounty toward them. Such people might be said to rise from ordinary love to special love. Then there are those who are so in love with God as absolute truth that even God's favors are veils between them and God. Instead of being led to loving God by regarding God's favors, these people are led to the favors by regarding the Benefactor. For these people, the beauty of ordinary love is an outcome of special love.

While ordinary love and special love are distinct, nevertheless they are still interrelated in some way. In a metaphysical sense, ordinary love could not exist without divine love, if divine love is understood as the power that created the universe. Even if completely unaware of its divine origins, therefore, in this sense ordinary love is completely dependent upon the reality of divine love.

This inner relationship is illustrated in Qashani's definition of primal love (*al-muhabbat al-asliyya*). Primal love, he says, is love of essence. This is the basis of all kinds of love, he explains, and of all that is between a couple, be it by affinity in their essence, or by harmony of characteristic, class, condition, or function.

Primal love, as the Sufi perceives it, is what keeps the universe together, in the marriage that pervades all creation. Qashani calls this "the compassionate favor" of "the Living," that is, God, in reference to the creation of the universe through God's desire to be known. This is how both ordinary conscience and mystical vision can use the ordinary world to cultivate consciousness of God: "I was a hidden treasure," says God to explain creation, "and I loved to be known."

According to Qashani, the words "I loved to be known" refer to basic affection and essential love that connect the concealed with the manifest, that is to say, connect God with the universe. This connection, he says, is the root of the marriage that pervades all creation. That is why the Qur'an refers to natural and human phenomena as being among the signs of God.

Qashani explains that the oneness required of love is the manifestation of the nature of unity through every level of the order of the universe of particulars, including all divisions of the whole. That is what maintains the unity of multiplicity in all its forms from division and dissolution. Thus the union (iqtiran, "marriage") of unity with multiplicity is the connection of the marriage that pervades all creation.

This is not very far, in philosophical terms, from the Taoist idea of universal and individual yin and yang, or from the Buddhist idea of the hidden presence of emptiness or absolute truth within the very essence of matter or relative reality. But the comparison means little if there is no way to apply these ideas to life in the world today. Connection, after all, is the essence of the matter.

To transpose this basic idea into terms of practical use in the context of the dimensions of human life we have explored, we can turn back to the Qur'an, where it mentions the creation of soul mates as a sign of God, soul mates with whom to feel at peace, between whom God has placed affection and mercy. This passage bespeaks a connection between ordinary love and special love in the experience of domestic bliss and tranquillity; the next passage broadens the context of human conviviality: "And among the signs of God is the creation of the heavens and the earth and the diversity of your languages and your complexions. Surely in that is a sign for the knowing" (30:22).

This particular pathway to perception of essential unity underlying factual multiplicity is perfected in a later verse, with an address to all humanity: "O humankind! We created you from a male and a female, and We made you races and tribes, that you may know one another" (49:13).

It is in this spirit that the book now finished has taken shape, inspired by the belief that in truth we human beings, male and female, members of all races and peoples, should know one another, in our diverse forms as well as our universal nature. One way we can do this is to observe the beliefs and attitudes different people of various cultures have in regard to their connections with heaven and earth, with all beings, and especially with each other. Our part in composing these observations and reflections has been to witness and wonder, more than to criticize or judge. Our aim throughout, however, has been understanding, which we believe is of the essence of love.

Select Bibliography

Adi Bangali: nritattik o samajtattik bislesan. Ajoy Roy. Dhaka: Bangla Academy, 1997.

Adventures in Afghanistan. Louis Palmer. London: Octagon, 1990.

Ahkam al-Qur'an. Abu Bakr Muhammad bin Abdallah (al ma'ruf bi ibn al Arabi). Beirut: Dar al Kitab al 'Alamiyya, 1988.

The Ajanta Caves: Artistic Wonder of Ancient Buddhist India. Benoy K. Behl. New York: Harry N. Abrams, 1998.

Alaoler kabye Hindu-Muslim Sanskriti. Amrita Lal Bala. Dhaka: Bangla Academy, 1991.

The Art of Wealth. Translated from the Sanskrit, with commentary, by Thomas Cleary. Deerfield Beach, Florida: Health Communications, 1998.

Among the Dervishes. O. M. Burke. London: Octagon, 1973.

Awakening to the Tao, Liu I-ming. Translated by Thomas Cleary. Boston: Shambhala, 1988.

Bankei Zenji hogoshu. Compiled by Fujimoto Tsuchishige. Tokyo: Shunjusha, 1971.

Bengali Literature. J. C. Ghosh. Oxford: Clarendon, 1948.

Bikuni shi. Araki Ryosen. Tokyo: Toyo Shoin, 1929.

The Book of Balance and Harmony. Translated by Thomas Cleary. San Francisco: North Point, 1989.

Borobudur: Golden Tales of the Buddhas. John Miksic. Photographs by Marcello Tranchini. Boston: Shambhala, 1990.

A Brief History of Tantric Literature. S. C. Banerji. Calcutta: Naya Prokash, 1988.

Buddhist Yoga. Translated by Thomas Cleary. Boston: Shambhala, 1995.

The Carnal Prayer Mat. Li Yu. Hertfordshire: Wordsworth Editions, 1995.

Caryagitikos. Edited by Nilratan Sen. West Bengal: Dipali Sen, 1978.

257

Chang San-feng t'ai-chi lien-tan pi-chueh. Attributed to Chang San-feng. Taipei: Hsin Wenfeng, 1978.

Chang San-feng wu-shu hui-tsung. Compiled and annotated by Hsu Ying. Taipei: Chen Shanmei, 1970.

Chen-chiu-hsue. Compiled by the Jiangli Institute of New Medicine. Hong Kong: Medicine and Health Publications, 1973.

China's Muslims. Michael Dillon. Oxford: Oxford University Press, 1996.

Chung-kuo ku-tai hsing-hsueh chi-ch'eng. Lung I-yin. Hong Kong: Pa Lung, 1991.

Chung-kuo ta-tsang-ching fan-i k'e-yin shih. (Shih) Tao An. Lushan, China: Lushan Publishing, 1978.

The Code of the Samurai. Translated by Thomas Cleary. Boston: Tuttle, 1999.

Convivencia: Jews, Muslims, and Christians in Medieval Spain. Edited by Vivian Mann, Thomas Click, and Jerrilynn Dodds. New York: George Baziller in association with the Jewish Museum, 1992.

Dakini Teachings. Translated by Erik Pema Kunsang. Boston: Shambhala, 1990.

Daojia yangsheng biku. Edited by Hong Jianlin. Beijing: Dalian, 1991.

Daojiaoshi ciliang. Compiled by the Research Center of the Chinese Taoist Cooperative. Shanghai: Shanghai Ancient Books, 1991.

The Dark Side of Christian History. Helen Ellerbe. San Rafael: Morningstar Books, 1995.

Dasabhumisvara nama mahayanasutram. Edited by Ryuko Kondo. Tokyo: Daijyo Bukkyo Kenyo-kai, 1936.

Devi: The Goddess. Written and directed by Satyajit Ray, from a story by Prabhat Kumar Mukherjee, based on a theme of Rabindranath Tagore. Sony Picture Classics, 1960.

Dream Conversations: On Buddhism and Zen. Muso Kokushi. Translated by Thomas Cleary. Boston: Shambhala, 1996.

Early Christian Heresies. Joan O'Grady. New York: Barnes and Noble, 1985.

The Ecstasy of Enlightenment. Translated from the Old Bengali with commentary by Thomas Cleary. York Beach, Maine: Samuel Weiser, 1998.

Erh-nu ying-hsiung chuan. Edited by Hu Shih-chih. Taipei: Hsin Wenfeng, 1979.

Fang-chung yang-shu. Edited by Chou I-mou et al. Hong Kong: Haifeng, 1990.

Fang Tao yu-lu. Compiled by Li Luo-ch'iu. Taiwan: Chen Shanmei, 1966.

The Flower Ornament Scripture. Translated by Thomas Cleary. Boston: Shambhala, 1993.

Founders of India's Civilization. P. L. Bhargava. Berkeley: Asian Humanities Press, 1992.

Gandavyuhasutram. Edited by P. L. Vaidya. Darbhanga: Mithila Institute, 1960.

A Glossary of Sufi Technical Terms. 'Abd al-Razzaq al-Qashani. Arabic text with translation by Nabil Safwat, revised and edited by David Pendlebury. London: Octagon, 1991.

Goddesses in Art. Lanier Graham. New York: Artabras, 1997.

Guhyasamaja-tantra. Edited by Matsunaga Yukei. Tokyo: Toho Shuppan, 1978.

The Guide for the Perplexed. Maimonides. Translated by M. Friedlander. New York: Dover, 1956.

Han Fei-tzu. Shanghai: Shanghai Ancient Books, 1989.

Handbook of Chinese Herbs and Formulas. Him-che Yeung. Los Angeles: Institute of Chinese Medicine, 1983.

High Religion: A Cultural and Political History of Sherpa Buddhism. Sherry B. Ortner. Princeton: Princeton University Press, 1989.

Hsi yu chi. Wu Ch'eng-en. Taipei: Shih-chieh shu-chu, 1974.

Huangdi yinfujing quanshu. Compiled by Wang Yi and Sheng Ruiyu. Sian: Xiaxi luyou, 1992.

Hsien-shu pi-k'u. Yu-shu Chen-jen. Taipei: Hsin Wenfeng, 1978.

Hsien-tsung tan-tao chen-ch'uan. Li-ch'en. Taipei: Hsin Wenfeng, 1984.

Hsing-ming yao-chih. Wang Tung-ting. Taipei: Hsin Wenfeng, 1978.

The Human Zoo. Desmond Morris. New York: Kodansha, 1996.

The Hundred Tales of Wisdom. Translated from the Persian by Idries Shah. London: Octagon, 1978.

Ikkyu. Mizugami Tsutomu. Tokyo: Chuokoronsha, 1978.

Ikkyu shokoku junyu ki. Aoki Hanpo. Tokyo: Seikokan, 1938.

Imaginary Muslims: The Uwaysi Sufis of Central Asia. Julian Baldick. New York: New York University Press, 1993.

Immortal Sisters: Secret Teachings of Taoist Women. Translated and edited by Thomas Cleary. Berkeley: North Atlantic, 1996.

The Inner Teachings of Taoism. Translated by Thomas Cleary. Boston: Shambhala, 1986.

Ippen Shonin goroku. Ippen. Tokyo: Toho Shoin, 1936.

Islam in Tribal Societies: From the Atlas to the Indus. Edited by Akbar S. Ahmed and David M. Hart. London: Routledge and Kegan Paul, 1984.

Islamic Art and Spirituality. Seyyed Hossein Nasr. Ipswich, Suffolk: Golgonooza, 1987.

The Japanese Art of War. Thomas Cleary. Boston: Shambhala, 1991.

The Complete Kama Sutra. Translated by Alain Danielou. Rochester, Vermont: Park Street, 1994.

Kanjinkakumu-sho. Ryoben. Tokyo: Toho, 1937.

Kaoseng chuan i-chi. Hui-hsiao. Taipei: Taiwan Sutra Printing, 1973.

Kashf al-Mahjub of Al Hujwiri: The Oldest Persian Treatise on Sufism. 'Ali B. Uthman Al-Jullabi Al Hujwiri. Translated by Reynold A. Nicholson. London: Luzac, 1976.

Kinsei kijinden. Tomo Kokei. Tokyo: Iwanami Shoten, 1980.

Kinsei Zenrin genkoroku. Mori Keizo. Tokyo: Nihon Tosho Senta, 1977.

Kon-tai ryobu shingon kaiki. Yoshida Keikou. Kyoto: Heiryakuji, 1979.

Kuang-ch'eng-tzu chieh. Su Shih. Taipai: Tzu-yu, 1980.

Kuan-tzu. Shanghai: Shanghai Ancient Books, 1989.

Laksmi-Tantra. Edited by V. Krishnamacharya. Madras: Adyar, 1959.

Li-tai shen-hsien shih. Compiled by Wang Chien-chang. Taiwan: Hsin Wenfeng, 1979.

Lieh-tzu. Taipei: Hsi-wen, 1975.

Living and Dying with Grace: Counsels of Hadrat 'Ali. Translated by Thomas Cleary. Boston: Shambhala, 1996.

The Lost Books of the Bible. William Hone. New York: Bell, 1979.

The Lotus Transcendent: Indian and Southeast Asian Art from the Samuel Eilenberg Collection. New York: Metropolitan Museum of Art, 1991.

Lu-men-tzu. P'i Jih-hsiu. Taiwan: Tzu-yu, 1980.

Lu-tsu hui-chi. Attributed to Lu Ch'un-yang. Taiwan: Hsin Wenfeng, 1975.

Luo-yu-t'ang yu-lu. Huang Yuan-ch'i. Taiwan: Chen Shanmei, 1974.

Madhyayuger Bangla shahitye Muslim kabi. Azhar Islam. Dhaka: Bangla Acadamy, 1992.

The Manipulated Mind. Denise Winn. London: Octagon, 1983.

Mahanirvana Tantra, with the commentary of Hariharananda Bharati. Delhi: Motilal Banarsidass, 1989.

Manusmrti with the Manubhasya of Medhatithi. Edited by Ganganath Jha. Delhi: Motilal Banarsidass, 1999.

Ming I yen-an lei pien. Compiled by He Lien-ch'en. Shanghai: Tungfang Shu-chu, n.d.

Mongolia: The Legacy of Chinggis Khan. Patricia Berger, Terese Tse Bartholomew et al. Photographs by Kazuhiro Tsuruta. San Francisco: Asian Art Museum, 1995.

The Muqaddimah: An Introduction to History. Ibn Khaldun. Translated from the Arabic by Franz Rosenthal, edited and abridged by N. J. Dawood. Princeton: Princeton University Press, Bollingen Series, 1967.

Myoe Shonin shu. Edited by Kubota Jun and Yamaguchi Akiho. Tokyo: Iwanami, 1981.

The Nazis and the Occult. Dusty Sklar. New York: Dorset, 1977.

A New History of India. Second edition. Stanley Wolpert. Oxford: Oxford University Press, 1982.

New Light on Tantra. S. C. Banerji and Sures Chandra. Calcutta: Punthi Pustak, 1992.

Niso no kokuhaku. Annotated translation of Therigatha from Pali into Japanese by Nakamura Gen. Tokyo: Iwanami Bunko, 1981.

Nu-hsien wai-shi. Lu Hsiung. Taipei: T'ien-I, 1976.

Opening the Dragon Gate: The Making of a Modern Taoist Wizard. Chen Kaiguo and Zheng Shunchao. Translated by Thomas Cleary. Boston: Tuttle, 1998.

Oriental Magic. Sayed Idries Shah. London: Octagon, 1968.

From Paracelsus to Newton: Magic and the Making of Modern Science. Charles Webster. Cambridge University Press, 1982.

Persian Painting. Text by Basil Gray. Geneva: Editions d'Art Albert Skira, 1995.

Physicians' Desk Reference for Herbal Medicine. Montvale, New Jersey: Medical Economics, 1998.

Plant Intoxicants. Ernst von Bibra. Rochester, Vermont: Healing Arts, 1995.

Practical Taoism. Translated by Thomas Cleary. Boston: Shambhala, 1996.

Psychology: The Study of Human Experience. Third edition. Robert Ornstein and Laura Carstensen. New York: Harcourt Brace Jovanovich, 1991.

Qigong jingxuan. Beijing: People's Physical Education, 1984.

Ramaseeana. Sir Wm. H. Sleeman. Calcutta: G. H. Huttman Military Orphan Press, 1836.

Religions of the Silk Road: Overland Trade and Cultural Exchange from Antiquity to the Fifteenth Century. Richard C. Foltz. New York: St. Martin's, 1999.

Rokujo engi: Ippen Hijirie. Edited and annotated by Asayama Ensho. Tokyo: Sankibo Busshorin, 1941.

The Original Rubaiyyat of Omar Khayyam. Translation and critical commentaries by Robert Graves and Omar Ali-Shah. New York: Doubleday, 1968.

The Sacred Knowledge of the Higher Functions of the Mind. Translated by G. N. Jalbani. Edited by David Pendlebury. London: Octagon, 1982.

San-feng ch'uan-shu. Attributed to Chang San-feng. Taiwan: Hsin Wen-feng, 1978.

Scythian Gold. Edited by Ellen D. Reeder. New York: Harry N. Abrams in association with the Walters Art Gallery and the San Antonio Museum of Art, 1999.

In Search of the Cradle of Civilization: New Light on Ancient India. Georg Feuerstein, Subhash Kak, and David Frawley. Wheaton, Illinois: Quest Books, 1995.

The Secret of the Golden Flower. Translated by Thomas Cleary. San Francisco: Harper-SanFrancisco, 1991.

Secret Societies. Edited by Norman MacKenzie. London: Aldus Books, 1967.

Secret Societies: From the Ancient and Arcane to the Modern and Clandestine. David V. Barrett. London: Blandford, 1997.

Sex, Health, and Long Life. Translated by Thomas Cleary. Boston: Shambhala, 1999.

Shan nu-jen chuan. P'eng Chi-ch'ing. Taiwan: Hsin Wenfeng, 1976.

Shangyang-tzu yuan chu ts'an-t'ung-ch'i. Ch'en Chih-hsu. Taiwan: Hsin Wenfeng, 1978.

Shasekishu. Muju. Kyoto: Heiryakuji Shoten, 1933.

Shinto: The Unconquered Enemy. Robert O. Ballou. New York: Viking, 1945.

Sleepless Nights: Verses for the Wakeful. Translated by Thomas Cleary. Berkeley: North Atlantic, 1995.

The Spirit of Tao. Translated and edited by Thomas Cleary. Boston: Shambhala, 1998.

Sri Kalacakratantra-raja. Edited by Biswanath Banerjee. Calcutta: Asiatic Society, 1993.

Strange Sects and Curious Cults. Marcus Bach. New York: Barnes and Noble, 1993.

Sufi Studies East and West. Edited by L. F. Rushbrook Williams. New York: E. P. Dutton, 1974.

Sufi Thought and Action. Assembled by Idries Shah. London: Octagon, 1980.

The Sutra of Hui-neng, Grand Master of Zen. Translated by Thomas Cleary. Boston: Shambhala, 1998.

Suvikrantavikrami-Pariprccha Prajnaparamita-Sutra. Edited by Hikata Ryusho. Kyoto: Rinsen, 1983.

The Sword and the Flute. David Kinsley. Berkeley: University of California Press, 1997.

Ta chih-tu lun. Attributed to Nagarjuna. Translated by Kumarajiva. Taiwan: Hsin Wenfeng, 1981.

Ta Tao Chen-t'i. Edited by Hsiao Shih-t'ien. Taiwan: Tzu-yu, 1976.

Tadhkaratul-Auliya or Memoirs of Saints. Fariduddin Attar. Selected, abridged, and translated from Persian by Bankey Behari. Lahore: Muhammad Ashraf, 1975.

Tafsir al-Jalalayn. Jalaluddin Muhammad bin Ahmad al-Muhalli and Jalaluddin Abdurrahman bin abi Bakr as-Suyuti. Beirut: Dar el Marefah, 1990.

T'ai-chi-ch'uan chen chuan. Ch'en Yen-lin. Taiwan: Wu-chou, 1980.

Tain Bo Cualnge. Edited by Cecile O'Rahilly. Dublin: Dublin Institute for Advanced Studies, 1984.

T'ai-hsi-ching su-lueh. Wang Wen-lu. Taipei: Tzu-yu, 1980.

Tantraraja Tantra. Edited by Lakshmana Shastri. Delhi: Motilal Banarsidass, 1997.

Tantric Visions of the Divine Feminine: The Ten Mahavidyas. David Kinsley. Berkeley: University of California Press, 1997.

T'an-tzu. T'an Hsiao. Taipei: Tzu-yu, 1980.

The Taoist Classics: The Collected Translations of Thomas Cleary. 4 vols. Boston: Shambhala, 1999.

Tao-chiao yen-chiu tz'u-liang. Compiled by Yen I-p'ing. Taiwan: Hsi-wen, 1974.

Tao te ching chu-chieh. Huang Yuan-ch'i. Taiwan: Chen Shanmei, 1978.

Tao-tsang chi-yao. Compiled by P'eng Wen-ch'in et al. Taiwan: Hsin Wenfeng, 1977.

Tao-tsang yuan-liu k'ao. Ch'en Kuo-fu. Taipei: Hsiang-sheng, 1975.

Tao-t'ung ta-ch'eng. Compiled by Wang Tung-ting. Taiwan: Hsin Wenfeng, 1975.

Thunder in the Sky: On the Acquisition and Exercise of Power. Translated by Thomas Cleary. Boston: Shambhala, 1993.

T'ien-chi pi-wen. Compiler anonymous. Taiwan: Chen Shanmei, 1984.

In the Tradition of Moses and Mohammed: Jewish and Arab Folktales. Banche L. Serwer-Bernstein. Northvale, New Jersey: Jason Aronson, 1994.

Transmission of Light: Zen in the Art of Enlightenment. Zen master Keizan. Translated by Thomas Cleary. Tokyo: Weatherhill, 1992.

Travels in the Unknown East. John Grant. London: Octagon, 1992.

Understanding Reality: A Taoist Alchemical Classic. Chang Po-tuan, with commentary by Liu I-ming. Translated by Thomas Cleary. Honolulu: University Press of Hawaii, 1987.

Unlocking the Zen Koan. Thomas Cleary. Berkeley: North Atlantic, 1997.

Views from the Jade Terrace: Chinese Women Artists 1300-1912. Marsha Weidner, Ellen Johnston Laing, Irving Yucheng Lo, Christina Chu, and James Robinson. Indianapolis: Indianapolis Museum of Art and New York: Rizzoli International, 1988.

Vitality, Energy, Spirit: A Taoist Sourcebook. Translated and edited by Thomas Cleary. Boston: Shambhala, 1991.

Wakan meishi sanzen shu. Presented by Nukariya Kaiten. Tokyo: Hinoe-uma, 1922.

Wen-tzu: Understanding the Mysteries. Attributed to Lao-tzu. Translated by Thomas Cleary. Boston: Shambhala, 1992.

The Wisdom of the Prophet: Sayings of Muhammad. Translated by Thomas Cleary. Boston: Shambhala, 1994.

The Wisdom of the Prophets (Fusus al-Hikam). Muhyi-d-din ibn 'Arabi. Translated from Arabic to French with notes by Titus Burckhardt, translated from French to English by Angela Culme-Seymour. Gloucestershire: Beshara, 1975.

The Wrong Way Home: Uncovering the Patterns of Cult Behavior in American Society. Arthur J. Deikman, M.D. Boston: Beacon, 1994.

Wu tai chien-k'ang hsiu-lien-fa. Hung Wan-hsiang. Taiwan: Chen-shan-mei, 1973.

Women and Education: Bangladesh. Edited by Parveen Ahmad et al. Dhaka: Women for Women, 1978.

Yang-hsing pien. He Huai-ching. Taipei: Hsin Wenfeng, 1978.

The Yonitantra. Critically edited with an introduction by J. A. Shoterman. New Delhi: Manohar, 1980.

Yuzu nembutsu shinge sho. Yukan. Tokyo: Toho Shoin, 1936.

Yuzu nembutsu sho. Daitsu. Tokyo: Toho Shoin, 1936.

Zen and the Art of Insight. Selected and translated by Thomas Cleary. Boston: Shambhala, 1999.

Zenmon hogo shu. Edited by Yamada Kodo. Tokyo: Koyukan, 1905.

Zhongguo fangshu dazidian. Edited by Chen Yingzheng et al. Guangdong: Zhongshan University, 1991.

Zhou Yi ji-jieh. Compiled by Li Ding-zuo. Beijing: Beijing shi Zhongguo shudian, 1984.

INDEX

265

Female roles, as temporary vs. absolute,
142
Femaleness, as universal emptiness and in-
tuitive insight, 164
Females, 142
suppression of self-expression, 95–96
Feminine culture, 16. *See also* Matriarchal
cultures
Feminine Harmony, 61–62
Feminine integrity, exemplars of, 230
Femininity, 142
negative meanings, 22
Feminism, 166, 192, 200, 202, 203, 205
spiritual, 3, 222
Fertility, 16, 48, 116, 224
Fertilization, 45
"Fetal breath," 89–90, 92
"Fetal education," 72, 93–94, 102, 235,
237
Fire, 45, 61, 88, 177, 178
as consciousness, 88
mating of water and, 88
Fist, Madame, 102–3
Fixations, 136, 138, 142, 147, 155, 164,
171, 178
Flower Ornament Scripture, 143, 161, 162, 171,
188–95, 199, 209, 212, 213
Flowers, 139–40, 169, 183
Foot binding, 128
Foundation/Mu'assissa, 228–29
Four Exemplary Women, 230
Freedom, 13, 22, 141, 147, 153, 168,
185. *See also* Liberation
Fu Hao, Queen, 71

Gaels, 99
Gandhara Buddhism. *See* Kushan-Gandhara
Buddhism
Gender difference, Buddhist relationship
to, 131–33
Gender stereotypes, origin of, 167
Genitals, male vs. female, 199
Gestation, imagery and symbolism of, 86,
88, 91–92, 166, 168
"Gestation" meditative process, 90, 93
Gestation theme, 93
Ghora, 48

God(s), 249, 254
contemplated in men *vs.* women, 247
images of, 2
God/goddess pairs, 66, 218
Goddess(es), 3. *See also specific topics*
gross, subtle, and ultimate forms of, 21
images of, 2
names, 8–9
twilight imagery of, 3
warlike and peaceful/benevolent, 17
Goddess worship, 21, 57–58. *See also* Indian
Goddess worship; *specific goddesses*
Golden Mother, 97–100, 110
Goodness, 146, 165–66, 226
Gopa ("Cowherd"), 151, 165
Government, 96–97. *See also specific societies*
spirituality in, 100
Taoism and, 125–27
Grace, 13, 14
Grandmothers, 71
Gratitude and ingratitude, 224–25

"Hairy woman," 107
Hakuin, Zen master, 156
Han dynasty, 83–85, 87, 190, 201
Hasan, 243, 244
Heaven, 12, 13
and earth, 87–88, 91
Hidden Breath, 62, 63
"Hidden woman," 72. *See also* "Mysterious
female"
Higher Power, Goddess as, 15
Himiko (Pimiko), 69
Hinayana Buddhism, 132, 138, 163, 190
Hindu Goddess worship
for empowerment and success, 136
priesthood and, 5, 6
Hindu gods. *See also specific gods*
gender dualism in, 217–18
Hindu society, 10
Hindu women, restricted freedoms of, 6,
17
Hindu worldview, triads of, 45
Hinduism, 6, 10. *See also specific topics*
exclusion of women, 131, 229
influenced by Buddhism, 22–23, 45
"Holy woman," 178